ROUTLEDGE LIBRARY EDITIONS: JAPAN'S INTERNATIONAL RELATIONS

Volume 4

U.S./JAPAN FOREIGN TRADE

U.S./JAPAN FOREIGN TRADE
An Annotated Bibliography of Socioeconomic Perspectives

RITA E. NERI

LONDON AND NEW YORK

First published in 1988 by Garland Publishing, Inc.

This edition first published in 2018
by Routledge
2 Park Square, Milton Park, Abingdon, Oxon OX14 4RN

and by Routledge
711 Third Avenue, New York, NY 10017

Routledge is an imprint of the Taylor & Francis Group, an informa business

© 1988 Rita E. Neri

All rights reserved. No part of this book may be reprinted or reproduced or utilised in any form or by any electronic, mechanical, or other means, now known or hereafter invented, including photocopying and recording, or in any information storage or retrieval system, without permission in writing from the publishers.

Trademark notice: Product or corporate names may be trademarks or registered trademarks, and are used only for identification and explanation without intent to infringe.

British Library Cataloguing in Publication Data
A catalogue record for this book is available from the British Library

ISBN: 978-1-138-30279-2 (Set)
ISBN: 978-1-315-14875-5 (Set) (ebk)
ISBN: 978-1-138-55019-3 (Volume 4) (hbk)
ISBN: 978-1-138-55021-6 (Volume 4) (pbk)
ISBN: 978-1-315-14717-8 (Volume 4) (ebk)

Publisher's Note
The publisher has gone to great lengths to ensure the quality of this reprint but points out that some imperfections in the original copies may be apparent.

Disclaimer
The publisher has made every effort to trace copyright holders and would welcome correspondence from those they have been unable to trace.

U.S./JAPAN FOREIGN TRADE
An Annotated Bibliography of Socioeconomic Perspectives

Rita E. Neri

GARLAND PUBLISHING, INC. • NEW YORK & LONDON
1988

© 1988 Rita E. Neri
All rights reserved

Library of Congress Cataloging-in-Publication Data

Neri, Rita E., 1942–
U.S./Japan foreign trade: an annotated bibliography of
socioeconomic perspectives / Rita E. Neri.
p. cm.—(Garland reference library of social science; vol.
403)
Bibliography: p.
Includes indexes.
ISBN 0–8240–8471–3 (alk. paper)
1. Japan—Economic conditions—1945- —Bibliography. 2. Industry
and State—Japan—Bibliography. 3. Japan—Social conditions—1945-
—Bibliography. 4. Japan—History—1945- —Bibliography. 5. Law—
Japan—Bibliography. 6. Japan—Foreign economic relations—United
States—Bibliography. 7. United States—Foreign economic relations—
Japan—Bibliography. I. Title. II. Series: Garland reference
library of social science; v. 403.

Z7165.J3N36 1988   [HC462]   016.382'0973'052—dc19
87–34805 CIP

Printed on acid-free, 250-year-life paper
Manufactured in the United States of America

CONTENTS

Preface	ix
Introduction	xi

I. History and General Works
    A. History   3
    B. General Works   7

II. Culture and Society
    A. Culture   11
        1. Art and Cinema   11
        2. Cultural Dimensions   12
        3. Folk Literature and Mythology   18
        4. Language   19
    B. Social Dynamics   20
        1. Crime and Crime Control   20
        2. Education   21
            a. Educational Policy   24
            b. Higher Education   26
            c. Nursery Schools   27
            d. Secondary Education   27
            e. Teachers   27
        3. Family   28
        4. Human Rights   30
        5. Medical Care   32
        6. National Characteristics   33
        7. Religion   37
        8. Social Conditions   40
        9. Women   47

III. Science, Technology and Environment
    A. Science   51
    B. Technology   52
    C. Environment   53

IV. Law and Politics
    A. Law   55
        1. Antitrust Law   57
        2. Civil Liberties and Civil Procedure   60
        3. Commercial Law   61
        4. Constitutional Law   64
        5. Courts and Judicial System   65
        6. Criminal Law   66
        7. Environmental Law   66
        8. Intellectual Property Law   67
        9. International Law   67
       10. Labor Law   68
       11. Securities Law   68
       12. Tax Law   69
    B. Politics and Government   70
        1. Elections   82
        2. Local Politics and Government   86
        3. Political Participation   89
        4. Political Parties   90
    C. Foreign Relations   94
        1. Treaties   96
        2. Defenses   96
        3. Military Policy   98

V. General Works on the Economy
    A. Economic Conditions   101
    B. Social Effects of Economic Growth   122

VI. Economic Planning
    A. Economic Policy   127
    B. Industry and State   137

VII. Finance
    A. Banks and Banking   143
    B. Finance   144
    C. Taxation   148

VIII. Commerce, Business and Industry
    A. Commerce and Business   149
        1. Commerce   149
        2. Commercial Policy   152
        3. Cultural Aspects of Business   152
        4. Corporations   153
            a. Foreign Business Enterprises   155
            b. General Trading Companies   155
            c. Industrial Groups   158
            d. International Business Enterprises   159
            e. Small Business   161

Contents   vii

                    5. Marketing   161
                    6. Transfer Pricing and Venture Capital   165
                    7. Foreign Economic Relations   165
                        a. Import Quotas and Joint Ventures   166
                        b. Negotiation   167
              B. Industry   168
                    1. Industries   168
                        a. Automobile Industry   171
                        b. Beef Industry   172
                        c. Computer Industry   173
                        d. Electronics Industry   174
                        e. Manufacturing Industry   175
                        f. Steel Industry   176
                    2. Technological Innovation   177
                        a. Industrial Robots   178

  IX. Industrial Management, Organization and Productivity
        A. Industrial Management   181
              1. Employees   204
              2. Employment System   207
        B. Industrial Organization   212
        C. Industrial Productivity   214
              1. Quality Circles   217
              2. Quality Control   219
              3. Research and Development   219

   X. Industrial Relations   221

  XI. U.S.-Japan Relations (General)   225

 XII. U.S.-Japan Economic Relations   233

Author Index   257

Title Index - Books   269

Title Index - Articles   287

Subject Index   301

PREFACE

This bibliography consists of annotated entries of monographs and journal articles published in English that discuss socioeconomic aspects of Japanese society as well as the general and economic dynamics of United States-Japan trade relations. Emphasis is on the Japanese perspective. It does not include materials on Japanese investments or companies in the United States. Nor does it contain works on American or Japanese responses to the trade situation. The contents are selective rather than comprehensive, and the majority of materials fall within the publication period from 1970 to early 1987.

The entries are arranged in alphabetical order by author. The Japanese names are given in the Western style, with surname last, rather than in the traditional Japanese manner of surname first. All index entries refer to citation numbers.

The resources of the following institutions were used in the preparation of this work: Baruch College Library, CUNY; the East Asian and International Law libraries of Columbia University; the Japan Society Library; the MidManhattan Library; the Fogelman Library of the New School for Social Research; the New York Law School Library; the Elmer Holmes Bobst Library of New York University; and the Graduate School of Business Administration Library of New York University.

Special thanks go to the staff of the Access Services and Interlibrary Loan departments of Baruch College Library for their cheerful assistance and patience.

I would like to acknowledge the invaluable assistance of Pamela Chergotis, Managing Editor of Garland Publishing, who was always available to answer questions and offer advice and encouragement. I would also like to express my appreciation to Lynette Reed for her excellent skill in preparing the manuscript and for her good cheer; she made Ames seem a little bit closer.

Finally, I would like to extend my gratitude to Professor Raymond Chang of Baruch College Library, not only for suggesting the idea for this work, but also for his continued advice and encouragement while it was in progress.

INTRODUCTION

The major premise of this work is that no single factor is responsible for the troubled state of United States-Japan trade relations. Instead, a myriad of interrelated factors exist, all of which have created, and continue to create, a very serious situation not only for the two countries but for the entire international economic scene. These factors include economic, political, legal, cultural, social, geographical and historical aspects present in both the United States and Japan. The Japanese perspective is emphasized here since there is much to be learned in this area.

At the end of World War II, Japan was completely devastated. However, during the postwar period it achieved an unprecedented rate of economic growth, often referred to as the "economic miracle," and by 1971 its gross national product (GNP) in the categories of exports and imports, investment, government expenditure, and consumption was approximately five times as large as it had been in 1954. Much has been written on the reasons for Japan's postwar economic success, and we would like to briefly discuss some of them.

The major force behind Japan's rapid industrial progress was the industrial policy developed by the government and implemented by the Ministry of International Trade and Industry (MITI), the Ministry of Finance, and the Economic Planning Agency, together with the corporate sector. The relationship between government and business has frequently been referred to as "Japan, Incorporated." This industrial policy was directed primarily towards the development of certain industries and companies and towards the encouragement of the national propensity for saving in order to create a large amount of capital that could be used to invest in and develop industrial growth. The policy directed the flow of investments into various businesses and industries and also into research and development (R&D) in various ways. A few major commercial "city" banks financed large well established Japanese businesses and held high levels of permanent stock ownership in them as well. Many specialized banks, such as the Japan Development Bank and the Industrial Bank of Japan provided long-range financing

of important industries. The Ministry of Finance and the Bank
of Japan were responsible for directing bank loans to industries and companies with high growth potential and for deny-
ing loans to deteriorating industries. In order to make certain that capital would be available for industrial investment,
the government instituted a system of capital controls that
prevented large amounts of money from leaving Japan. It also
maintained tight control of the home market by minimizing the
importation of manufactured goods from abroad by establishing
stringent protectionist policies, which included tariffs, quotas, inspections, and administrative delays. The policy also
emphasized the development and use of technology in industrial
manufacturing, and this was accomplished both by assimilating
Western technology and by developing its own technology. And
finally, defense spending was kept to a minimum in order that
more funds would be available for industrial development.

Other factors that have been responsible for Japan's rapid
postwar economic growth are the sogoshosha, or general trading
company, which have promoted Japan's export-based economic
growth; the concern of the Japanese firm with the long run
rather than short-term profits (they can do this because most
of their financial backing comes from bank loans rather than
from the sale of securities, and therefore they are not under
pressure by stockholders to show an annual profit); management
techniques and the employment system; cooperation between unions and management; emphasis on industrial productivity and
quality control; and an educated and highly motivated work
force. Among the cultural factors that are responsible are
the work ethic (willingness to work because the job is there);
preference for working in groups; sense of loyalty by workers
to their company; the combination of Confucianism, Shinto,
Taoism, and Buddhism which created the familism that is the
basis of Japanese industrialization and management practices;
and cultural homogeneity.

While Japan was experiencing its postwar economic boom,
the United States was beginning to undergo economic setbacks,
and in 1971 incurred its first annual trade deficit since 1893.
In 1980 the United States trade deficit with Japan was $1.6
billion, and by 1985 it had reached $40.7 billion. By now it
had become a net debtor nation and was borrowing from Japan.
The 1980s saw a progressive widening of the United States-Japan
trade imbalance and an increase in trade friction. Japanese
exports to the United States, the majority of which were manufactured goods, increased much more rapidly than did American
exports to Japan, which consisted primarily of food and raw
materials. In addition to the increased trade imbalance, other
factors have heightened the economic and social tension between
the two countries, and among these are the following: inade-

Introduction xiii

quate consultative mechanisms between the two governments; erroneous or outdated perceptions of each country in the other country; inadequate performance of the American economy; slow liberalization of market access in Japan; a failure by the government and private sector in both countries to deal with difficult problems; Japan's preoccupation with economic matters that results in gaps in other areas, such as foreign relations; threats by the United States of protectionist measures; the influence of Japan's homogeneous culture on its national behavior; the yen exchange rate; problems in negotiations between the Americans and Japanese; difficulties in doing business in Japan; fundamental differences in value systems between the two countries; Japan's low rate of defense spending; Japan's emergence as world leader in certain markets formerly dominated by the United States, such as the automobile and semiconductor industries; Japan's complex distribution system; and Japan's huge trade surplus and capital reserve from savings, much of which has been invested in American securities and real estate.

The increased tension in United States-Japan economic relations has become a major media issue, and "Japan bashing" has become a popular topic. This is contrary to the positive treatment of Japan by writers during the postwar era. Various articles written in the last few years exemplify the current situation. Karel G. van Wolferen, in an article in the 1986/87 issue of *Foreign Affairs*, discusses the cynical manner in which the Japanese have dealt with foreigners by the use of powerless intermediaries to tell the foreigners what they want to hear. Theodore H. White's article, published in the *New York Times Magazine* in 1985, regards Japan's economic policies as being equivalent to a counterattack against the United States after America's victory in 1945. Japan has become aware of America's growing cultural and political negativism, and this has been expressed in various writings. In one such article entitled "Stepping on the Tiger's Tail," published in the *Japan Economic Journal*, the author, Masahiko Ishizuka, stresses that Japan needs its own defense and economic strategy in order to insure its own survival and in order not to be "pushed around by the U.S." This statement is illustrative of the view popular in Japan and expressed in the Japanese media that Japan is a unique nation and is misunderstood and unfairly treated by the rest of the world.

Trade relations between the United States and Japan have also been influenced by the political environment of each country. During the five year term of former prime minister Yasuhiro Nakasone relations deteriorated primarily because Mr. Nakasone had little control over the Liberal Democratic Party (LDP, which is the ruling political party in Japan) and had trouble in dealing with the bureaucracy and the party.

On October 31, 1987, Mr. Nakasone's successor, Noboru Takeshita was confirmed as party leader of the LDP and was elected Prime Minister on November 6. Mr. Takeshita, who is known to have more control over the LDP, favors painstaking consensus within the LDP, and among the bureaucracy, business and farming interests. Because of the outdated voting system, rural votes have up to three times the weight of an urban vote. As a consequence of this, farmers, who comprise a very small part of the population, receive huge subsidies, and LDP ministers have made agricultural protection a non-negotiable topic in diplomatic and trade talks, which has been an additional strain on United States-Japan trade relations.

The United States and Japan have become the two major components of a complex world economy, and they both influence and are influenced by this economy, which consists of global markets, international interdependence among countries, and the combination of economic forces with domestic politics and foreign policy. This international interdependence was amply illustrated by the stock market crash of October 19, 1987, in which all the major world markets suffered record losses. It is therefore of the utmost importance that the United States and Japan maintain favorable economic and diplomatic relations by acknowledging their interdependence and by attempting to lessen tensions in their trade relationship.

BIBLIOGRAPHY

Buruma, Ian. "A New Japanese Nationalism." *New York Times Magazine*, 12 April, 1987.

Darlin, Damon. "The Adjuster." *Wall Street Journal*, 8 October, 1987, 1.

Drucker, Peter F. "Japan's Choices." *Foreign Affairs* 65 (1986/87):923-941.

Helm, Leslie. "Will Japan Really Change?" *Business Week* no. 2946 (May 12, 1986):47-58.

Kristof, Nicholas D. "Japan Trade Barriers Called Mainly Cultural." *New York Times* 4 April, 1985, A1, D5.

Makin, John H. "Our Japan Problem--and Japan's." *New York Times* 30 August, 1987, 27.

Mayer, Martin. "Japan Rolls the Market." *New York Times Magazine*, 20 September, 1987.

Wayne, Leslie. "Japanese Thrust in Wall Street." *New York Times*, 25 March, 1987, D1, D4.

White, Theodore H. "The Danger from Japan." *New York Times Magazine*, 28 July, 1985.

Wolferen, Karel G. van. "The Japan Problem." *Foreign Affairs* 65 (1986/87):288-303.

U.S./Japan Foreign Trade

I
HISTORY AND GENERAL WORKS

A. HISTORY

1. Beasley, W.G. *The Modern History of Japan.* 3d ed. New York: St. Martin's, 1981.

    An updated edition of a classic history of the social, economic, and political aspects of Japan. Covers the period from the early nineteenth century to the 1970s.

2. Beasley, W.G., ed. *Modern Japan: Aspects of History, Literature and Society.* Berkeley: University of California Press, 1975.

    Selected papers presented at a Conference on Modern Japan, held in Oxford and London in 1973, which concentrate on the problems stemming from modernization. The history papers deal with various aspects of the political and international tensions created by specific political and historical events from the period of the civil war of 1868 to the Tokyo Air Raid of March 1945. The literature papers examine national attitudes as expressed in drama and the novel in the context of the relationship between modern ideas and institutions and traditional culture and society. The papers contained in the society section discuss new postwar religions, the use of leisure, industrial relations, balance of payments, and the problems of urbanization.

3. Buckley, Roger. *Japan Today.* Cambridge: Cambridge University Press, 1985.

    An introductory survey of the political, economic and social aspects of contemporary Japan. Discusses the positive factors behind Japan's economic success as well as political and social problems. Also examines the gradual changes in Japan's foreign and defense policies that have resulted from its increasing industrial power.

4. Busch, Noel F. *The Horizon Concise History of Japan.* New York: American Heritage, 1972.

   A brief historical overview. The illustrations demonstrate the character of Japan's historic art tradition, and they convey an idea of the look of the land and the people over the centuries.

5. Downs, Ray F., ed. *Japan Yesterday and Today.* New York: Praeger, 1970.

   Discusses various periods in Japanese history, beginning with prehistoric times and ending with the contemporary era, by means of excerpts from writings by prominent scholars. Among the topics included are the importation of Chinese culture, the feudal age, modernization, World War II, and contemporary Japan.

6. Duus, Peter. *The Rise of Modern Japan.* Boston: Houghton Mifflin, 1976.

   Examines Japan's rise to world prominence over the past one hundred years, with reference to political, social, economic, and diplomatic events.

7. Entwistle, Basil. *Japan's Decisive Decade: How a Determined Minority Changed the Nation's Course in the 1950s.* London: Grosvenor Books, 1985.

   Presents a study of Entwistle's work and experiences in Japan as a representative of Moral Re-Armament during the 1950s. Discusses the ideological developments in politics, industrial relations, and economics as well as the international relations of the postwar period.

8. Hall, John Whitney. *Japan: From Prehistory to Modern Times.* New York: Delacorte, 1970.

   A history of Japan from prehistoric times through the Allied Occupation and recovery. Hall explains the manner in which Japan's political and social institutions have changed and diversified over time, and how this gave rise to Japan as a modern world power. Emphasis is on the premodern period.

9. Hane, Mikiso. *Japan: A Historical Survey.* N.p.: Charles Scribner's Sons, 1972.

   Encompasses traditional and modern Japan and includes political, social, economic, cultural, and intellectual aspects. Much attention is paid to the social conditions

History and General Works

of the peasants and workers, and emphasizes cultural and intellectual developments. Chapters are arranged according to major events and developments in Japanese history rather than to chronological events.

10. Hunter, Janet, comp. *Concise Dictionary of Modern Japanese History*. Berkeley: University of California Press, 1984.

    Contains brief, basic information on the individuals, organizations and events that have played significant roles in Japan's history. The time span covered by the entries is from 1853 through 1980, but the postwar period has been given relatively less coverage than the earlier years. Focus is on political, diplomatic, and socioeconomic developments.

11. Isenberg, Irwin, ed. *Japan, Asian Power*. New York: H.W. Wilson, 1971.

    Sketches some of the major historical events that have shaped the Japanese economy and society. Offers a broad view of the political, economic, and sociological aspects. Also provides a detailed analysis of the economy and a view of Japan's relations with the world.

12. Iwao, Seiichi, ed. *Biographical Dictionary of Japanese History*. Tokyo: International Society for Educational Information, 1978.

    Focuses on those persons who have played outstanding roles in economic, political, social, religious, and scientific life. The volume is divided into four chronological sections: (1) Ancient period, (2) Medieval period (1185-1572), (3) Early Modern period (1572-1868), and (4) Modern period (1868-   ).

13. Lehmann, Jean Pierre. *The Roots of Modern Japan*. New York: St. Martin's, 1982.

    Underscores the extent to which culture and economy have exerted reciprocal influences on Japan's modernization process. Examines the economic, political, social, intellectual, and moral dimensions of Japanese society. Emphasis is on two major historical periods: the Tokugawa period (1600-1868) and the Meiji period (1868-1912).

14. Livingston, Jon, Joe Moore and Felicia Oldfather, eds. *Postwar Japan: 1945 to the Present.* New York: Pantheon Books, 1973.

    This is volume two in the series *The Japan Reader*, and it begins with the American Occupation following World War II; volume one ends with 1945. Consists of a collection of writings that include contemporary accounts, fiction, documents, and scholarly writings, all of which illustrate the central issues of modern Japanese history. Particular emphasis is placed on social and economic questions.

15. Lu, David John. *Sources of Japanese History.* New York: McGraw-Hill, 1974.

    These two volumes contain selected documents about Japanese history that reflect the spirit of the times and the lifestyles of the people of the age, and that emphasize the development of social, economic, and political institutions. Some of the documents were written by unknown common people or minor officials. The writings cover the period from the beginnings of Japan's history through the early 1970s.

16. Mason, R.H.P. and J.G. Caiger. *A History of Japan.* New York: Free Press, 1974.

    Emphasis is on politics, economics, and culture. The following periods are covered: archaic, ancient, medieval, and early modern.

17. Morton, W. Scott. *Japan: Its History and Culture.* New York: McGraw-Hill, 1984.

    Reprint of a work originally published in 1970. Includes a new chapter that updates events to early 1984. Covers the following topics: art, religion, economic and social life, politics, and military history.

18. Reischauer, Edwin O. *Japan: The Story of a Nation.* 3d ed. New York: A.A. Knopf, 1981.

    A general history covering premodern times to the 1970s. Originally published in 1946 under the title *Japan, Past and Present*. Examines the following aspects: the feudal system, the transition to a modern state, economic and political growth, the rise of militarism, World War II, the American Occupation, and the postwar era.

19. ———— and Albert M. Craig. *Japan: Tradition and Transformation.* Boston: Houghton Mifflin, 1978.

    A detailed history that begins with early Japan and the absorption of Chinese civilization and continues up to the 1970s. Emphasis is on social and economic development and change, and politics and government.

20. Wray, Harry and Hilary Conroy, eds. *Japan Examined: Perspectives on Modern Japanese History.* Honolulu: University of Hawaii Press, 1983.

    A collection of essays written by American and Japanese scholars on controversial issues in modern Japanese history. They cover the period from 1868 to the postwar era.

B. GENERAL WORKS

21. Bunge, Frederica M., ed. *Japan: A Country Study.* 4th ed. Washington, D.C.: GPO, 1983.

    Written by a multidisciplinary team of social scientists. Describes and analyzes the economic, national security, political, and social systems and institutions and their interrelationships. Also looks at how these systems are affected by cultural factors.

22. Burks, Ardath W. *Japan: A Postindustrial Power.* 2d, updated ed. Boulder, Colo.: Westview Press, 1984.

    A study of the Japanese and their culture, with emphasis on Japan's post-industrial status. Covers the following subjects: the landscape, history and tradition, art, modernization, postwar politics and economy, post-industrial society, national character, and Japan in the world. Estimates political trends through the election of Yasuhiro Nakasone as prime minister. Contains an annotated bibliography.

23. De Mente, Boye. *The Whole Japan Book.* Phoenix, Ariz.: Phoenix Books, 1983.

    An informal, eclectic listing, with brief descriptions, of various topics related to Japanese culture and history. Designed to serve as an introduction to Japan.

24. Jansen, Marius B. *Japan and Its World: Two Centuries of Change*. Princeton, N.J.: Princeton University Press, 1980.

    Collected lectures on the changes in the intellectual and psychological aspects of the Japanese world view that have occurred in the two hundred years since 1776, which coincide with Japan's emergence from isolation to world power.

25. Japan Center for International Exchange, ed. *The Silent Power: Japan's Identity and World Role*. Tokyo: Simul Press, 1976.

    Essays by leading Japanese social scientists selected from *The Japan Interpreter*, which focus on the cultural and socio-political aspects of Japan's foreign relations. The selections in Part One present and explain features of Japanese culture that affect behavior in international affairs. The essays in Part Two discuss the actual mechanics of policy formation, and those in Part Three deal with Japan's relations with other countries, especially with the United States.

26. *Japan Echo* 1 (1974)- . Tokyo: Japan Echo, Inc.

    A periodical which contains full or partial translations of important articles on various topics written by prominent Japanese critics and commentators which have appeared in leading Japanese publications. Published quarterly.

27. *Journal of Japanese Studies* 1 (1974)- . Seattle: Society for Japanese Studies, University of Washington.

    Contains scholarly articles on various subjects as well as sections on opinion and comment and book reviews. Published semi-annually.

28. *Kodansha Encyclopedia of Japan*. Tokyo: Kodansha, 1983.

    The largest and most comprehensive encyclopedia about Japan to appear in English to date. Its nine volumes and 9,417 entries contain articles by Japanese and non-Japanese scholars that cover thirty-seven categories of information from the fields of history, literature, art, religion, economy, geography, science, technology, law, women, leisure, among others.

29. Ohta, Thaddeus Y., comp. *Japanese National Government Publications in the Library of Congress: A Bibliography.* Washington, D.C.: Library of Congress, 1981.

    Contains 3,376 unannotated entries which include some bilingual or English-only documents. The majority of materials listed are serials, but other types are included as well, such as catalogs, directories, handbooks, and statistical surveys. The largest part of these holdings have been acquired since 1956, although the collection includes a number of works dating from the years prior to, during, and immediately following World War II. Included are works that have been published by ministries and agencies of the three branches of Japan's government (viz., legislative, executive, and judicial), and commercial publishers serving these agencies or quasi-governmental bodies.

30. O'Neill, P.G., ed. *Tradition and Modern Japan.* Tenterden, Kent, England: Paul Norbury Publications, 1981.

    Based on papers given at the Second International Japanese Studies Conference, held in Florence, Italy in 1979. The book is divided into five sections: (1) people and society, (2) early Western and Christian elements, (3) politics and war, (4) art and architecture, and (5) literature, theater and language.

31. Tiedemann, Arthur E., ed. *An Introduction to Japanese Civilization.* Lexington, Mass.: D.C. Heath, 1974.

    Essays on Japanese history and on aspects of Japanese civilization. The history essays cover early Japan to the postwar era. The civilization essays discuss religion, art, literature, economics, politics, law, and society.

II
CULTURE AND SOCIETY

A. CULTURE

1. ART AND CINEMA

32. Kato, Shuichi. *Form, Style, Tradition: Reflections on Japanese Art and Society.* Berkeley: University of California Press, 1971.

    Discusses ideas concerning the meaning of art in the context of Japanese culture. The essays deal with Japanese art of various periods, and they are related to fundamental problems of art in general. Among the topics covered are: the relationship between the artist and society; the question "what is art?", in which the essays are concerned with the evolution of style in Buddhist sculpture; the significance of visual art in the development of national culture and a particular type of attitude towards art and life; and the difficulties that can emerge for the artist in a situation of culture conflict in contemporary Japan.

33. Mellen, Joan. *The Waves at Genji's Door: Japan through Its Cinema.* New York: Pantheon Books, 1976.

    Mellen argues that we are able to penetrate Japan's society and history through its film because the Japanese cinema is constantly preoccupied with history, and therefore it re-creates the Japanese experience. In addition, Japanese films reconsider the social institutions of Japan, the workings of the family, the status of women, the nature and effects of the educational system, and the uses to which the press, police and military have been put. The Japanese film has been in search of the inner dynamic of Japan's ancient culture, its patterns of industrial development, and the crisis of identity that resulted from development, and it has recorded the historical tensions of society. Mellon places the Japanese film in its historical, social, and political context. The work is divided into six parts: (1) at Genji's door, (2) being Japanese, the quest through history, (3) the Second World War and its aftermath, (4) woman in Japan, (5) the family under siege, and (6) alternatives.

34. Richie, Donald. *Japanese Cinema: Film Style and National Character.* Garden City, N.Y.: Doubleday, 1971.

    A succinct history of Japanese film, from its beginnings in 1896 through 1970, as well as an exploration of the Japanese culture and mind. Richie relates the films discussed here to other art forms and to the traditions and attitudes of the Japanese people. Examines well-known classics as well as the popular "entertainment" films, and the unique vision of the Japanese film-makers.

35. Sato, Tadao. *Currents in Japanese Cinema.* New York: Kodansha International, 1982.

    A collection of essays by Sato, a film critic, who favors popular culture over traditional in his treatment of Japanese film. These essays reflect Sato's social concerns, and they present the reader with a rare view of modern Japanese history, as well as his knowledge of cinematic technique. Among the topics discussed here are film heroines, war films, the family, the villain, American-Japanese relations in Japanese films, and developments in the 1960s and 1970s.

2. CULTURAL DIMENSIONS

36. Aoki, Michiko Y. and Margaret B. Dardess, comps. *As the Japanese See It: Past and Present.* Honolulu: University Press of Hawaii, 1981.

    A collection of readings written by Japanese individuals that include folk legends, sermons, short stories, excerpts from novels, biographical material, as well as other forms. They are designed to help Western readers understand Japanese ways of thinking and acting. Selections range from the eleventh century to 1976 and are arranged by the following topics: religion, the family, the community, and the state.

Culture and Society

37. Bailey, Jackson H., ed. *Listening to Japan: A Japanese Anthology*. New York: Praeger, 1973.

    Essays covering various aspects of Japanese life and areas of concern. Discusses such topics as cultural ideas and values, politics and economics, and ideals and education of young people.

38. Barthes, Roland. *Empire of Signs*. New York: Hill and Wang, 1982.

    Barthes offers a unique interpretation of the Japanese culture and language. He analyzes visual signs, images and gestures in order to grasp the significance of Japan's unknown culture and language. He considers the exchange of signs to have a fascinating richness, mobility, and subtlety, which do not require words in order to be understood; instead, one can "read" the meanings which are "written" on these signs.

39. Befu, Harumi. *Japan: An Anthropological Introduction*. San Francisco: Chandler, 1971.

    An anthropological introduction to Japanese society that emphasizes processes of change, development, and modernization. Views the process of modernization against the background of traditional Japan: how traditional cultural patterns and institutions have aided or hindered the modernization process, and how these traditional patterns and institutions have been changed by the forces of modernization. Begins with the cultural origins and historical background of prehistoric Japan, then moves on to the study of kinship systems and rural communities. Following this is a discussion of religious beliefs and systems in both rural and urban Japan, and then an analysis of how the social stratification system changed during the transitional agrarian period to modern industrial times. Also examines certain selected aspects of the Japanese personality, and concludes with a discussion of modernization.

40. Caudill, William A. "The Influence of Social Structure and Culture on Human Behavior in Modern Japan." *Journal of Nervous and Mental Disease* 157 (1973):240-257.

    Examines the implications of tradition and modernity on the psychological and behavioral characteristics of the Japanese people.

41. Cleaver, Charles Grinnell. *Japanese and Americans: Cultural Parallels and Paradoxes*. Minneapolis: University of Minnesota Press, 1976.

    Cultural differences and similarities between the United States and Japan are discussed with the author's goal of dispelling stereotypes and misunderstandings. Among the subjects discussed here are fictional writing and architecture, political and military nationalism, international economic reputations of both countries, attitudes towards nature, and the organization of work and leisure.

42. Craig, Albert M., ed. *Japan: A Comparative View*. Princeton, N.J.: Princeton University Press, 1979.

    Papers presented at a conference that compare various aspects of Japanese society and culture with those of both Western and non-Western countries. Among the topics discussed are history, political change, culture and personality, and economy and society.

43. Ellwood, Robert S., Jr. *An Invitation to Japanese Civilization*. Belmont, Calif.: Wadsworth, 1980.

    A survey of the essence of Japanese culture and history, which includes discussions of religion, philosophy, visual arts, architecture, and the literary, musical, and dramatic arts.

44. Fields, George. *From Bonsai to Levi's: When West Meets East: An Insider's Surprising Account of How the Japanese Live*. New York: Macmillan, 1983.

    English language version of a book originally written for a Japanese audience by a Western-oriented market researcher working in Japan. Examines the problems Western firms marketing their products in Japan have had in adapting their business practices to the Japanese way of doing things. Fields argues that in order to be successful, business people doing business in Japan need to consider the unique features of Japanese society and culture in conducting their affairs. Most of the chapters consist of case studies of how an awareness or lack of awareness of Japanese culture led to successes or failures for foreign firms trying to sell their products in Japan. Fields offers a cultural analysis of the Japanese market and the attempts to penetrate it with Western products.

45. Gibney, Frank. *Japan: The Fragile Superpower*. Rev. ed. New York: W.W. Norton, 1979.

    A description of the characteristics and qualities of the Japanese that have contributed to Japan's economic success, and which are compared with those of the United States.

46. Grossberg, Kenneth A., ed. *Japan Today*. Philadelphia: Institute for the Study of Human Issues, 1981.

    Selected papers by Japanese authorities from panel discussions presented at the 1979 "Japan Today" cultural program that took place in the United States. They address cultural, political, economic, and social issues of contemporary Japan as well as its place in the future.

47. Hoover, Thomas. *Zen*. New York: Random House, 1977.

    Traces the history and characteristics of both Zen and the Zen arts. Covers the beginnings of Zen (prehistoric times) through the present. Among the Zen arts discussed are archery and swordsmanship, landscape and stone gardens, architecture, the No Theater, the tea ceremony, haiku poetry, and ceramic art. Hoover contends that Zen culture, together with the already highly developed vocabulary and capacity for perception developed in the Heian era (794-1185), has made Japanese culture unique in world civilization.

48. Ishida, Eiichiro. *Japanese Culture: A Study of Origins and Characteristics*. Tokyo: University of Tokyo Press, 1974.

    Lectures by a distinguished ethnologist and cultural anthropologist on the relationship between the origins of the Japanese and the contemporary Japanese people, together with their distinctive cultural traits. Ishida contends that a continuous pattern exists that does not easily change, and he supports this by presenting evidence from certain significant trends in Japanese history.

49. Kojima, Kazuto. "Public Opinion Trends in Japan." *Public Opinion Quarterly* 41 (1977):206-216.

    A quantitative study of changes in the Japanese ways of thinking and the continuity of tradition since the end of World War II in such areas as daily life, culture, politics, and society.

50. Kumon, Shumpei. "Some Principles Governing the Thought and Behavior of Japanists (Contextualists)." *Journal of Japanese Studies* 8 (1982):5-27.

    An integration of various aspects of Japanese culture into a cohesive and unique whole. Among the topics included are world outlook, language, and social relations.

51. Kuwabara, Takeo. *Japan and Western Civilization: Essays on Comparative Culture*. Tokyo: University of Tokyo Press, 1983.

    Collected essays by a Japanese intellectual and scholar on such topics as the social effect of art, tradition versus modernization, the classics in contemporary Japan, Europe and Japan, and the art of modern haiku.

52. Morsbach, Helmut. "Aspects of Nonverbal Communication in Japan." *Journal of Nervous and Mental Disease* 157 (1973):262-277.

    Describes the characteristics of nonverbal behavior in relation to the historical and social factors unique to Japan.

53. Murakami, Hyoe and Edward G. Seidensticker, eds. *Guides to Japanese Culture*. Tokyo: Japan Culture Institute, 1977.

    A bibliography containing summaries and commentaries of forty-five works by modern Japanese scholars on major areas of Japanese culture. Included are such topics as language, spiritual life, intellectual tradition, social relations, literature, history, and the arts.

54. Nishibe, Susumu. "Japan As a Highly Developed Mass Society: An Appraisal." *Journal of Japanese Studies* 8 (1982):73-96.

    Nishibe discuses his observation that the Japanese are becoming increasingly ethnocentric and self-complacent as the result of Japan's economic success, and that this must be a part of the essential nature of mass societies.

55. Ono, Setsuko. "Fragile Blossom, Fragile Superpower: A New Interpretation?" *Japan Quarterly* 23 (1976):12-27.

    Contemporary Western images of Japan are seen by Ono as resembling those images created at the end of the nineteenth century by two authors, Pierre Loti and Lafcadio Hearn.

56. Pollack, David. *The Fracture of Meaning: Japan's Synthesis of China from the Eighth through the Eighteenth Centuries.* Princeton, N.J.: Princeton University Press, 1986.

   Examines the history of the interpretation (hermeneutics) of China's cultural influence on Japan, with emphasis on particularly crucial periods and issues. The author is concerned with the Japanese interpretations of what they saw as essentially Chinese, rather than our own interpretations or those of the Chinese. Among the topics discussed are the problem of writing, early medieval Zen, and Tokugawa aesthetics.

57. Reischauer, Edwin O. *The Japanese.* Cambridge, Mass.: Harvard University Press, 1981.

   Originally published in 1977. Contains a brief general background of Japan's history. More attention is given to the social organization, values, and politics of the Japanese, and their relationship with the outside world.

58. Tazawa, Utaka. *Japan's Cultural History: A Perspective.* Tokyo: Ministry of Foreign Affairs, 1973.

   A brief presentation that attempts to understand contemporary Japan and its culture by studying the process by which the ancestors of today's Japanese adapted other cultures. Divided into five distinctive cultural epochs: Archaic age, Early Historic age, Medieval age, Pre-modern age, and Modern age. The development of the formative arts is traced through these periods.

59. Varley, H. Paul. *Japanese Culture.* 3d ed. Honolulu: University of Hawaii Press, 1984.

   A survey of the history of Japanese cultural developments, as related to political and institutional trends, from the earliest times to the present.

60. Watanbe, Masao. "The Conception of Nature in Japanese Culture." *Science* 183 (1974):279-282.

   Examines the Japanese love of nature in traditional Japan that has existed from the very early days of Japan's history. This love of nature is exemplified in the appreciation of beauty of nature in, for example, landscapes, miniature gardens and trees, flower arrangement, the tea ceremony, and haiku poetry. Man is considered a part of nature and the art of living in harmony with nature is the wisdom of life. However, Watanbe contends that since the introduction of modern science and technology, the Japanese people are more directly exposed to and more helpless in the current environmental crisis because they are still immersed in nature itself and do not realize what is happening to nature and to themselves.

61. Welch, Theodore F. and Hiroki Kato. *Japan Today: A Westerner's Guide to the People, Language and Culture of Japan*. Lincolnwood, Ill.: Passport Books, 1986.

    Consists of an alphabetic arrangement of a wide range of topics on Japanese cultural concepts, customs, and terms. Provides basic information for those doing business with the Japanese as well as for others. Includes a section on Japanese language basics and an appendix with travel information. A revised edition of *Japan Connections*, published in 1983.

3. FOLK LITERATURE AND MYTHOLOGY

62. Algarin, Joanne P. *Japanese Folk Literature: A Core Collection and Reference Guide*. New York: R.R. Bowker, 1982

    Provides an introduction to the folklore and folktales of Japan (including myths, legends, and fairy tales) by means of English language sources. Divided into the following sections: works on Japanese folklore; Japanese folktale anthologies; and classic folktales, which lists and abstracts classic folktales. The appendices include Japanese language sources and a glossary of Japanese terms.

63. Piggott, Juliet. *Japanese Mythology*. Rev. ed. New York: P. Bedrick Books, 1983.

    A well illustrated collection of Japanese myths, legends, folktales, and folklore. Japan's indigenous legends are deeply embedded in the minds of its people, and the well known tales of gods, goddesses, heroes, and talking animals are repeated in books, in drama, and within the family.

4. LANGUAGE

64. Goldstein, Bernice Z. and Kyoko Tamura. *Japan and America: A Comparative Study in Language and Culture.* Rutland, Vt.: Charles E. Tuttle, 1975.

    Focuses on the differences in language patterns between American English and Japanese in relation to cultural and personality variations between the United States and Japan.

65. Miller, Roy Andrew. *The Japanese Language in Contemporary Japan: Some Socio-Linguistic Observations.* Washington, D.C.: American Enterprise Institute for Public Policy Research, 1977.

    Some of the inner workings of Japanese society are brought out through this examination of the Japanese language. Surveys contemporary socio-linguistic writings by Japanese intellectuals that deal with the relationship between language and society, and with the problems that are caused by the use of the language by foreigners as well as by the Japanese.

66. ———. *Japan's Modern Myth: The Language and Beyond.* New York: Weatherhill, 1982.

    An analysis of the myth that the Japanese language is unique and is equated with the Japanese and their culture and therefore is virtually impossible for anyone to learn, whether Japanese or foreigner. The nature and role of this myth in contemporary Japan and its importance for understanding the country are discussed as well.

67. ———. *Nihongo: In Defence of Japanese.* London: Athlone Press, 1986.

    Miller attempts to answer the principal questions that Western readers generally have about the Japanese language. He addresses the following topics: the Japanese writing system; the grammatical structure of the modern Japanese language; an evaluation of the criticisms of the language by Japanese critics, observers, and foreign observers; interlinguistic semantic congruence and incongruence; semantic divergencies between Japanese and other major world languages; and translation of Japanese literature into English. Miller strongly recommends that the Japanese language should be defended from its critics: otherwise the study of Japanese and the language itself might disappear.

B. SOCIAL DYNAMICS

1. CRIME AND CRIME CONTROL

68. Ames, Walter L. *Police and Community in Japan.* Berkeley: University of California Press, 1981.

    Written by an anthropologist who worked directly with police officers in Japan from 1974 to 1975 for dissertation research purposes. Examines how the police develop their approach in different kinds of communities and in response to various problems and complexities in Japanese society. Emphasis is on actual operations and on the informal aspects of policing.

69. Amnesty International. *The Death Penalty in Japan: Report of an Amnesty International Mission to Japan, 21 February-3 March 1983.* London, 1983.

    A reproduction of a memorandum, with minor amendments, that was sent to the Minister of Justice in Japan on May 31, 1983. Contains the findings of the Amnesty International delegates on the use of the death penalty in Japan and Amnesty International's recommendations to the Japanese government on the subject.

70. Clifford, William. *Crime Control in Japan.* Lexington, Mass.: Lexington Books, 1976.

    Clifford maintains that Japan's "social miracle" of actually containing and reducing the amount of crime committed during a period of industrial growth and rapid urbanization has yet to be appreciated by the Japanese themselves as well as by foreigners. He discusses the reasons for this phenomenon, which are primarily due to cultural factors, such as the Japanese self-image, toleration and dependence, and conflict and consensus. Also discussed here are the criminal justice system, the police, correctional services, public participation, juvenile delinquency, gangsters, female crime, drugs, and suicide.

71. Kaplan, David E. and Alec Dubro. *Yakuza: The Explosive Account of Japan's Criminal Underworld.* Reading, Mass.: Addison-Wesley, 1986.

    A study of the history, operations, and influence of the Yakuza, a three hundred year old organized crime group. The authors maintain that the group is connected with the ultranationalist right in Japan, and often this coalition has served as a paramilitary force for Japan's ruling Liberal Democratic Party, the LDP. They also contend that the Yakuza is becoming institutionalized on the West Coast of the United States because of its involvement with criminal activities here.

2. EDUCATION

72. Anderson, Ronald S. *Education in Japan: A Century of Modern Development.* Washington, D.C.: U.S. Dept. of Health, Education, and Welfare, Office of Education, 1975.

    Focuses on the contemporary issues in Japanese education seen in the perspective of the last one hundred years of educational development. The present method of education at each major level is described, and the attitudes of teachers and students as well as the fundamental values resulting from the present system are assessed. Also discusses major problem areas, among which are teacher status, administration, supervision and finance, instructional media and special programs, and student protest.

73. Aso, Makoto and Ikuo Amano. *Education and Japan's Modernization.* Tokyo: Japan Times, 1983.

    Traces the development process of Japanese education and clarifies the role education has played in the modernization of Japan. Begins with the history of the educational system prior to 1872 (in 1872 the modern educational system was originated in the fundamental Code of Education promulgated by the government), and continues up through the 1980s. Includes such topics as industrial progress and expansion of educational opportunities, failure of nationalistic education and the creation of a democratic educational system, the impact of technological innovation, and the period of educational reform.

74. Beauchamp, Edward R., ed. *Learning to Be Japanese: Selected Readings on Japanese Society and Education.* Hamden, Conn.: Linnet Books, 1978.

    The articles in this collection deal not only with formal education, but with other ways in which people learn, and have learned, to be Japanese. Covers the time span from 1603 to the present, and the approach is both historical and sociological. Part One is concerned with the roots of contemporary Japanese education. Part Two provides an overview of selected dimensions of contemporary Japanese education, and Part Three summarizes some possible future directions of Japanese education.

75. Bowman, Mary Jean with the collaboration of Hideo Ikeda and Yasumasa Tomoda. *Educational Choice and Labor Markets in Japan*. Chicago: University of Chicago Press, 1981.

    Examines the plans and expectations of students concerning future education and career options. These perceptions are explored with respect to how much they are influenced by family backgrounds and geographic location, as well as how they affect and are affected by the type of upper-secondary curriculum in which a student is enrolled and by related aspects of secondary school experiences. Includes data relating fathers' attitudes concerning labor market structures and job opportunities to students' perceptions of how labor markets operate. The data come primarily from a special survey of Japanese male high school students who were in their senior year in 1966 to 1967.

76. Cummings, William K. *Education and Equality in Japan*. Princeton, N.J.: Princeton University Press, 1980.

    Cummings contends that postwar Japan provides an example of a society that has been transformed by education. He presents a study of Japanese education, particularly on the primary level, and describes how it is promoting egalitarian social change. A detailed analysis is provided of the historical, political, and social background of postwar education and of the contemporary egalitarian educational process. Also examined is the impact of youth and their egalitarian social values on adult institutions.

77. ————, ed. *Educational Policies in Crisis: Japanese and American Perspectives*. New York: Praeger, 1986.

    Compares the educational systems of Japan and the United States, and addresses the following topics: educational crises, educational structure, transition from school to work, and each country's perception of the educational system of the other.

78. ———— and Victor Nobuo Kobayashi. "Education in Japan." *Current History* 84 (1985):422-433.

    Discusses Prime Minister Nakasone's proposal for educational reform, which is the third comprehensive reform

Japan has had. Also discusses the previous two reforms. The authors contend that these attempts at educational reform are signs of Japan's dissatisfaction with the educational system.

79. Duke, Benjamin C. *The Japanese School: Lessons for Industrial America.* New York: Praeger, 1986.

    Based on Duke's conviction that the economic growth of modern Japan has depended extensively on the role of the educational system, which produces loyal, literate, competent, and diligent industrial workers. Analyzes the ethical teachings and basic subject matter of mathematics, reading, and writing, which reflect the cultural traditions of Japan and which Duke regards as major contributing factors leading to Japan's economic development. Duke also compares the educational traditions and systems of Japan and the United States, and examines what the two countries can learn from each other.

80. Kiefer, Christie W. "The Psychological Interdependence of Family, School, and Bureaucracy in Japan." *American Anthropologist* 72 (1970):66-75.

    Looks at the role that the educational system plays in sustaining the emotional habits learned in childhood and in channeling them into the bureaucratic values of adult roles.

81. Kobayashi, Victor Nobuo. "Tradition, Modernization, Education: The Case of Japan." *Journal of Ethnic Studies* 12 (1984):95-118.

    The author illustrates his thesis that in contemporary Japan tradition has developed along with, and is a part of, modernization. Emphasis is on education, which utilizes the practices of rote and imitation, which have long since been deemed outmoded, in the teaching-learning of traditional arts in a nation considered the most modern and industrial in Asia.

82. Morton, W. Scott. "Educational and Cultural Trends in Japan Today." *Current History* 60 (1971):213-217.

    Morton posits that in contrast to Japan's economic progress and modernization, not much change has occurred in either education or cultural trends; that the old ways have not been abandoned for the new.

83. Shimahara, Nobuo K. *Adaptation and Education in Japan.*
    New York: Praeger, 1979.

    Japanese education is examined within the framework of
    adaptation, with emphasis on group orientation, a sig-
    nificant aspect of the Japanese adaptation pattern. The
    author maintains that the response of education to the
    needs of the social, economic, and political institutions
    of society is guided by culture, which determines the
    pattern of adaptation for individuals. An anthropological
    and sociological approach.

84. White, Merry I. "Japanese Education: How Do They Do It?"
    Public Interest 76 (1984):87-101.

    White argues that there is a powerful relationship be-
    tween Japanese educational achievement and social and eco-
    nomic success, and she observes Japanese education here
    in order to ascertain its motive forces. Among the topics
    discussed are national consensus, institutional central-
    ization, fiscal support, the role of mothers, pedagogy,
    the role of competition, and problems.

85. ―――――. *The Japanese Educational Challenge: A Commit-
    ment to Children.* New York: Free Press, 1987.

    The success of Japanese education is attributed to deep-
    seated psychological, cultural, and historical traditions
    rather than to educational policies, which White still
    considers to be important. Japanese attitudes towards
    child rearing and the complicated relationship between
    mother and child motivate children to learn. White also
    discusses such topics as the homogeneity of the Japanese
    culture; the highly centralized system of education; the
    relatively high social and economic status of teachers;
    the tremendous pressure to fit into one's social group;
    and the Japanese view that education is the key to in-
    dustrial development, national cohesion, and international
    political stature, which is the result of Japan's lack
    of natural resources and the necessity of living by its
    wits.

a. Educational Policy

86. Organization for Economic Co-operation and Development.
    Reviews of National Policies for Education: Japan.
    Paris, 1971.

    Consists of the report on Japanese educational policies,
    prepared by the group of OECD Examiners who visited Japan
    in 1970, and the confrontation meeting between the OECD

Examiners, Japanese authorities, and members of the OECD Education Committee held in Paris in 1970. During the confrontation meeting the following issues were discussed: basic issues in educational policy and planning in Japan, autonomy and flexibility in education, education and democracy, and the process and objectives of educational reform. The report touches upon some of the following topics: early childhood and school education, the university system and its reform, financing and restructuring higher education, university entrance procedures, and internal governance of universities.

87. ----------. Directorate for Scientific Affairs. *Educational Policy and Planning: Japan.* Paris, 1973.

    Contains the major background documents for the OECD examination of educational policy in Japan conducted in 1970. Emphasis is on three general aspects of policy which underlie the future development of Japanese education; the first aspect is the response of Japanese education to national and social demand; the second one involves internal qualitative concerns in the delivery of education to the Japanese people; and the third aspect addresses the question of how this educational service is paid for. The second part of the book presents the general conclusions and recommendations of the Central Council for Education of Japan.

88. Park, Yung Ho. "'Big Business' and Education Policy in Japan." *Asian Survey* 22 (1982):315-336.

    Park argues that the assumption of domination by a business elite in education policymaking is not valid. Rather, he contends that the Japanese education policy is much more pluralistic than commonly believed, with various groups exercising considerable power over the official policy makers (the Liberal Democratic Party, and the government).

89. Pempel, T.J. *Patterns of Japanese Policymaking: Experiences from Higher Education.* Boulder, Colo.: Westview Press, 1978.

    Pempel contends that the dominant perceptions of policymaking in Japan to date are inadequate. He examines in detail the way in which the Japanese government has, since the end of World War II, formulated state policy in three areas of higher education: university administration, specialization and differentiation, and enrollment expansion. Based on the results of his analysis, Pempel concludes that there is little to confirm and much to challenge in existing interpretations of how policy is made in Japan. Focus is on the isolation of the three ideal typical patterns of policymaking: policymaking by camp conflict, incremental policymaking, and pressure group policymaking.

b. Higher Education

90. Cummings, William K. "The Japanese Private University." *Minerva* 11 (1973):348-371.

    Addresses the problem of the state of deterioration of the Japanese private universities and the need for reform. Cummings contends that public universities have much higher standards and are more selective in their admissions procedures.

91. ―――――. "Understanding Behavior in Japan's Academic Marketplace." *Journal of Asian Studies* 34 (1975):313-340.

    The labor market approach is used in this study of mobility of professors and inbreeding in the Japanese university system.

92. ―――――, Ikuo Amano and Kazuyuki Kitamura. *Changes in the Japanese University: A Comparative Perspective*. New York: Praeger, 1979.

    Essays that describe and analyze recent changes in Japan's university system. Among the topics included here are finance, mass higher education, the Japanese student and the labor market, the productivity of the Japanese scholar, and the organization and administration of individual universities.

93. Japan. Central Council for Education. "The Reform of Japanese Higher Education." *Minerva* 11 (1973):387-414.

    A slightly abridged version of the sections relating to higher education of the Council's report which was submitted to the Minister of Education in 1971.

94. Morton, W. Scott. "Japanese Universities and Students Today." *Current History* 75 (1975):174-185.

    Discusses the history of university development, the curriculum, and student activism.

95. Zeugner, John F. "What Can We Learn from the Japanese? The Puzzle of Higher Education in Japan." *Change* 16 (1984):24-31.

   Zeugner, who has taught at various universities in Japan, presents a critical assessment of the university system. He contends that there exists in Japan a generalized social expectation that universities do not, and should not, accomplish anything beyond their initial credential screening, and that Japanese life will generate whatever compensatory mechanisms that might be needed to overcome the expected failures of university education. Also discussed are faculty re-interpretation of the academic calendar, classroom lateness, faculty control and factionalism, socializing, and the failure of faculty and students to take the university seriously.

c. Nursery Schools

96. Lewis, Catherine C. "Cooperation and Control in Japanese Nursery Schools." *Comparative Education Review* 28 (1984):69-84.

   Identifies potentially interesting areas for future research in nursery school socialization and aims at stimulating American thinking about two aspects of early education: school practices which influence the development of cooperative behavior in children, and adult strategies for controlling children's behavior. Provides observational data from fifteen Japanese nursery schools on early socialization.

d. Secondary Education

97. Rohlen, Thomas P. *Japan's High Schools*. Berkeley: University of California Press, 1983.

   Discusses secondary education in Japan within the social context. Based on Rohlen's fieldwork in Japan in 1974 and on observations made during later visits.

e. Teachers

98. Duke, Benjamin C. *Japan's Militant Teachers: A History of the Left-Wing Teachers' Movement*. Honolulu: University Press of Hawaii, 1973.

   A study of Nikkyoso, the Japan Teachers Union, which is the largest union in Japan, and one of the largest unions of teachers in the world. Duke traces the evolution of the left-wing teachers' movement from 1919 to 1947, which led to the formation of Nikkyoso in 1947.

Also discussed is the period of militancy from 1947 to 1967, and the causes for the union's militant role. Nikkyoso has had a hostile relationship with the Japanese Ministry of Education, and Duke maintains that this mutual antagonism provides the key to an understanding of developments within postwar Japanese education.

99. Thurston, Donald R. *Teachers and Politics in Japan.* Princeton, N.J.: Princeton University Press, 1973.

    Evaluates the influence Nikkyoso, the Japan Teachers' Union, has had as an interest group on its own members and on the formulation and implementation of educational policies. Also assesses the significance of Nikkyoso on postwar Japanese politics and society. Nikkyoso represents elementary and lower secondary teachers and is the largest of the teachers' organizations.

3. FAMILY

100. Caudill, William A. and Carmi Schooler. "Child Behavior and Child Rearing in Japan and the United States: An Interim Report." *Journal of Nervous and Mental Disease* 157 (1973):323-338.

     Report of the results of a study in which the behavior of infants and their mothers in Japan and the United States was observed. Subsequent observations of the same children at 2 1/2 and 6 years of age are also reported.

101. Coleman, Samuel. *Family Planning in Japanese Society: Traditional Birth Control in a Modern Urban Culture.* Princeton, N.J.: Princeton University Press, 1983.

     Discusses the birth control methods Japanese couples use. The Japanese pattern stands out among affluent industrialized countries because of the heavy reliance on induced abortion and the small proportion of couples who make use of the postwar period advances in contraceptive technology that were developed in the 1930s. This stands in obvious contrast to Japan's ultramodernity in so many other respects.

102. Conroy, Mary. "Maternal Strategies for Regulating Children's Behavior." *Journal of Cross-Cultural Psychology* 11 (1980):153-172.

     Report of a study of the comparison of control strategies used by mothers in Japan and the United States to gain compliance from young children. Examines two aspects of the responses to the control items, cognitive structuring and psychological space. Cognitive structuring refers to the basis of appeal the mother used in her response to gain compliance from her child, and includes appeals to authority, rules, feelings, or consequences other than punishment. Psychological space refers to the external conditions for compliance that are established by the mother's response. Discusses the cultural contexts that contribute to the differences in responses between the Japanese and American mothers.

103. Hendry, Joy. *Becoming Japanese: The World of the Pre-School Child.* Honolulu: University of Hawaii Press, 1986.

    Examines the interactions of adults with pre-school children, a time which most Japanese regard as a vitally important time of preparation for later development. Hendry's research involved working with Japanese mothers and other caretakers, and with kindergartens and day nurseries. The theoretical framework is drawn from social anthropology.

104. Kitaoji, Hironobu. "The Structure of the Japanese Family." *American Anthropologist* 73 (1971):1036-1057.

    Kitaoji argues that such concepts as positional terminology, sociocentric organization, rules of succession and inheritance, physical and social kinship, fosterage and adoption, and perpetual kinship, which characterize the stem family, are more useful tools in understanding the logic of Japanese kinship and family organization than the concepts of descent, which characterizes the patriarchal extended family, and residence rules, which characterize the nuclear family.

105. Shigaki, Irene S. "Child Care Practices in Japan and the United States: How Do They Reflect Cultural Values in Young Children?" *Young Children* 38 (1983):13-24.

    Discusses data pertaining to socialization of the young gathered during the author's one year stay in Japan, during which time visits were made to nurseries and kindergartens. Shigaki contends that Japan serves as a good cultural opposite to the United States, and that this study can serve as a useful counterpoint in helping to better understand the relationship between American socialization practices and the values that they foster.

The following topics are included: cultural values, the group and interdependence, and the spirit of perseverance.

106. Stevenson, Harold, Hiroshi Azuma and Kenji Hakuta, eds. *Child Development and Education in Japan.* New York: W.H. Freeman, 1986.

    Chapters written by Japanese and American scholars in the fields of psychology, education, sociology, and anthropology. Among the topics included here are the roles of Japanese children in society and culture, child rearing practices, the family, education, and the Japanese language.

107. Wagatsuma, Hiroshi. "Some Aspects of the Contemporary Japanese Family: Once Confucian, Now Fatherless?" *Daedalus* 106 (1977):181-210.

    Looks at the postwar decline of authority of the Japanese father in the family, which has been caused by the following factors: changes in values, the increased number of nuclear families, crowded housing conditions, the influence of the media, and the father's weakened financial position in marriage.

4. HUMAN RIGHTS

108. Beer, Lawrence Ward. "Group Rights and Individual Rights in Japan." *Asian Survey* 21 (1981):437-453.

    Considers the Japanese preference for asserting, promoting, and violating human rights in groups rather than as individuals acting alone, in relation to some contemporary human rights problems. Among the areas discussed are women's rights; refugees; and discrimination against resident Koreans, Chinese, Okinawans, atom bomb victims, Ainu (proto-Caucasians), Burakumin (descendants of Japanese engaged in outcaste tasks), and mixed-blood children.

109. ———— and C.G. Weeramantry. "Human Rights in Japan: Some Protections and Problems." *Universal Human Rights* 1 (1979):1-33.

    Emphasis is on the work of the Civil Liberties Bureau and its commissioners, and on problems which have been written about very rarely, or not at all, in English language academic sources. Covers the issue from the perspectives of law, sociology, history, and economics.

110. De Vos, George A. *Japan's Outcastes: The Problem of the Burakumin.* London: Minority Rights Group, 1971.

    Briefly discusses the discriminatory treatment of the Burakumin, an indigenous segment of the Japanese population. Among the topics covered are origins of caste, discrimination, social deviancy, process of passing, and political activity.

111. ———— and Hiroshi Wagatsuma, eds. *Japan's Invisible Race: Caste in Culture and Personality.* Rev. ed. Berkeley: University of California Press, 1972.

    A collection of writings which examine the general nature of caste segregation and racist ideology and their significant incidence in Japan by means of various social science methods. Explores the political, social, economic, and psychological conditions of the Japanese outcaste. Also includes a comparative structural analysis of caste in society.

112. ———— and William O. Wetherall. *Japan's Minorities: Burakumin, Koreans, Ainu, and Okinawans.* New 1983 ed. London: Minority Rights Group, 1983.

    Provides a brief sketch of the discrimination experiences of the Burakumin, Koreans, Ainu, and Okinawans living in Japan. More attention is given to the Burakumin here because the authors contend that the least is known about them outside Japan. However, De Vos and Wetherall also state that much of what the Burakumin have experienced also holds true for the other minority groups.

113. Hah, Chong-do and Christopher C. Lapp. "Japanese Politics of Equality in Transition: The Case of the Burakumin." *Asian Survey* 18 (1978):487-504.

    Discusses the current political situation of the Burakumin, the genetic descendants of the "eta," who were relegated to the social position of outcastes during the Tokugawa period, and who were forced by law to practice a variety of "impure" professions, such as butchery, grave tending, and executions. Explores recent ideological shifts in the leadership of the Buraku Liberation League (BLL) and the tactical maneuvers which helped produce momentous gains during the past decade. Also analyzes the crucial role of the state or authoritative political power in establishing and institutionalizing a particular pattern of majority-minority relations.

114. Lee, Changsoo. *Koreans in Japan: Ethnic Conflict and Accommodation*. Berkeley: University of California Press, 1981.

Presents a scholarly analysis of the minority-majority relations of Koreans in Japan, which are influenced by legal restrictions and discriminatory social attitudes inherited from the past. Traces the history of the Korean-Japanese relationship, which from earliest historical times has manifested both cooperation and conflict. Also examines contemporary legal and educational issues, and presents case studies of Koreans living in Japan.

5. MEDICAL CARE

115. Steslicke, William E. *Doctors in Politics: The Political Life of the Japan Medical Association*. New York: Praeger, 1973.

Steslicke states that he had two basic objectives in writing this book. The first is to provide a more intimate view of the specific issues and controversies related to medical care in contemporary Japan. The second objective is to contribute to a better understanding of Japanese politics. He presents a detailed, narrative case study of the Japan Medical Association's 1960-61 campaign to obtain favorable governmental action on its "Four Demands": abolition of restrictions on medical treatment, a rise in the value of the point unit, simplification of paperwork, and integration of schedules A and B and an end to regional differences in medical fees.

116. ─────. "Doctors, Patients, and Government in Modern Japan." *Asian Survey* 12 (1972):913-931.

The Japanese government plays a leading role in the affairs of the medical profession through its regulation of the system of medical care in general, through the administration of health insurance, as well as through other means. Steslicke discusses the effects this has had on the traditional doctor-patient relationship developed during the Meiji Restoration, and the new pattern of involving doctors, patients, and government which has gradually emerged.

Culture and Society 33

6. NATIONAL CHARACTERISTICS

117. Barnland, Dean C. *Public and Private Self in Japan and the United States: Communicative Styles of Two Cultures.* Tokyo: Simul Press, 1975.

    A preliminary report of studies investigating the character of interpersonal communication in Japan and the United States. Special emphasis is on the distinctiveness of Japanese patterns of interaction. Develops the notion that the "public self" and "private self" have unique relationships in both countries, and discusses the consequences of this idea. Examines national differences in communicative patterns in detail, including both verbal and nonverbal patterns, as well as defensive techniques favored when threatening interpersonal situations occur. Underlying the entire work is Barnlund's premise that the human personality and the social structure are interlocking systems.

118. Christopher, Robert C. *The Japanese Mind: The Goliath Explained.* New York: Linden Press/Simon & Schuster, 1983.

    A "psychic" and institutional guidebook to contemporary Japan, which looks at the following topics: the Japanese tribe, growing up Japanese, the social animal, work and power, and the future. Christopher believes that the way the United States deals with Japan in the decades ahead is likely to affect our national well-being greatly. He also has the conviction that the United States has not dealt very intelligently with Japan in recent years, and this is primarily because most Americans have very little understanding or knowledge of Japan.

119. Condon, John C. *With Respect to the Japanese, a Guide for Americans.* Yarmouth, Me.: Intercultural Press, 1984.

    Written primarily for American businesspeople living and working in Japan. Discusses Japanese values and behavior which affect communication, social and business relations, and management styles, and contrasts them with American values and characteristics. Recommendations are given on how to deal with the Japanese during face to face encounters.

120. Courdy, Jean-Claude. *The Japanese: Everyday Life in the Empire of the Rising Sun.* New York: Harper & Row, 1984.

   Observations of the Japanese by a French journalist who re-visited Japan after having lived there in the 1960s. Includes the author's perceptions of the Japanese, the dualities of the Japanese culture (the coexistence of myth and reality, tradition and modernism), the realities of the Japanese at home, in society, and in business. Also discusses the threats and challenges to Japan, among which are foreigners, the war, and democracy.

121. De Vos, George A. *Socialization for Achievement: Essays on the Cultural Psychology of the Japanese.* Berkeley: University of California Press, 1973.

   A collection of essays that discuss the relationship between the cultural psychology of the Japanese and the importance of the need for achievement and success. Also includes essays on failure and deviant behavior.

122. Doi, Takeo. *The Anatomy of Dependence.* Tokyo: Kodansha International, 1973.

   Explains the interpersonal relations aspect of Japanese organizational behavior in terms of the concept of "amae," or the feeling of dependence and the desire to be passively loved that infants have towards the mother. Doi argues that the Japanese prolong these feelings into adulthood and that they influence their relationships. On the personal level, the Japanese seek relationships that enable them to presume the goodwill of other people. Doi maintains that "amae" has far reaching effects on the life of the individual and on Japanese society.

123. ————. *The Anatomy of Self: The Individual Versus Society.* Tokyo: Kodansha International, 1986.

   Offers insights into the relationships between the study of psychology and culture, between language and mind, and between the Americans and the Japanese. Also explains the Japanese concepts of "omote" and "ura" in terms of Western ideas in order to find in them a universal significance.

124. Lebra, Takie Sugiyama. *Japanese Patterns of Behavior.* Honolulu: University Press of Hawaii, 1976.

   Looks at the beliefs and values generally shared by

the Japanese and shows how they place great importance on social interactions and relationships, and less emphasis on individuality. This cultural theme is used throughout the book as a means to understanding the way the Japanese interact with others and how they see themselves as individuals. Also discusses child rearing practices, selected features of deviant behavior, and therapy.

125. ———— and William P. Lebra, eds. *Japanese Culture and Behavior: Selected Readings*. Rev. ed. Honolulu: University of Hawaii Press, 1986.

The editors have completely revised their original work (1974) in response to the rapid changes taking place in contemporary Japanese culture, as well as to new developments in the social sciences. This edition presents a diversity of perspectives and topics from various disciplines, including anthropology, psychology, psychiatry, and linguistics. It is divided into four parts, an arrangement that reflects the theme of interrelationships between culture and behavior. Part One focuses on morality; Part Two presents patterns of interaction, communication, and grouping; Part Three addresses some aspects of child rearing and of adult training; and Part Four is concerned with pathology.

126. Lee, O-young. *Smaller Is Better: Japan's Mastery of the Miniature*. Tokyo: Kodansha International, 1984.

Analyzes the Japanese cultural principle of reductionism, in which objects and concepts are reduced to their bare essentials. Lee discusses some examples of this principle, among which are the folding fan and the No mask, as well as its manifestations in nature, society, and in contemporary technology. Lee also contrasts and compares Japan with the rest of Asia.

127. Mannari, Hiroshi and Harumi Befu, eds. *The Challenge of Japan's Internationalization: Organization and Culture*. Tokyo: Kodansha International, 1983.

Essays which present the research results and thoughts of various Japanese and Western scholars who attended an interdisciplinary conference at Kwansei Gakuin University, Japan, in 1981. They explore the phenomena of the internationalization of Japanese business, politics, industrial organization, culture, and personal character.

128. Minami, Hiroshi. *Psychology of the Japanese People.* Toronto: University of Toronto Press, 1971.

   Originally published in Japanese in 1953. Minami has written a new preface for this English edition in which he discusses the changes the Japanese mind has undergone since the book was first published, and he follows the themes described in the previous edition. These themes (viz., the Japanese self, the sense of happiness and of unhappiness, irrationalism and rationalism, spiritualism and physicality, and human relationships) are present here and are used to answer questions concerning the Japanese psychology as seen in historical perspective. Some examples of these questions are the kinds of negative functions premodern elements of the Japanese mentality performed in the modernization of Japan following World War II, and how much had modern elements been able to grow within the feudalistic society since the Meiji restoration.

129. Murakami, Yasusuke. "Ie Society As a Pattern of Civilization." *Journal of Japanese Studies* 10 (1984):281-363.

   An essay based on Murakami's book *Ie Society As a Pattern of Civilization* published in Japanese in 1979. An interdisciplinary analysis of the fundamental "ie" (or group oriented) form of Japanese social organization, which attempts to define and identify this characteristic of Japanese society and to examine its manifestations.

130. Ozaki, Robert S. *The Japanese: A Cultural Portrait.* Rutland, Vt.: Charles E. Tuttle, 1978.

   Ozaki states that this book is an unofficial guide to Japan and to the Japanese character, and that there is no guarantee of the accuracy of information or interpretation. It contains the author's views on Japanese culture, its development, and its characteristics. The approach is eclectic in that he has included whatever he found useful for his purposes.

131. Taylor, Jared. *Shadows of the Rising Sun: A Critical View of the "Japanese Miracle."* New York: William Morrow, 1983.

   A critical look behind the accomplishments of Japan, and at how the Japanese think and behave. Taylor states that the work concentrates on those aspects of Japan that the Japanese might be least eager to publicize.

The first part examines those elements of Japanese thinking that seem most different from that of the West, while the second part focuses on specific areas of contemporary Japanese life. Among the topics discussed are uniqueness; hierarchy; the group; conformity; reason, feeling, and religion; the corporation; sex and sex roles; culture and language; Japan at play; Japan and the world; and lessons for America. Taylor argues that although the Japanese have been very successful, they have not been successful in all the ways that matter, at least to the West. Many of their successes are based on what makes them different from Westerners and have been achieved at a psychological cost Westerners might not be willing to pay.

7. RELIGION

132. Bellah, Robert N. *Tokugawa Religion: The Cultural Roots of Modern Japan*. New York: Free Press, 1985.

Originally published in 1957. The text is the same as the previous edition, but a new subtitle has been used, and a new introduction included. Bellah applies a Weberian sociological perspective in his analysis of Japan's modernization process. He emphasizes the modernizing social and economic consequences of religious belief (Buddhism, Confucianism, and Shinto) and action of the Tokugawa period (1600-1868).

133. Davis, Winston. *Dojo: Magic and Exorcism in Modern Japan*. Stanford, Calif.: Stanford University Press, 1980.

Presents the True-Light Supra-Religious Organization (Sukyo Mahikari) gospel as it is preached, believed, and practiced in a provincial congregation in Japan. Mahikari is a new folk religion that is based on miracles and magic. Davis is concerned with how new religions, ideas, and behavior patterns become established in members' lives, how people change as a result of their participation in the sect, and how social, religious, and magical criteria determine status within the group. His ultimate goal is to relate the worldview of the sect to the cognitive orientation of the mainstream of Japanese society and therefore to arrive at a better understanding of the function of cognitive deviance in modern society. The word "dojo" that appears in the title refers to a building or place set aside for the purposes of exorcism of evil spirits and the performance of miracles.

134. Drummond, Richard Henry. *A History of Christianity in Japan*. Grand Rapids, Mich.: William B. Eerdmans, 1971.

   Surveys the history of the totality of Christianity in Japan: Roman Catholic, Protestant, and Orthodox, from the sixteenth century to the present. Drummond spent thirteen years in Japan as a Protestant missionary, and has incorporated his personal understanding along with the results of both Japanese and Western scholars and missionaries over the entire period of this study.

135. Earhart, H. Byron. *Japanese Religion: Unity and Diversity*. 3d ed. Belmont, Calif.: Wadsworth, 1982.

   A general history of Japanese religion and its dynamics, which offers an interpretation of persistent themes through three historical periods: (1) formative period (prehistoric to 710-84), (2) period of development and elaboration (794-1185 to 1568-1600), and (3) period of formalism and renewal (1600-1867 to the postwar era). Covers Shinto, Buddhism, Confucianism, Taoism, folk religion, Christianity, Tenrikyo, and Soka Gakkai. Includes an annotated bibliography.

136. ―――. *Religions of Japan: Many Traditions within One Sacred Way*. San Francisco: Harper & Row, 1984.

   An introduction to Japanese religion within a historical-cultural context. Earhart explains the major traditions and objects of worship; interprets Japanese concepts of worship reflected in views on society, space, time, and human life; and assesses the general world view created by the individual traditions taken as a whole.

137. Hardacre, Helen. *Lay Buddhism in Contemporary Japan: Reiyukai Kyodan*. Princeton, N.J.: Princeton University Press, 1984.

   Reiyukai Kyodan (the Society of the Friends of the Spirits), which is derived from the Buddhist tradition, is one of the largest and most vital of Japan's new religions. Hardacre analyzes Reiyukai ancestor worship and veneration of the Lotus Sutra. Also included here are chapters on the history of Reiyukai, its contemporary activities and organization, its relationship with the family, the role of women, and ritual, witnessing, and healing.

138. Japan. Agency for Cultural Affairs. *Japanese Religion: A Survey*. Tokyo: Kodansha International, 1972.

    Describes the various religions and major religious organizations in Japan. Includes statistical tables.

139. Morioka, Kiyomi. *Religion in Changing Japanese Society*. Tokyo: University of Tokyo Press, 1975.

    A collection of research reports and theoretical papers concerning the changes religion is undergoing in contemporary Japan. Arranged under three headings that represent the major streams of religion: folk religion and Shinto, Buddhism, and Christianity. Morioka analyzes these religions in terms of the effects that the enormous population shifts and changes in the traditional structure of the family since World War II have had on their social foundations.

140. Murakami, Shigeyoshi. *Japanese Religion in the Modern Century*. Tokyo: University of Tokyo Press, 1980.

    Explores the relationship between modern religion and social, economic and political conditions from the Meiji Restoration (1868) to the 1970s. Looks at the effects of these conditions on religion and the impact of religion on them.

141. Picken, Stuart D.B. *Shinto: Japan's Spiritual Roots*. Tokyo: Kodansha International, 1980.

    Shinto has run persistently through Japan's history from its beginnings up to the present, and has consistently influenced the attitudes of the Japanese towards life and the world around them. It has no clear philosophy or ethics, but it expresses an attitude of joyful acceptance of life and a feeling of closeness to nature. It pervades the sophisticated, highly developed society of contemporary Japan, yet has remained unchanged from its beginnings. In this well illustrated book, the image of Shinto is conveyed as the living spiritual root of the Japanese. It identifies what is unmistakably Shinto, and detects some of its influences both in obvious and less obvious places.

142. Powles, Cyril. "'Yasukuni Jinja Hoan': Religion and Politics in Contemporary Japan." *Pacific Affairs* 49 (1976):491-505.

   Powles argues that the attempts to re-establish the Yasukuni Shrine, which honors those who died in World War II for the Emperor's cause, represents one aspect of a large-scale drift on the part of Japan's ruling elites back toward the emperor-centered authoritarian society that existed before 1945. Between 1969 and 1974 they introduced into the Diet a bill for the national re-establishment of the Shrine, but had to withdraw it each time because of public opposition. Religion has traditionally been a powerful reinforcer of politics in Japan, and has tended to legitimate the authority of existing regimes, and at the pinnacle of the religio-political establishment is the sacred institution of the imperial household.

143. White, James W. *The Sokagakkai and Mass Society*. Stanford, Calif.: Stanford University Press, 1970.

   A study of the membership and ideology of the Sokagakkai, which is a militant and nationalistic religious movement in Japan. Discusses its political significance as well, since it is also a strong political party.

8. SOCIAL CONDITIONS

144. Austin, Lewis, ed. *Japan: The Paradox of Progress*. New Haven: Yale University Press, 1976.

   Papers from a seminar held at Yale University in 1983 that deal with the paradoxical relationship between tradition and social change. The ultimate concern of the contributors is to point to some of the interlocking consequences, direct and longer term, of action and inaction within a framework of political, economic, and sociocultural parameters.

145. Edelstein, Alex S., John E. Bowes and Sheldon M. Harsel, eds. *Information Societies: Comparing the Japanese and American Experiences*. Seattle: International Communication Center, School of Communications, University of Washington, 1978.

   Consists of papers delivered at a conference which was sponsored jointly by the School of Communications of the University of Washington and the Battelle Seminars and Studies Program in Seattle. Focus is on communication policies, policymaking, and on research of mutual concern to both Japan and the United States. The volume is organized into five major sections: Part One is devoted to national policies and international cooperation; Part Two deals with development and functioning of information societies; Part Three addresses communication problems in information societies; Part Four is concerned with challenges of policy and comparative research; and Part Five consists of rapporteurs' commentaries.

146. Fodella, Gianni, ed. *Social Structures and Economic Dynamics in Japan up to 1980*. Milano: Universita Bocconi, 1975.

   A collection of papers by sociologists, historians, economists, political scientists, writers, and government officials presented at an international symposium in Milan in 1974, on the future changes in Japan's socioeconomic system up to 1980. Discusses the following aspects: family, labor, society, domestic economy, and external economy.

147. Fukutake, Tadashi. *The Japanese Social Structure: Its Evolution in the Modern Century*. Tokyo: University of Tokyo Press, 1982.

   Concerned with changes in the nature of Japanese society from prewar to contemporary times that have resulted from modernization and democratization. Begins with the modernization process in the prewar period from 1868, a period characterized by peasant households and family enterprises in both manufacturing and commerce, and by the importance of the family, the village, and the urban neighborhood. Following this, discussion centers on change in postwar society, on the democratization process, industrialization, urbanization, on changes in the agrarian employment structures, and on the development of mass society. Finally, Fukutake analyzes contemporary Japanese society, the product of all this social change, and looks at the stratification system, politics, economic and social development, social security and social welfare, and future problems facing Japanese society.

148. ―――. *Japanese Society Today*. 2d ed. Tokyo: University of Tokyo Press, 1981.

   Fukutake contends that in its attempts to become a modern, industrial society, Japan has achieved impressive economic goals at the expense of social development. He examines the severe problems with which Japanese society is faced, with reference to structure, the family, rural and urban society, industrialization, mass society, social problems and development, and the future of Japanese society.

149. Fuse, Toyomasa, ed. *Modernization and Stress in Japan*. Leiden: E.J. Brill, 1975.

   Collected essays written by scholars in the fields of history, political science, and sociology, which discuss the process and some specific cases of stress and tension in contemporary Japanese society resulting from Japan's modernization experience. Among the topics covered here are roots of Japan's modernization experience, economic development, relations with Asia, protest and the political system, and tradition and modernity.

150. Hane, Mikiso. *Peasants, Rebels and Outcastes: The Underside of Modern Japan*. New York: Pantheon Books, 1982.

   Hane reviews the lives and thoughts of the rural populace and the poor, who came out of the villages to enter the mines, factories, and brothels. Much of the information is based on personal testimony, eyewitness accounts, memoirs, diaries, and individual recollections gathered by Japanese social scientists. Covers the period from the beginning of the Meiji era (1868) to the outbreak of war in the Pacific.

151. Iga, Mamoru. *The Thorn in the Chrysanthemum: Suicide and Economic Success in Modern Japan*. Berkeley: University of California Press, 1986.

   A comprehensive analysis of the contributions of social structure and national character to success and suicide in Japan.

152. Ishida, Takeshi. *Japanese Political Culture: Change and Continuity*. New Brunswick, N.J.: Transaction Books, 1983.

   A collection of articles by Ishida that emphasize continuity and change in modern Japan. Focus is on the value system and organizational structure. Part One delineates continuity and change in modern Japan. Part Two presents case studies that shed light on various aspects of modern Japan in comparative perspective. Part Three is devoted to essays on peace research.

153. ———. *Japanese Society.* New York: Random House, 1971.

   Considers how the two sides of Japanese society (viz., rapid economic development, and the "miserable" circumstances under which the individual lives) are able to coexist and how they have been reconciled. Looks at those features of Japanese society that have prevailed in prewar, postwar, and contemporary Japan.

154. Kinmonth, Earl H. *The Self-Made Man in Meiji Japanese Thought: From Samurai to Salary Man.* Berkeley: University of California Press, 1981.

   The author contends that the ethos, institutions, and status of the contemporary Japanese white-collar worker, or salaryman ("saraiiman"), are the products of nineteenth century developments. He describes the changes that occurred as the ideal of self-advancement through education and salaried employment spread from its samurai origins to the general populace, a development which led to the emergence of Japan's new middle class.

155. Kirkpatrick, Maurine A. "Consumerism and Japan's New Citizen Politics." *Asian Survey* 15 (1975):234-246.

   Examines the origins and character of the new interest in consumer interest activism and its relation to the current popular search for a new form of citizen power.

156. Koschmann, J. Victor, ed. *Authority and the Individual in Japan: Citizen Protest in Historical Perspective.* Tokyo: University of Tokyo Press, 1978.

   Essays written by contemporary Japanese intellectuals on the criticism of authority and protest movements from prewar to postwar Japan. Emphasis is on the relationship between individuals and authority. Consists of two parts. Part One deals with the individual as subject in prewar Japan. Part Two is concerned with the individual as citizen in postwar Japan.

157. Koyano, Shogo. "Sociological Studies in Japan: Prewar, Postwar and Contemporary Stages." *Current Sociology* 24 (1976):7-208.

   A description of studies of Japanese society conducted by Japanese sociologists with emphasis on fact finding research on social problems and theoretical studies directly related to it. Does not include the fields of educational sociology, sociology of law, or social psychology.

158. Krauss, Ellis S., Thomas P. Rohlen and Patricia G. Steinhoff, eds. *Conflict in Japan*. Honolulu: University of Hawaii Press, 1984.

   Essays by sociologists, anthropologists, and political scientists that are concerned with the sources of social and political conflict in postwar Japan and on the ways in which conflict is expressed and managed. This conflict approach is applied to studies of the major institutions of Japanese society: family, village, school, workplace, bureaucracy, and to studies of the relations between institutions and organized groups in the political process.

159. Masatsugu, Mitsuyuki. *The Modern Samurai Society: Duty and Dependence in Contemporary Japan*. New York: AMACOM, 1982.

   A brief review of Japanese culture and management development, written by a consultant. Discusses the characteristics of the Japanese culture, based on short historical notes, as well as psychological and sociological concepts related to individual behavior and personal interactions. Also examines quality control of human resources, the company man, and Japanese leadership.

160. Morley, James William, ed. *Prologue to the Future: The United States and Japan in the Postindustrial Age*. Lexington, Mass.: Lexington Books, 1974.

   Papers written by Japanese and American economists, political scientists, sociologists, philosophers, and communications experts that speculate on Japan and the United States as the world's first postindustrial societies. Changes and problems related to this new stage of history are discussed, where information and intelligence will play the key role in production rather than labor and capital, and the educated person will be the focus of social life and leadership. The following areas are included as topics of discussion: the economy, politics, the city, and information.

161. Nakane, Chie. *Japanese Society*. Berkeley: University of California Press, 1972.

   A structural analysis of Japanese group organization, in which the basis of discussion is Nakane's vertical principle theory. According to this theory, the most characteristic feature of Japanese social organization arises from the single bond in social relationships; an individual or a group always has one single distinctive relation to the other, which is in contrast to that of caste or class societies. This basic social relationship reveals the core of the vertical structure principle, in which an intricate hierarchical order of ranking takes place, based on seniority. Examines the following topics: criteria of group formation, the internal structure of the group, the overall structure of Japanese society, and characteristics and value orientation of the Japanese.

162. Organisation for Economic Co-operation and Development. *Towards an Integrated Social Policy in Japan.* Paris, 1977.

    A report that presents the views of the Japanese government and its role in the development and coordination of social policies. Addresses the following issues: the background of social policy, the present state of social policy integration, and analysis and evaluation of social policy.

163. Palmore, Erdman B. *The Honorable Elders: A Cross-Cultural Analysis of Aging in Japan.* Durham, N.C.: Duke University Press, 1975.

    Addresses the question of the extent to which traditional respect for the aged continues in Japan's modern industrial society. Using both quantitative and nonquantitative methods, Palmore analyzes the present status and social integration of the aged.

164. ———— and Daisaku Maeda. *The Honorable Elders Revisited: A Revised Cross-Cultural Analysis of Aging in Japan.* Durham, N.C.: Duke University Press, 1985.

    A revision of Palmore's *The Honorable Elders: A Cross-Cultural Analysis of Aging in Japan* (1975). Compares the differences in the social status of the aged in Japan, the United States, Great Britain, and France by means of both quantitative and qualitative methods.

165. Plath, David W. "'Ecstasy Years'--Old Age in Japan." *Pacific Affairs* 46 (1973):421-429.

    Discusses newfound concern with the problems and needs of the aging in Japan. Among the factors contributing to this concern are compulsory retirement at age fifty-five in most Japanese enterprises, austere pensions and old-age benefits, and increased life-expectancy.

166. Smith, Robert J. *Ancestor Worship in Contemporary Japan*. Stanford, Calif.: Stanford University Press, 1974.

    Examines the history and contemporary status of ancestor worship. The conjugal family is replacing the household as the primary domestic unit, and this has affected ancestor worship as the household has been the center of ancestral rites for centuries. Many conjugal families are not obligated to the ancestors on the bases of inheritance of property or of extensive co-residence as the household members were. Also discussed is the nature of various spirits, ghosts, and gods.

167. ─────. *Japanese Society: Tradition, Self, and the Social Order*. Cambridge: Cambridge University Press, 1985.

    Smith views Japan's complex industrial society as being unique from the Western world because of its fundamentally different historical and cultural traditions. Failure to understand these differences has led to misinterpretations of Japanese society and culture.

168. Steven, Rob. *Classes in Contemporary Japan*. Cambridge: Cambridge University Press, 1983.

    Analyzes the structure and composition of the various social classes and their relationships with capitalism. Also discusses the possibilities of revolutionary social change.

169. Tsurumi, Kazuko. *Social Change and the Individual: Japan Before and After Defeat in World War II*. Princeton, N.J.: Princeton University Press, 1970.

    Examines the relationship between societal change (viz., modernization) and its resulting effects on the values and attitudes of individuals.

170. Vogel, Ezra F. *Japan As Number 1: Lessons for America*. New York: Harper & row, 1980.

    Vogel discusses the factors responsible for Japan's success in achieving economic productivity, high educational and health standards, and crime control. He considers these factors as potential models that America

could emulate in order to adapt more successfully to
the postindustrial age.

171. ―――. *Japan's New Middle Class: The Salary Man and
His Family in a Tokyo Suburb.* 2d ed. Berkeley: University of California Press, 1971.

A study of white collar employees of large business
corporations and government bureaucracies and their families. Based on field research done in Japan from 1958
to 1960.

9. WOMEN

172. Cook, Alice H. and Hiroko Hayashi. *Working Women in
Japan: Discrimination, Resistance, and Reform.* Ithaca,
N.Y.: New York State School of Labor and Industrial
Relations, Cornell University, 1980.

Cook and Hayashi contend that the practice of permanent
employment and seniority wages has created an employment
system that is more discriminatory towards women than
those of other industrialized countries. Examines the
relevance of court cases relating to equal pay, retirement policies, job transfer, and maternity leave.

173. Jones, H.J. "Japanese Women and Party Politics." *Pacific Affairs* 49 (1976):213-234.

Explores, within a social context, the position of
Japanese women in the politics of the seventies. Although there has been a gradual increase of women participating in the Citizens Movement, the number of women
entering and remaining in politics is still small.

174. ―――. "Japanese Women and the Dual-Track Employment
System." *Pacific Affairs* 49 (1976-77):589-606.

Jones maintains that a sex based dual-track employment
system persists in all areas of employment in postwar
Japan, despite legal reforms and denouncement of discrimination on the basis of sex. This system is characterized by the short-term employment of primarily women
who do not have security or welfare benefits, and by
the lifetime employment system for males which is made
possible since women can be hired on a short-term basis
to bolster the labor force when necessary. During child
rearing years women drop out or are pushed out of the
labor market and they return in their forties, to part-

time work. In addition, women's wages are less than those of men, on the whole.

175. ———. "Japanese Women in the Politics of the Seventies." *Asian Survey* 15 (1975):708-723.

   Examines the Public Opinion Survey of the Women's Vote in the 33rd General Election (1972), in which the following suggestions are made: (1) elections are not just for parties, (2) sex appeal of male candidates is no longer relevant, (3) policy and issues are alive, (4) the women's vote is severing family kinship ties, and (5) there may be political potential in "my-homeism."

176. Keller, Sherry Yajima. "Sex Discrimination in Employment: The Legal Status of the Working Woman in Japan." *Loyola of Los Angeles International and Comparative Law Annual* 3 (1980):83-97.

   The author argues that the employment system has changed very little over the years, despite the postwar reforms that gave women the right to equality. Discriminatory employment practices are still prevalent in contemporary Japan. In addition, women seldom turn to the legal system for assistance. Keller looks at the role of the courts in Japan together with the Japanese culture in order to provide a better understanding of the many obstacles the Japanese woman faces in her struggle for equality.

177. Lebra, Joyce, Joy Paulson and Elizabeth Powers, eds. *Women in Changing Japan.* Boulder, Colo.: Westview Press, 1976.

   Collected essays that address the issue of the degree to which women in contemporary Japan are departing from the traditional feminine ideal, an ideal that prescribed a domestic, subordinate, and often subservient role. The essays are the result of both extensive research and interviews with women in the following occupational categories: housewife, office woman, factory worker, service industry worker, professional woman, women in the media, and women in politics.

178. Lebra, Takie Sugiyama. *Japanese Women: Constraint and Fulfillment.* Honolulu: University of Hawaii Press, 1984.

   Based on the results of fieldwork done by the author in Japan. The primary source of data consists of life histories given by Japanese women. Among the topics covered are marriage, motherhood, careers, and later years.

179. Nishikawa, Shunsaku and Yoshio Higuchi. "Determinants of Female Labor-Force Participation." *Japanese Economic Studies* 9 (1980-81):62-87.

    Discusses the reasons for the increase in the female labor force participation rate between 1976 and 1978; until 1975 it had been in continuous decline for more than a half century. Also questions the possibilities of the continuation of this increase for the immediately foreseeable future.

180. Pharr, Susan J. "Women in Japan Today." *Current History* 68 (1975):174-184.

    Looks at the impact the legal guarantees of full political rights and equality of the postwar period have had on women. Focus is on education, employment, marriage, and political activity. Also examines their impact on customs and traditional ways of thinking.

181. Robins-Mowry, Dorothy. *The Hidden Sun: Women of Modern Japan.* Boulder, Colo.: Westview Press, 1983.

    The author focuses on the effort of women leaders in the development of a more coherent and self-respecting role for women in modern Japan from the 1870s to the 1980s. Japanese women's attitudes and activities and their effect on women, society and Japan's policies are studied, as well as the influence of women and how they exert it.

III
SCIENCE, TECHNOLOGY, AND ENVIRONMENT

A. SCIENCE

182. Anderson, Alun M. *Science and Technology in Japan.* Harlow, Essex, UK: Longman, 1984.

    A guide to the major research programs going on in Japan. Provides a detailed directory of the research institutes, universities, and industrial companies where they are being carried out. Also contains a comprehensive description of the major cooperative research ventures between the Japanese government and private industry.

183. Nakayama, Shigeru, David L. Swain and Yagi Eri, eds. *Science and Society in Modern Japan: Selected Historical Sources.* Cambridge, Mass.: MIT Press, 1974.

    A collection of papers considered as being representative of the main areas of concern among Japanese science historians. They are also considered typical of the varied interests in and approaches to the relations of science and society among those most active in this field during the last few decades. Divided into three parts. The first part is concerned with emergent ideologies of science; the second part deals with exploratory research concerns; and the third part discusses Japanese scientists and their social context. Includes an annotated bibliography of English language works on the social history of modern Japanese science.

B. TECHNOLOGY

184. Buzbee, B.L., R.H. Ewald and W.J. Worlton. "Japanese Supercomputer Technology." *Science* 218 (1982):1189-1193.

    To meet the foreseeable domestic need for large-scale computing capabilities for nuclear fusion, image analysis, and other areas, Japan has begun an ambitious program to advance supercomputer technology. Concepts of national projects are being used to advance this development, and one such project is the National Superspeed Computer Project. The authors discuss this project and also comment on the Fifth-Generation Computer Project. They also describe some of the implications of these projects, which are under the auspices of MITI (Ministry for International Trade and Industry), for the United States.

185. Holden, Constance. "Innovation: Japan Races Ahead as U.S. Falters." *Science* 210 (1980):751-754.

    Discusses the reasons for Japan's success in the high technology sector. Among the reasons included are the following: national industrial policy, well coordinated government policies that affect industry, management strategies of long-range planning and quality control, emphasis on quality control, a national dedication to economic growth, and an ability to absorb and improve foreign technologies. The U.S. is lagging behind Japan in industrial productivity and innovation, and Holden suggests that perhaps the U.S. should learn and adapt from the Japanese, just as the Japanese once learned so much from the U.S.

186. Lynn, Leonard H. "Japanese Technology at a Turning Point." *Current History* 84 (1985):418-432.

    In spite of its technological strength, Lynn states that Japan continues to spend much more to purchase foreign technology than it receives for the sale of its own technology. In addition, the image persists (even in Japan) that the Japanese are better able to copy than to create technology. Lynn addresses the factors responsible for these problems.

187. ─────────. "Japanese Technology: Successes and Strategies." *Current History* 82 (1983):366-390.

    Probes the reasons behind Japan's technological successes, among which are the following: the Japanese ability to find out about technological developments so effectively, and their talents in using new production technologies quickly, such as robots.

188. Moritani, Masanori. *Japanese Technology: Getting the Best for the Least.* Tokyo: Simul Press, 1982.

   Masanori attempts to track down, from a comparative technology perspective, the secret behind Japan's ability to produce outstanding industrial products at very low cost. He stresses the positive aspects and strengths of Japan's technological environment and points out the problems of Europe and the United States.

C. ENVIRONMENT

189. Hibino, Kazuyuki. "Tokyo: The Overpopulated Megalopolis." *Japan Quarterly* 20 (1973):203-212.

   The negative effects of Japan's rapid economic growth on Tokyo are discussed, among which are overcrowding and environmental pollution.

190. Huddle, Norie and Michael Reich. *Island of Dreams: Environmental Crisis in Japan.* New York: Autumn Press, 1975.

   Examines the environmental problems which have been caused by Japan's economic success. The authors state that Japan's experiences should serve as a warning to other highly industrialized countries, and that it will be necessary to develop a global effort for ecological survival, which will require a strictly monitored international consensus. There is a 1987 edition, which was not available for examination.

191. Organisation for Economic Co-operation and Development. *Environmental Policies in Japan.* Paris, 1977.

   Concentrates on the pollution control aspect of Japan's environmental policies. Investigates four main themes: (1) setting of standards, (2) compensation, (3) control of the location of industrial projects, and (4) economic consequences.

192. ———. Group on Urban Affairs. *Urban Policies in Japan: A review by the OECD Group on Urban Affairs Undertaken in 1984/5 at the Request of the Government of Japan.* Paris, 1986.

Focuses on those aspects of Japanese urban policy considered to be of particular interest to other OECD countries. Includes the following aspects: balanced development, the rational use of land, housing and urban revitalization, provision and financing of urban infrastructure, and the environment in urban areas. The report has four objectives: (1) to describe the urban situation, policies and prospects; (2) to provide an evaluation of urban policies; (3) to assist the Japanese government by making urban policy recommendations; and (4) to assist other OECD countries by identifying comparisons with their own urban trends and policies.

193. Ui, Jun. "The Singularities of Japanese Pollution." *Japan Quarterly* 19 (1972): 281-291.

Analyzes the factors responsible for Japan's severe environmental pollution problem. According to Ui, the major factors are the development of Japanese capitalism and industry, and resistance and obstruction to solving the problem.

194. White, James W. *Political Implications of Cityward Migration: Japan As an Exploratory Test Case.* Beverly Hills, Calif.: Sage Publications, 1973.

Report of a study of the effects of urbanization and modernization on urban migrants in the city of Uji, a suburb of Kyoto, which was conducted in 1962.

195. ——— and Frank Munger, eds. *Social Change and Community Politics in Urban Japan.* Chapel Hill: Institute for Research in Social Science, University of North Carolina at Chapel Hill, 1976.

Papers that address some of the questions that arise from city size and density, with emphasis on social and community politics. Includes chapters on the following areas: leadership, sociability and social change in a white-collar apartment complex, the impact of rapid urban change on neighborhood solidarity, citizens' protest movements in urban and rural Japan, and social change and community involvement in metropolitan Japan.

IV
LAW AND POLITICS

A. LAW

196. Beer, Lawrence Ward and Hidenori Tomatsu. "A Guide to the Study of Japanese Law." *American Journal of Comparative Law* 23 (1975):284-324.

An introductory guide that provides information on the academic field of Japanese law and information that will assist in the acquisition of basic knowledge and in the conduct of research. It suggests where additional information and the necessary Japanese language materials in both Japan and the United States can be found. Includes an annotated bibliography of source materials.

197. Benjamin, Roger W. "Images of Conflict Resolution and Social Control: American and Japanese Attitudes Toward the Adversary System." *Journal of Conflict Resolution* 19 (1975):123-137.

Benjamin examines the question of whether cross-national differences in images and assumptions about conflict resolution and social control inhibit international conflict resolution of important political, economic and military matters. He presents an ideal type model of conflict resolution and social control in Japan and the United States in one area, the legal system, and presents data on the question developed from a comparative study of the Tokyo and Minnesota district courts.

198. Fujita, Yasuhiro. "Procedural Fairness to Foreign Litigants As Stressed by Japanese Courts." *International Lawyer* 12 (1978):795-811.

In dealing with international litigation, Fujita contends, Japanese judges have often tried to interpret the law very liberally so as to ensure procedural fairness and substantial justice to foreign litigants. He also maintains that Japanese judges have paid due consideration to the protection of aliens in court in the area of procedural law, sometimes in contradiction to the code and statutory provisions.

199. Haley, John Owen. "Sheathing the Sword of Justice in Japan: An Essay on Law Without Sanctions." *Journal of Japanese Studies* 8 (1982):265-281.

   A discussion of the weak formal law enforcement aspects of Japan's legal system, which results in strong group and community cohesion and the endurance of patron-client relationships through which individuals receive the security and protection the law is unable to provide. In addition, community consensus and sanctions function as extralegal substitutes in the maintenance of social control.

200. *Law in Japan: An Annual* 1 (1967)-   . Tokyo: Faculty of Law, University of Tokyo.

   Consists of articles on various aspects of Japanese law. The articles are translations that have appeared previously in other publications. The 1975 special issue consists of *An Index to Japanese Law: A Bibliography of Western Language Materials, 1867-1973*, compiled by Rex Coleman and John Owen Haley. The 1978 issue contains "Index to Japanese Law," Supplement no. 5, by Matthias Scheer.

201. Noda, Yosiyuki. *Introduction to Japanese Law*. Tokyo: University of Tokyo Press, 1976.

   A general survey of the subject. Includes discussion of the following topics: legal history, Western law, government organization, the legal profession in Japan, Japanese and the law, and sources of law (viz., legislation, custom cases and legal theory).

202. Stevens, Charles R. "Japanese Law and the Japanese Legal System: Perspectives for the American Business Lawyer." *Business Lawyer* 27 (1972):1259-1273.

   A synopsis written for the American business lawyer involved with Japanese legal matters. Includes a brief history of Japanese law, the sources of law, administrative guidance, the judicial system, and the legal profession.

203. ———. "Modern Japanese Law as an Instrument of Comparison." *American Journal of Comparative Law*. 19 (1971):665-684.

Stevens contends that the teaching of Japanese law as an instrument of comparison should be included in American law school curricula. He presents three reasons for his contention. The first is that Japanese law is a blend of the civil law system, American law, and Japanese characteristics, and therefore is of interest to comparativists. The second reason is the Japanese law is a developing legal system in the process of dynamic change. And the third reason is the commercial importance of Japan.

204. Tanaka, Hideo, ed. *The Japanese Legal System: Introductory Cases and Materials*. Tokyo: University of Tokyo Press, 1976.

An introduction to the general structure of Japanese law. Consists of cases and articles that illustrate the various areas of the law. The following topics are included: outline of the constitutional and legal system, legal process, development of Japanese law since 1867, role of law and lawyers in Japanese society, courts and procedure, the legal profession, constitutional history since 1867, judicial review, the "Renunciation of War" clause, constitutional guarantee of human rights, and research in Japanese legal materials.

1. ANTITRUST LAW

205. Hadley, Eleanor M. *Antitrust in Japan*. Princeton, N.J.: Princeton University Press, 1970.

A study of monopolies and antitrust law from the Occupation to 1970. Divided into two parts: Part One discusses what was done during the Occupation toward breaking up concentrated businesses and the reasons for doing so, and Part Two analyzes the contemporary scene in Japan.

206. Higgins, Mary Faith. "Japanese Fair Trade Commission Review of International Agreements." *Loyola of Los Angeles International and Comparative Law Annual* 3 (1980):43-66.

Addresses a few of the most common problems encountered under the Antimonopoly Act in international license and distributorship agreements with Japanese parties. The Act requires that all international agreements be submitted to the Japanese Fair Trade Commission (FTC) for review within thirty days of conclusion, and the Commission has the option of raising objections with which the parties involved then have to deal.

207. Hildebrand, James L. and Mitsuo Matsushita. "Antimonopoly Law of Japan--Potential Consequences of International Contract Violations under Article 6." *New York University Journal of International Law & Politics* 6 (1973):215-243.

    A brief analysis of the potential legal effects and consequences of the Antimonopoly Law of Japan. Emphasis is on Article 6, which prohibits the conclusion of an international agreement or contract containing provisions deemed to constitute an "unreasonable restraint of trade or unfair business practice." The Article also requires an entrepreneur who has entered into an international agreement or contract to file a report with the Japanese Fair Trade Commission (FTC) within thirty days after the date of its formation.

208. Iyori, Hiroshi and Akinori Uesugi. *The Antimonopoly Laws of Japan*. 2d ed. New York: Federal Legal Publications, 1983.

    Provides insight into the history, development and structure of Japan's contemporary antimonopoly jurisprudence. Among the topics covered are history of the policies concerning cartels and monopolies, the Antimonopoly Act as amended, exemption laws, and statistics. The appendix includes the text of various antimonopoly acts.

209. Matsushita, Mitsuo. "Export Control and Export Cartels in Japan." *Harvard International Law Journal* 20 (1979):103-125.

    Examines the legal regulation of exports through the Control Law, through export cartels created under the Transactions Law, and through the maintenance of fair competition in exporting under the Antimonopoly Law.

210. ———— and James L. Hildebrand. "Antimonopoly Law of Japan Relating to International Business Transactions." *Case Western Reserve Journal of International Law* 4 (1972):124-160.

    A general introduction to the Antimonopoly Law of

Japan. Describes its general structure and the related enforcement agencies, and clarifies certain aspects of the law that are relevant to Japan-United States business transactions. Among the relevant aspects are the licensing of patents and technology, the acquisition and control of Japanese business enterprises, and the utilization of distribution agreements.

211. Ramseyer, J. Mark. "The Costs of the Consensual Myth: Antitrust Enforcement and Institutional Barriers to Litigation in Japan. *Yale Law Journal* 94 (1985):604-645.

Ramseyer contends that there are few lawyers and lawsuits in Japan because of institutional barriers to litigation. He approaches antitrust law as a case study in the role of litigation in Japan. The role of private litigation in deterring illegal behavior is summarized and the relation between cultural attitudes toward litigation and institutional barriers to the use of the courts is described. The American and Japanese frameworks for private antitrust litigation are compared and the various antitrust damage actions in Japan to date are analyzed. In addition, the major institutional barriers to such suits are outlined and discussed with reference to their implications for the distribution of power and wealth in Japanese society. Ramseyer argues that the barriers have eliminated virtually all deterrents to cartelization in Japan, and that the barriers to antitrust suits are examples of barriers to litigation that have helped to reinforce a nonlitigious ethos and have thereby played an important part in assuring the continued legitimacy of bureaucratic rule.

212. ———. "Japanese Antitrust Enforcement after the Oil Embargo." *American Journal of Comparative Law* 31 (1983):395-430.

Summarizes the handling by Japan's leading appellate court in economic litigation in 1980 of the oil embargo criminal antitrust case in which twelve oil companies were convicted of criminal antitrust violations, and fourteen of their top executives were sentenced to prison. The defendants had acted as they did only after obtaining the approval of MITI (Ministry of International Trade and Industry). Also traces the implications of the decisions for criminal and civil liability.

213. "Trustbusting in Japan: Cartels and Government-Business Cooperation." *Harvard Law Review* 94 (1981):1064-1084.

   Traces the postwar development of Japanese antitrust enforcement, and analyzes the effects of the Japanese High Court's conviction decision in the 1980 Oil Cartel Criminal Case on the future of the relationship between MITI (Ministry of International Trade and Industry) and the business community.

214. Tsuji, Yoshihiko. "Regulation of Resale Price Maintenance in Japan." *New York Law Forum* 18 (1972):397-410.

   Discusses Japanese policy toward resale price maintenance. The Antimonopoly Act, whose laws are enforced by the Fair Trade Commission (FTC), makes almost all resale price maintenance illegal.

2. CIVIL LIBERTIES AND CIVIL PROCEDURE

215. Beer, Lawrence Ward. *Freedom of Expression in Japan: A Study in Comparative Law, Politics, and Society.* Tokyo: Kodansha International, 1984.

   Beer analyzes the status of civil liberties in Japanese law, society and politics. He discusses some aspects of the history of freedom in contemporary Japan, some relevant patterns of social thought and behavior, official and unofficial regulatory systems and norms, and judicial decisions, and the views of Japanese legal scholars are referred to. In addition, comparisons are made with other democracies and with authoritarian systems.

216. Hattori, Takaaki and Dan Fenno Henderson. *Civil Procedure in Japan.* New York: M. Bender, 1983-

   Presents Japanese procedures for civil dispute resolution, which involves means other than litigation as well. Japanese civil procedure is based, to a large extent, on German civil procedure, and therefore presents a unique opportunity for studying the requirements and problems involved in the importation of foreign procedural institutions. Includes a discussion of the history, the political organization, and the history of Japanese civil procedure, as well as its authoritative sources. The work is in loose-leaf format and is updated when necessary.

3. COMMERCIAL LAW

217. Foster, Mark Edward. "Analysis of the Newly Amended Commercial Code of Japan." *Case Western Reserve Journal of International Law* 15 (1983):587-600.

    On October 1, 1982, the most extensive revisions ever made to the Japanese Commercial Code went into effect. Extensive amendments to its key sections, namely the sections on corporate shares, shareholders, directors, accounting, and auditing, have been made. Foster compares the pre-amendment and the new Code revisions in order that the significance of the new provisions can be effectively summarized.

218. Fujita, Yasuhiro. "Japanese Regulation of Foreign Transactions and Private-Law Consequences." *New York Law Forum* 18 (1972):317-353.

    Examines Japanese case law that deals with the private-law consequences of statutory violations of government regulations (public law) of foreign transactions. Among the government regulations are the Control Law, the Foreign Investment Law, the Antimonopoly Law, and foreign corporations law.

219. Goldsmith, Scott K. "Japanese Business Entities." *Case Western Reserve Journal of International Law* 6 (1974): 257-278.

    Delineates the essential features of Japanese business organization available to foreign enterprise. Goldsmith advises that choice of the appropriate form of business organization by a foreign business is usually a matter for consultation with Japanese lawyers experienced in Japanese labor and commercial law. The laws of Japan permit the United States business person to do business there in several forms, among which are licensing and royalty arrangements, export operations to Japan, and temporary operations in Japan. In addition, business relations may be established through the utilization of a branch of an organization formed under foreign law or through the formation of one or more of several types of qualifying business entities recognized under Japanese law.

220. Hahn, Elliott J. *Japanese Business Law and the Legal System.* Westport, Conn.: Quorum Books, 1984.

    Written for those who need to learn more about the major areas of the Japanese business law system and how to work within it. Includes references to Japanese cultural, sociological, and economic dynamics. Among the topics discussed are lawyers, legal education, quasi-lawyers, the court system, negotiating with the Japanese, doing business in Japan and its legal aspects, the role of the government in the Japanese business law system, and antitrust.

221. Haley, John Owen, ed. *Current Legal Aspects of Doing Business in Japan and East Asia*. Chicago: American Bar Association, 1978.

   Primary emphasis is on recent developments and emerging areas of concern. Divided into ten sections. Section One deals with the changing political and economic context of trade and investment; Section Two contains articles on contrasting approaches toward law and the legal profession; Section Three is concerned with corporate structure; Section Four addresses antitrust regulation; Section Five is involved with securities regulation; Section Six covers litigation; Section Seven is concerned with taxation; Section Eight contains articles on pollution and land use controls; and Sections Nine and Ten involve legal aspects of doing business with Korea and Southeast Asia.

222. Hartman, F.L. "Japanese Foreign Investment Regulation: Semantics and Reality." *New York Law Forum* 18 (1972): 355-376.

   Hartman argues the premise that although efforts have been made to liberalize the Foreign Investment Law and other Japanese foreign investment policies, the scope of such liberalization remains to be seen. The government, largely through MITI (Ministry of International Trade and Industry), continues to control and screen private agreements for the investment of foreign capital in new and existing Japanese enterprises.

223. Hildebrand, James L. "Establishing a Joint Venture Company in Japan: Legal Considerations." *Case Western Reserve Journal of International Law* 6 (1974):199-236.

   A general introduction to certain legal considerations relating to the establishment of a joint venture company in Japan based on the conventional arrangements entered into between non-Japanese and Japanese corporations. Briefly outlined are the following: (1) the structure and documentation of a typical joint venture company in Japan established by a non-Japanese and Japanese corporation, (2) some of the more important Japanese government controls, and (3) the normal legal steps that must be taken in connection with the establishment of an equity joint venture in Japan.

224. Johnson, Mark S. "The Japanese Legal Milieu and Its Relationship to Business." *American Business Law Journal* 13 (1976):335-353.

Written for the American investor seeking to enter the Japanese business world. Explores the three major components of the Japanese legal legacy: the Japanese foundation, the European contribution, and the American addition. Also analyzes administrative guidance (viz., the Japanese way of guiding business) in terms of its definition, justification, function, and limitation. Also briefly points out the legal assistance available to foreigners wanting to do business in Japan.

225. King, Henry T., Jr. "Corporate Divorce--Japanese Style." *Case Western Reserve Journal of International Law* 6 (1974):250-255.

King offers his advice on terminating a joint venture in Japan for the American business person. He maintains that this raises special problems for the foreign investor, which are unique to Japan, and he discusses these problems as well.

226. *Legal Aspects of Doing Business with Japan, 1985.* New York: Practising Law Institute, 1985.

Originally distributed at a program sponsored by the Practising Law Institute, 1985, New York City. Contains articles on various related topics, including the Japanese financial system; alternatives for entering the Japanese market; corporate acquisitions; the tax system; dispute resolution; and new developments in the telecommunications industry. There is also a 1981 edition.

227. Matsumoto, Keiji. "Management Responsibility to Minority Shareholders in Japan: Derivative Suit in West-East Melting Pot." *New York Law Forum* 18 (1972):377-395.

Discusses the Japanese version of the derivative suit and the reasons why it is not used in Japan as it is in the United States. Also examines the historical, social, and financial aspects of the Japanese corporation and the legal system, with reference to the derivative suit.

228. McKinnon, Jill L. *The Historical Development and Operational Form of Corporate Reporting Regulation in Japan.* New York: Garland, 1986.

Originally issued as the author's dissertation, Macquarie University, 1984. The objective is to examine the historical development of the Japanese system of corporate reporting regulation from its formal inception in 1899, and environmental influences on the development and contemporary state of the system. Among the topics discussed are social environment and political, legal, and corporate systems in Japan; introduction to the commercial code; depression and war; the Allied Occupation; modification of the audit component; and the introduction of consolidated financial statements.

4. CONSTITUTIONAL LAW

229. Itoh, Hiroshi and Lawrence Ward Beer. *The Constitutional Case Law of Japan: Selected Supreme Court Decisions, 1961-70.* Seattle: University of Washington Press, 1978.

This may be considered a sequel to *Court and Constitution in Japan: Selected Supreme Court Decisions, 1948-60*, by John M. Maki (1964). It contains thirty-two Supreme Court cases that were selected according to one or more of the following guidelines: (1) a landmark decision, (2) considered legally, socially and/or politically important by specialists in Japan, and (3) of special interest to the foreign legal scholar and/or social scientist. It does not include commentary or analysis of the legal, socioeconomic or political significance of these decisions.

230. Kim, Chin. "Constitution and Obscenity: Japan and the U.S.A." *American Journal of Comparative Law* 23 (1975):255-283.

The Japanese Constitution of 1947 is very similar to the United States Constitution in many areas, including the Bill of Rights and judicial review clauses. However, the respective highest courts have taken different approaches in solving problems that have emerged in constitutional litigation. One example of this is the area of obscenity, which provides a basis for Japanese and American comparative jurisprudence. This article discusses and compares specific obscenity cases of both countries.

231. Maki, John M., ed. and trans. *Japan's Commission on the Constitution: The Final Report.* Seattle: University of Washington Press, 1980.

A selected translation of the final report of Japan's Commission on the Constitution, which held meetings from 1957 to 1964. During this period the Commission conducted a massive study of the Constitution of Japan, which came into effect on May 3, 1947. The following areas are covered: the establishment and organization of the Commission; its duties, organization, and operation; its investigations and deliberations; and the opinions of the Commission.

5. COURTS AND JUDICIAL SYSTEM

232. Bolz, Herbert F. "Judicial Review in Japan: The Strategy of Restraint." *Hastings International and Comparative Law Review* 4 (1980):88-142.

Concentrates on those social, historical, and political factors that have impeded the development in Japan of powerful American-style judicial review, and on postwar influences that have nonetheless gradually increased the use of judicial review. Bolz contends that the restrained use of judicial review by the Japanese Supreme Court has been the result of a rational strategy designed to preserve or increase the Court's political power.

233. Japan. Supreme Court. *Outline of Japanese Judicial System.* Tokyo, 1983.

A brief outline of the judicial system that covers the following topics: historical background, judicial system under the Constitution of 1946, kinds of courts and their jurisdiction, judges, court officials other than judges, and participation of laymen in judicial proceedings. Includes the Constitution of Japan.

234. Lorenzo, Richard M. "The Judicial System of Japan." *Case Western Reserve Journal of International Law* 6 (1974):294-303.

Briefly summarizes the Japanese judicial system. The contemporary legal system is a combination of civil and common law brought about by the voluntary adoption of civil law from Europe and the imposition of common law on Japan after World War II by the United States. However, civil law remains the dominant source of Japanese law.

6. CRIMINAL LAW

235. Koshi, George M. *The Japanese Legal Advisor: Crimes and Punishments*. Rutland, Vt.: Charles E. Tuttle, 1970.

    Presents Japanese criminal law and procedure as actually practiced in contemporary Japan. Designed to be used as a practical reference handbook. The chapters address the following topics: background of Japanese law; jurisdiction; safeguards for individual rights; investigation; arrest and trial procedures; punishment, parole, and amnesty; and description of major crimes. The appendices consist of the following: the Constitution, major legal and judicial institutions, index of statutes containing penal provisions which were in force on 1 January 1969, tables of maximum punishments, and a list of important statutes in criminal law.

236. Suzuki, Yoshio. "The Politics of Criminal Law Reform: Japan." *American Journal of Comparative Law* 21 (1973):287-303.

    Suzuki discusses reform of the Penal Code and its relationship to politics. In Japan, reform of procedural law and juvenile law is very difficult because of disagreement among the legal profession on the basic direction of change. There is, however, relative agreement among the legal profession and among political parties regarding reform of substantive criminal law.

7. ENVIRONMENTAL LAW

237. Gresser, Julian, Koichiro Fujikura and Akio Morishima. *Environmental Law in Japan*. Cambridge, Mass.: MIT Press, 1981.

    A comprehensive assessment of Japan's environmental law and policy, which establishes an analytic framework grounded in law, economics, and public administration. The authors have two principal objectives: (1) Japan's response to environmental problems, both domestic and international, offers insight into the role of law and legal institutions in Japan, and (2) Japan's successes and failures can help Western industrialized nations design more effective pollution controls. The book is divided into four sections: (1) historical perspective, (2) development of the judicial role, (3) environmental protection legislation and its administration, and

Law and Politics

    (4) Japan's environmental law and policy in international perspective.

238. Upham, Frank K. "Litigation and Moral Consciousness in Japan: An Interpretive Analysis of Four Japanese Pollution Suits." *Law and Society Review* 10 (1976):579-619.

    Focuses on the cultural and social factors that influenced the course of litigation of four pollution injury cases which the Japanese courts decided from 1971 to 1973.

8. INTELLECTUAL PROPERTY LAW

239. Doi, Teruo. *The Intellectual Property Law of Japan.* Germantown, Md.: Sijthoff & Noordhoff, 1980.

    A comprehensive treatise on the intellectual property law of Japan. Written for foreign inventors, authors, and business people seeking protection for their intellectual property in Japan, as well as for lawyers and patent agents representing such clients. Cites important court decisions and statutory provisions, with explanations. Includes the following topics: the patent system, the Utility Model Law, protection of unpatented know-how and trade secrets, the Design Law, the Trademark Law, the Unfair Competition Law, the Copyright Law, and regulation of licensing agreements under the Antimonopoly Law.

9. INTERNATIONAL LAW

240. *Japanese Annual of International Law* 1 (1957)- Tokyo: Japan Branch of the International Law Association.

    Contains articles on various aspects of Japanese international law as well as judicial decisions in public and private international law. Includes annual chronological lists of Japanese foreign affairs, treaties and other international agreements concluded by Japan, multilateral treaties and other agreements, and texts of international documents. Also includes the names and addresses of individual and corporate members of the International Law Association of Japan.

10. LABOR LAW

241. Hanami, Tadashi A. *Labour Law and Industrial Relations in Japan.* 2d rev. ed. Deventer, The Netherlands: Kluwer Law and Taxation, 1985.

   Hanami, a public commissioner with the Tokyo Metropolitan Labour Relations Commission, systematically and concisely describes and analyzes the Japanese industrial relations and labor law systems in order to reflect the significant changes that took place in Japanese industrial relations after 1979. These changes were caused by strains in the Japanese economy that resulted from the oil crisis and the international reactions against the tremendous expansion of Japanese business activities abroad. Originally written as a national labor law monograph for the *International Encyclopaedia for Labour Law and Industrial Relations.*

11. SECURITIES LAW

242. Loss, Louis, Makoto Yazawa and Barbara Ann Banoff, eds. *Japanese Securities Regulation.* Tokyo: University of Tokyo Press, 1983.

   The Japanese edition was published in two volumes in 1975 under the title *Securities Regulation in the United States and Japan.* In this edition, the greater part of the contents of the Japanese version dealing with the United States securities regulation has been omitted or condensed. The following topics are covered here: synopsis of securities regulation in the United States and Japan; the Japanese disclosure system and regulation of the distribution of securities; international securities transactions; regulation of broker-dealers and exchange markets; relations between securities corporations and customers; proxy regulation, tender offers, and insider trading; civil liability; and investment trusts. The appendices contain the text of various securities laws.

243. Tanikawa, Hisashi. *Credit and Security in Japan: The Legal Problems of Development Finance.* St. Lucia: University of Queensland Press, 1973.

   An investigation of the extent to which security laws hinder development finance in Japan. This study has been made in order to provide a comparison with the legal machinery for credit and security in those developing countries of Asia having civil law legal systems.

244. Tatsuta, Misao. "Enforcement of Japanese Securities Legislation." *Journal of Comparative Corporate Law and Securities Regulation* 1 (1978):95-138.

The author examines how the Japanese Securities and Exchange Law is enforced. Focus is on the following topics: (1) the sources of law upon which the enforcement is based and the organization of various regulatory bodies, (2) how the enforcement mechanisms operate to prevent securities fraud, and (3) some cases of securities fraud are described in order to show how the law has responded after the fact.

245. ―――――. *Securities Regulation in Japan*. Seattle: University of Washington Press, 1971.

Examines Japanese securities regulation through the analysis of texts of laws, Cabinet and ministerial rules, releases issued by the Department of Securities, and legal writings.

12. TAX LAW

246. Arthur Andersen & Co. *Tax and Trade Guide: Japan*. 3d ed. Chicago, 1978.

Presents basic information on the government, types of business organizations, taxes, labor and social laws, banking, finance, and incentives. This edition covers changes in Japanese law affecting business and taxes that have taken place to December 1977.

247. *Guide to Japanese Taxes, 1965-* . Tokyo: Zaikei Shoho Sha.

An annual publication that provides practical and up-to-date information on Japanese taxes. Is based on current laws, regulations, circulars. Covers the following topics: main features of Japanese national and local taxes, national income taxes, withholding income tax, assessment income tax, corporation tax, and inheritance and gift tax.

B. POLITICS AND GOVERNMENT

248. Allinson, Gary D. *Suburban Tokyo: A Comparative Study in Politics and Social Change.* Berkeley: University of California Press, 1979.

   Analyzes political changes that have accompanied the growth of suburbs in western Tokyo since the late nineteenth century. Underlying the study is the author's methodological purpose of explaining political change contextually, by depicting the social environment in which it occurs. In order to achieve this purpose, Allinson has selectively used the concepts, techniques, and methods of several social science disciplines, among which are anthropology, sociology, political science, and history. Focuses on the comparison of two suburbs, the cities of Musahino and Fuchu.

249. Austin, Lewis. *Saints and Samurai: The Political Culture of the American and Japanese Elites.* New Haven: Yale University Press, 1975.

   An inquiry into personal values in business and government (viz., political culture). Based on the results of Executive Consciousness Surveys administered to Japanese and American government administrators and business executives.

250. Baerwald, Hans H. *Japan's Parliament: An Introduction.* London: Cambridge University Press, 1974.

   A brief study of Japan's parliament, or Diet, which emphasizes what Baerwald considers to be its most important features. In addition, the author seeks to answer certain questions: (1) what are the origins of the Diet and how does this affect its place in Japanese politics, (2) what are the features of Japan's political parties that influence the manner of their operations in the Diet, (3) what is the internal organization of the Diet and how do its rules of procedure affect its capacity to fulfill its constitutional mandate, (4) why is the Diet the scene of periodic turmoil, and (5) what general conclusions can be made about the Diet as a parliamentary institution?

251. ─────. "Lockheed and Japanese Politics." *Asian Survey* 16 (1976):817-829.

   Discusses the 1976 Lockheed Corporation Senate hearings and Japanese Diet hearings, in which it was revealed that Lockheed had spent large sums of money in Japan to promote the sales of its aircraft, and that these illegal funds were paid to Japanese businessmen and government officials. On July 27, 1976, then Prime Minister Tanaka Kakuei was called in for questioning by the public procurators investigating the Lockheed scandal and he was then arrested. Baerwald examines the responses of the Japanese government and political parties to these events as well.

252. ——— and Akira Hashimoto. "Japan in 1982: Doing Nothing is Best?" *Asian Survey* 23 (1983):53-61.

For most of 1982, the adage of "doing nothing is best" was reflected in the world of Japanese politics. The authors discuss the reasons for this state of affairs, the most significant of which, they believe, is the structural situation among and inside the political parties.

253. Benjamin, Roger W. "Minerva and the Crane ('Tsuru'): Birds of a Feather? Comparative Research and Japanese Political Change--A Review Article." *Journal of Asian Studies* 40 (1980):69-76.

A critique of five works that represent the latest developments in scholarship on Japanese politics. The works are Ward, *Japan's Political System*; Pempel, ed., *Policymaking in Contemporary Japan*; Tsurutani, *Political Change in Japan*; Watanuki, *Politics in Postwar Japanese Society*; and Ike, *A Theory of Japanese Democracy*.

254. Bhuinya, Niranjan. *Parliamentary Democracy in Japan*. New York: Barnes & Noble Books, 1972.

Examines the changes that the adoption of the Constitution of 1947 created in the governmental structure. Among these changes were the transfer of sovereign power from the Emperor to the people, the supremacy of the legislature, separation of power, the guarantee of fundamental human rights, and the renunciation of war. Also looks at the various components of the revised governmental structure in relation to the Constitution. Included here are philosophy and basic principles of the Constitution, the Emperor, the Cabinet, the Diet, the Judiciary, rights and duties of the people, political parties, and local self-government.

255. Bowen, Roger Wilson. "The Narita Conflict." *Asian Survey* 15 (1975):598-615.

On September 16, 1971, during the Japanese government's drive to expropriate land that had been designated as the location for the Tokyo area's second international airport (the Sanrizuka-Narita region of the Chiba prefecture) from its recalcitrant owners, three policemen were murdered and many other persons injured. The opposition consisted of farmers and their allies, left-wing students. The events of that day and those of the five year period beginning July 1966, when the government announced its decision, constitute the "Narita Incident." Bowen sees this conflict as a manifestation of the problems created by economic growth in an advanced industrial society, and he discusses the history of the conflict and its various aspects.

256. Brzezinski, Zbigniew. *The Fragile Blossom: Crisis and Change in Japan.* New York: Harper & Row, 1972.

Based in part on observations made by the author during a brief stay in Japan in 1971 about changes the country is undergoing, and their domestic and international implications. With regard to domestic issues, the following topics are discussed: Japanese politics and government, the economy, and economic growth. With regard to external issues, Brzezinski discusses the new balance of power in Asia and its effect of the American role, and Japanese rearmament.

257. Cheng, Peter P. "The Japanese Cabinets, 1885-1973: An Elite Analysis." *Asian Survey* 14 (1974):1055-1071.

A study of the Japanese Cabinets and the political elite of cabinet rank from 1885 to 1973. A central issue is to see how the characteristics of these members have been conditioned by the Japanese political system.

258. Choi, Sung-il. "Politics-Economics-Public Policy Linkages in Japan, 1965-1969." *Asian Survey* 15 (1975):394-406.

A quantitative study that attempts to ascertain whether the environment or the political structure is more significant in explaining public policy. The author investigates the relationships between (1) political structure and the environment, (2) political outputs and the environment, and (3) political structure and political outputs.

259. Curtis, Gerald L. "Conservative Dominance in Japanese Politics." *Current History* 60 (1971):207-212, 246.

   Curtis contends that the conservative Liberal Democratic Party (LDP) has controlled the government since 1956, and as a consequence, Japan faces the danger of institutionalized one-party rule unless the Socialist opposition is revitalized. In addition, the majority of the LDP Diet members come from rural areas, and as a result the urban population is seriously underrepresented in national politics.

260. Dahlby, Tracy. "Anatomy of Japan: The Bureaucrats." *Far Eastern Economic Review* 111 (1981):34-40.

   An examination of the government bureaucracy. Describes how the bureaucrats are chosen and the team spirit and sense of loyalty to individual ministries that they possess. Dahlby considers these powerful government bureaucrats as successors to the samurai who founded Japan's bureaucracy in 1867.

261. Davies, Derek. "Japan '78: Time for Reflection, Kabuki-Style." *Far Eastern Economic Review* 100 (1978):37-44.

   A discussion of the contemporary political scene in Japan. Focuses on the political drama revolving around Prime Minister Takeo Fukuda's plan to dissolve the Diet in September, call a general election, and after the ruling Liberal Democratic Party (LDP) has been restored to power with an increased majority, get himself reelected to the presidency of his own party.

262. Elliott, James. "The 1981 Administrative Reform in Japan." *Asian Survey* 23 (1983):765-779.

   Looks at the steps the Japanese government took in 1981 to reform national finances and the administrative system that were precipitated by the very high and growing rate of government indebtedness and by pressure by business for administrative reform.

263. Endicott, John E. "The 1975-76 Debate over Ratification of the NPT in Japan." *Asian Survey* 17 (1977):275-292.

   Traces the course of the debate that surrounded the Nuclear Non-Proliferation Treaty (NPT) ratification drive of 1975 to 1976. Closely examines the decision-making process as revealed in the interaction between the Liberal Democratic Party (LDP) and the Japanese government. Also discusses the reasons why Japan did not ratify the

NPT in 1975, and why it was ratified in 1976, six years after Japan had signed it.

264. Flanagan, Scott C. "Value Change and Partisan Change in Japan: The Silent Revolution Revisited." *Comparative Politics* 11 (1979):253-278.

    A critique and modification of Ronald Inglehart's thesis that contends that traditional class-party political alignments in advanced industrial societies can be changed by the rise of affluence and its influence on value change.

265. Fukui, Haruhiro. "Japan's Nakasone Government." *Current History* 82 (1983):380-395.

    Fukui discusses the Nakasone government and contends that Nakasone is a nationalist ideologue and a political opportunist.

266. Harari, Ehud. "Japanese Politics of Advice in Comparative Perspective: A Framework for Analysis and a Case Study." *Public Policy* 22 (1974):537-577.

    Analyzes the functions of Japanese public advisory bodies and compares them with those in England and the United States. Includes a case study of the Japanese Advisory Council on the Public Personnel System.

267. Iga, Mamoru and Morton Auerbach. "Political Corruption and Social Structure in Japan." *Asian Survey* 17 (1977):556-564.

    Examines the income and expenses of members of the Japanese Diet in order to prove the suggestions that have been made that bribery is built into the Japanese political system. The results of this study, according to the authors, indicate that a tendency exists among members of the Japanese Diet to manipulate voters through direct or indirect forms of bribery and that this tendency is built into the political system.

268. Ike, Nobutaka. *Japanese Politics: Patron-Client Democracy*. 2d ed. New York: Alfred A. Knopf, 1972.

    The Japanese version of democracy, which stresses the group over the individual, is analyzed. This version is called patron-client democracy, and in it interpersonal and intergroup relations are based on vertical stratification by institution or group of institutions rather than on horizontal stratification by class or caste. As a consequence, individuals tend to relate to the political system through their patrons, who are usually local notables, political bosses, union leaders, local politicians and leaders of local organizations. Among the topics Ike discusses are the political structure, business, labor, agriculture, the bureaucracy, political parties, the electorate, political violence, public policy outputs, and Japan in the 1970s.

269. ———. *A Theory of Japanese Democracy.* Boulder, Colo.: Westview Press, 1978.

Proposes a model of the Japanese democratic system that is a rational choice model somewhat modified to correspond to Japanese empirical data. It is an investment model as well, which likens politicians to entrepreneurs and voters to investors. The theory is developed in the first part of the book, and is illustrated and elaborated upon in the second part. Ike argues that his model can be used to explain the political change of recent decades, in which the kinds of benefits sought by voters have been changing because of economic growth and urban migration, and that the democratic system has been slow to adapt to new demands.

270. Ishii, Ryosuke. *A History of Political Institutions in Japan.* Tokyo: University of Tokyo Press, 1980.

An outline of the history of political institutions in Japan, from their beginnings (ca. 250 B.C. to 603 A.D.) to the restoration of national independence following the end of World War II. Emphasis is on public law.

271. Itoh, Hiroshi, ed. and trans. *Japanese Politics—An Inside View: Readings from Japan.* Ithaca, N.Y.: Cornell University Press, 1973.

Selected empirical studies by Japanese scholars on various aspects of policy making through case studies or public opinion polls. The book is divided into four parts. The first two parts are concerned with the major political forces that govern decision-making at the national level. Part Three focuses on the study of the structure and process of decision-making at a subnational level, and Part Four examines the formulation of Japan's foreign policy.

272. Johnson, Chalmers. "Tanaka Kakuei, Structural Corruption, and the Advent of Machine Politics in Japan." *Journal of Japanese Studies* 12 (1986):1-28.

Discusses the significance of Tanaka Kakuei and the

Lockheed bribery case (1976) for governmental corruption and political machines, and the governance and democratization of Japan.

273. Kim, Chong Lim. "Socio-Economic Development and Political Democracy in Japanese Prefectures." *American Political Science Review* 65 (1971):184-186.

    A brief research note that tests the relationship between the socioeconomic development factors of levels of urban industrialism and of social overhead capital, and political democracy (viz., political competition and participation, and representation equality).

274. Kosaka, Masataka. *100 Million Japanese: The Postwar Experience*. Tokyo: Kodansha International, 1972.

    Presents the American Occupation and the political, economic, and social development of Japan from a Japanese point of view.

275. Kumon, Shumpei. "Japan Faces Its Future: The Political Economics of Administrative Reform." *Journal of Japanese Studies* 10 (1984):143-165.

    An analysis of the attempts by a former member of "Rincho" for administrative political and social reform. "Rincho" was a provisional commission for administrative reform formed by the government in 1980 and dissolved in 1983.

276. Massey, Joseph A. "The Missing Leader: Japanese Youths' View of Political Authority." *American Political Science Review* 69 (1975):31-48.

    Massey discusses the results of two surveys on the attitudes of Japanese youths towards political authority. Emphasis is on the following objectives: (1) whether a benevolent leader exists in the political imagery of contemporary Japanese youth, (2) whether a spillover of affect from the national leader to other important institutions of the political system takes place in later childhood, and (3) to consider some of the causes and consequences of the presence or absence of a benevolent leader in a political system.

277. McNelly, Theodore. *Politics and Government in Japan*. 2d ed. Boston: Houghton Mifflin, 1972.

    Political development in postwar Japan is analyzed through various structures in the political system.

278. Mitchell, Douglas D. *Amaeru: The Expression of Reciprocal Dependency Needs in Japanese Politics and Law.* Boulder, Colo.: Westview Press, 1976.

   Demonstrates, in a systematic and detailed way, the ways in which "amae" operates in the Japanese political realm, and its function as a motivational factor that underlies many characteristics and that explains much of Japanese political behavior. Mitchell defines "amaeru" as follows: "to avail oneself of some kindness or favor; to take advantage of a person's good will." It is related to "amai," which is defined as "not strict, indulgent, generous." Thus one person will be "amaeru," and the other "amai" in response; both roles are necessary for the dependency pattern known as "amae" to be in operation.

279. Murakami, Hyoe and Johannes Hirschmeier, eds. *Politics and Economics in Contemporary Japan.* Tokyo: Kodansha International, 1983.

   Essays by political scientists and economists on problems in Japan's political economy (viz., the political leadership, the bureaucracy, and the economic enterprises) stemming from the diminishing influence of its traditional social cohesiveness.

280. Murakami, Yasusuke. "The Age of New Middle Mass Politics: The Case of Japan." *Journal of Japanese Studies* 8 (1982):29-72.

   Explains the developments in Japanese politics in the past few years in terms of the changes that have occurred over the past two decades and in terms of basic political changes in other industrial democracies since 1960.

281. Najita, Tetsuo. *Japan: The Intellectual Foundations of Modern Japanese Politics.* Chicago: University of Chicago Press, 1974.

   Traces the development of Japan's political tradition from its beginning in 1600, to the Tokugawa period (1600 to 1868), during which time a bureaucratic order was established upon which much of modern Japan rests, up to the twentieth century. Najita presents an overall view of the history of modern Japan, which is full of dispute and intellectual tension rather than of unilinear achievement of high levels of nationality.

282. Park, Yung Ho. "The Governmental Advisory Commission System in Japan. *Journal of Comparative Administration* 3 (1972):435-467.

Surveys some of the salient aspects of the Japanese advisory commission system, among which are its composition, operations, methods of decision-making, and functions and uses of advisory commissions. Also identifies some of the major problems and weaknesses in the present system.

283. Pempel, T.J. "The Bureaucratization of Policymaking in Postwar Japan." *American Journal of Political Science* 18 (1974):647-664.

Examines the expanding public policymaking powers and influence of the bureaucracy.

284. Reed, Steven R. "The Changing Fortunes of Japan's Progressive Governors." *Asian Survey* 26 (1986):452-465.

Progressive (i.e., supported by leftist parties) mayors and governors have played a surprisingly large role in postwar Japanese politics. The election of opposition party governors and majors is important as a mechanism ensuring responsiveness in a dominant party system. Reed analyzes all postwar gubernatorial elections and argues that they are more sensitive to changes in the electorate than other elections in Japan, and therefore that they play an important role in guaranteeing government responsiveness to the electorate.

285. ———. "Is Japanese Government Really Centralized?" *Journal of Japanese Studies* 8 (1982):133-164.

Based on the results of research carried out in Japan from 1976 to 1977. Reed contends that the degree of centralization has been overestimated and that local governments have significant amounts of autonomy.

286. Richardson, Bradley M. *The Political Culture of Japan*. Berkeley: University of California Press, 1974.

A study of popular, or mass, political attitudes in postwar Japan. Excludes the opinions and actions of political groups or elites. One of the author's major concerns is to investigate the degree and scope of attitudinal change in Japan resulting from postwar political reforms. Most of the evidence consists of the results of public opinion surveys of political attitudes conducted between 1958 and 1967. Among the political attitudes analyzed here are political involvement, evaluative, participation, and voting attitudes; urban-rural differences; and the age factor and political culture.

287. ———— and Scott C. Flanagan. *Politics in Japan*. Boston: Little, Brown, 1984.

Studies Japanese politics using the structure-functional approach, which assumes that all countries perform the same political functions. This approach also pays special attention to the interaction between politics and society by stressing the importance of political culture, which is the aggregate of political values and attitudes in a particular system. The first part of the book focuses on system characteristics, such as the social and political setting and patterns of political behavior. The second part addresses system process and performance, which includes political recruitment, interest groups and policy-making, and an analysis of system performance.

288. Ryang, Key Sun. "Postwar Japanese Political Leadership: A Study of Prime Ministers." *Asian Survey* 13 (1973): 1010-1020.

An effort to examine the extent to which the postwar parliamentary cabinet contributed to the growth of democratic institutions and to determine the actual source of executive authority.

289. Shiratori, Rei, ed. *Japan in the 1980s*. Tokyo: Kodansha International, 1982.

Papers from a symposium on contemporary Japan, held at Sheffield University, England, in 1980. The chief purpose of the symposium was to analyze Japanese politics, economics, and related issues, in order to assist the British participants in understanding more fully the Japanese situation. The Japanese participants included persons involved in foreign relations, such as diplomats and government bureaucrats, as well as Parliamentary representatives of each political party.

290. Stockwin, J.A.A. *Japan: Divided Politics in a Growth Economy*. 2d ed. London: Weidenfeld and Nicolson, 1982.

Discusses the divisions within the Japanese polity from the 1950s up to 1981. The most well known division has been in policies towards defense and foreign affairs. Another important division concerns the distribution of wealth. And finally, at the root of Japan's divided polity, is the Constitution of 1947 and the lack of agreement about its revision. However, the political impact of these divisions has been partially blunted by the long rule of the Liberal Democratic Party, which has pursued a policy of rapid economic growth.

291. Suttmeier, Richard P. "The 'Gikan' Question in Japanese Government: Bureaucratic Curiosity or Institutional Failure?" *Asian Survey* 18 (1978):1046-1066.

    Explores the patterns of dominance of the central government bureaucracy by nontechnical personnel, or "gikan" (those having a general law background rather than one in science and engineering), and delineates some of the implications for understanding contemporary Japanese government. Suttmeier finds this situation to be an anomaly and a problem, since Japan is a highly industrialized society and presumably has a need for technically trained persons, especially in the central government bureaucracy, which has such a critical role in policy-making and implementation.

292. Tsuji, Kiyoaki, ed. *Public Administration in Japan*. Tokyo: University of Tokyo Press, 1984.

    Essays written by scholars and government agency representatives that describe the Japanese administrative system and its operation. Among the topics covered are public corporations, the civil service system, local administration and finance, legislative review, administrative guidance, and data processing in government.

293. Tsurutani, Taketsugu. *Political Change in Japan: Response to Postindustrial Challenge*. New York: David McKay, 1977.

    A study of the effects of Japan's transition from an industrial to a postindustrial society on its political system.

294. Valeo, Francis R. and Charles E. Morrison, eds. *The Japanese Diet and the U.S. Congress*. Boulder, Colo.: Westview Press, 1983.

    Papers resulting from a joint Japanese-United States comparative study of the Japanese Diet, or Parliament, and the United States Congress. They illuminate the details of the two systems in an integrated pattern so as to permit comparative study. Among the topics covered are the history of the two systems and the places they occupy in their respective constitutional structures; their organization and distribution of power; the lawmaking process and the role of political parties in both countries; the role of political parties in each; the role of the individual members of the Diet and the Congress; budgeting and finance; and defense, trade, and foreign policy.

295. Ward, Robert E. *Japan's Political System*. 2d ed. Englewood Cliffs, N.J.: Prentice-Hall, 1978.

   Elucidates the functioning and performance of the Japanese political system. Uses the following categories for the purpose of analysis: the foundations of politics, political dynamics, decision-making, and governmental performance. These categories are broken down further into more specific topics as follows: history, ecology, social structure, political culture, interest groups, parties, elections, leadership, organs of government, domestic affairs, and foreign relations.

296. ———— and Yoshikazu Sakamoto, eds. *Democratizing Japan: The Allied Occupation*. Honolulu: University of Hawaii Press, 1987.

   The result of the collaborative research efforts of a group of Japanese and American scholars, and much of it is based on government archival material made available only recently. Focuses on one of the principal objectives of the Occupation (1945 to 1952), the democratization of Japan's authoritarian political system. Attention is given to the new Constitution of 1946-1947, which was the most fundamental institutional change effected by the Occupation. Also looks at several of the Occupation's major programs of institutional and procedural reform, and the formation and early development of the conservative and reformist parties.

297. Watanuki, Joji. *Politics in Postwar Japanese Society*. Tokyo: University of Tokyo Press, 1977.

   Collected essays that discuss democracy in postwar Japan and the sociopolitical consequences of rapid economic growth. They also address the issues of the political system, with emphasis on the structure of political parties; political participation and voting behavior; and political attitudes toward Asia and the rest of the world.

298. White, James W. "Tradition and Politics in Studies of Contemporary Japan." *World Politics* 26 (1974):400-427.

   An essay review of five books that deal with the role of tradition in Japanese politics. The books under consideration here are Curtis, *Election Campaigning Japanese Style* (1971); Fukui, *Party in Power* (1970); Hellmann, *Japanese Domestic Politics and Foreign Policy* (1969); Takeshi, *Japan's Political Culture* (1970); and Thayer, *How the Conservatives Rule Japan* (1969).

1. ELECTIONS

299. Baerwald, Hans H. "Japan's December 1983 House of Representatives Election: The Return of Coalition Politics." *Asian Survey* 24 (1984):265-278.

    An examination of the results and significance of the 1983 House of Representatives Election, in which officially endorsed Liberal Democratic Party (LDP) candidates won only 250 seats, six below the minimum of 256. The projections of the leading newspapers had ranged from 260 seats to 278 seats for the LDP. However, within three days of the closing of the polls, the LDP had acquired 259 seats, and then ten additional seats. This was accomplished by the formation of the first coalition cabinet since 1948.

300. ―――. "Japan's 'Double' Elections." *Asian Survey* 20 (1980):1169-1184.

    In 1980 an unprecedented election was held for both the entire membership of the House of Representatives and one-half the membership of the House of Councillors. This was a unique situation, since a "double" election had never occurred on the same day. Baerwald analyzes the results and ramifications of the stunning victory of the Liberal Democratic Party, and the setbacks suffered by the opposition parties, with the exception of the Socialist Party.

301. ―――. "Japan's 35th House of Representatives Election: The LDP Toys with a Return to 1954." *Asian Survey* 20 (1980):257-268.

    Assesses the significance of the 1979 election in which only 248 of the officially endorsed candidates of the Liberal Democratic Party won seats in the House of Representatives. The Party had projected a target of 271 of the 511 House seats, and did not acquire the absolute minimum of 256 seats until ten "Independents" had joined its ranks after the election. The leadership of the LDP indulged in mutual recriminations for these results, almost bringing the conservatives back to where they had been in 1954, when they were organized into at least two separate parties.

302. ―――. "The Tanabata House of Councillors Election in Japan." *Asian Survey* 14 (1974):900-906.

    Examines the 1974 House of Councillors election. Baerwald maintains that the results indicate that although

Japan's society and economy are changing rapidly, the voters do not seem to want equally dramatic changes in their politics.

303. ——— and Nobuo Tomita. "Japan's 34th General Election: Cautious Change Amidst Incremental Instability." *Asian Survey* 17 (1977):221-236.

    The results of the House of Representatives election conducted in 1976 are analyzed within the context of selected aspects of recent political developments. Also discusses prospects for Japanese politics based on the election results.

304. Blaker, Michael K., ed. *Japan at the Polls: The House of Councillors Election of 1974*. Washington, D.C.: American Enterprise Institute for Public Policy Research, 1976.

    The election is examined against the backdrop of institutional, political, and social change in Japan. Consists of three essays. The first essay looks at several major themes in the historical evolution of the House of Councillors system. The second essay deals with the election campaign. And the third essay is primarily concerned with the election results and the impact of several key variables, particularly urbanization, upon political support structures and political party performance.

305. Brynildsen, Richard J. "A Decade of Japanese Diet Elections, 1967-1976: Conservatism and Radicalism Reevaluated." *Asian Survey* 17 (1977):967-977.

    Brynildsen looks back at the elections of 1967, 1969, 1972, and 1976 in order to determine what has occurred in Japan's unique multiparty system, and to speculate on its short-range and mid-range future.

306. Choi, Sung-il. "Systems Outputs, Social Environment, and Political Cleavages in Japan: The Case of the 1969 General Election." *American Journal of Political Science* 17 (1973):99-122.

    A quantitative study of the socioeconomic basis for the decline in support for the Liberal Democratic Party (LDP) and for the increased support for the opposition parties that emerged from the election results.

307. Copper, John F. "The Japanese Communist Party's Recent Election Defeats: A Signal of Decline?" *Asian Survey* 19 (1979):353-365.

    Analyzes the election results of 1976, in which the Communist Party (JCP) lost over half of the seats it held in the House of Representatives, the most important house of the Japanese Diet, and of 1977, in which the JCP lost four members in the House of Councillors (its strength dropped from 20 to 16 members). Also assesses the JCP's problems in terms of temporary difficulties and tactical errors as opposed to problems that may be long range and not easily overcome and that may ultimately reduce the importance of the Party in Japanese politics.

308. Curtis, Gerald L. *Election Campaigning: Japanese Style*. New York: Columbia University Press, 1971.

    The campaign strategy and organization of a candidate for the Japanese Diet from 1966 to 1967 is examined by Curtis, who observed the campaign first-hand. Gives insights into the characteristics of Japan's political structure and an understanding of the political process. Among the topics discussed are the politics of party endorsement, campaign organization, organizational strategy, and the official campaign.

309. ----------. "The 1969 General Election in Japan." *Asian Survey* 10 (1970):859-871.

    Delineates some of the significant trends in party support reflected in the 1969 election of members of the Lower House of the Diet, and explains certain characteristics of the electoral system.

310. Flanagan, Scott C. and Bradley M. Richardson. *Japanese Electoral Behavior: Social Cleavages, Social Networks, and Partisanship*. Beverly Hills, Calif.: Sage Publications, 1977.

    Applies the sociological paradigm to electorial behavior in contemporary Japan. This approach hypothesizes that people support parties on the basis of their social group memberships, and it pictures society as being divided into competing and antagonistic groups by one or more lines of cleavage, which are characterized as having strong partisan norms. This analysis is based primarily on the 1967 Japanese Election Study conducted by Robert E. Ward and Akira Kubota. Covers such issues as the Meiji Restoration of 1868 and segmental cleavages, Japan's industrial revolution and economic-functional cleavages, the structure of political competition in postwar Japan, class partisanship and voter mobilization, and socioeconomic status and the vote.

311. Hrebenar, Ronald J. "The Politics of Electoral Reform in Japan." *Asian Survey* 17 (1977):978-996.

    Hrebenar contends that the Japanese election system facilitates the continuance of Japan's one-party dominant system, and that this has been responsible for the recent fragmentation of the political party system. The basic elements of the election are discussed and their effects on the party system are analyzed. In addition, the issue of electoral system reform is examined.

312. Lee, Tosh. "Tokyo Metropolitan Assembly Election--1973." *Asian Survey* 14 (1974):478-488.

    Discusses the results of the Tokyo Metropolitan Assembly Election of 1973, which journalists called the most heated local election ever held in Japan, and which political experts regarded as a significant indicator of the changing trends in Japanese voting patterns.

313. Passin, Herbert, ed. *A Season of Voting: The Japanese Elections of 1976 and 1977.* Washington, D.C.: American Enterprise Institute for Public Policy Research, 1979.

    Japan's political system as seen through the elections for the House of Representatives in 1976 and for the House of Councillors in 1977. Both elections were dominated by two great national issues: the Lockheed scandal, which led to the downfall of the Cabinet and the indictment of former Prime Minister Tanaka Kakuei, and the bare margin of a victory by the Conservatives, who had held a majority in the lower house since 1955.

314. Stockwin, J.A.A. "Shifting Alignments in Japanese Party Politics: The April 1974 Election for Governor of Kyoto Prefecture." *Asian Survey* 14 (1974):887-899.

    Stockwin examines the 1974 election for governor of Kyoto Prefecture and its significance for party political alignments. Kyoto, usually considered traditional and conservative, had been a political stronghold of the left ever since Ninagawa Torazo was first elected prefectural governor in 1950. In the 1974 election, Ninagawa, dependent upon Socialist and, increasingly, upon Communist Party backing, was running for his seventh four-year term.

315. Tsurutani, Taketsugu. "The LDP in Transition? Mass Membership Participation in Party Leadership Selection." *Asian Survey* 20 (1980):844-859.

   In the fall of 1978, for the first time, the first mass membership primary for the biennial election for the president of the ruling Liberal Democratic Party and premier-designate took place. Prior to this selection procedure, LDP presidents had always been chosen by the Party's parliamentary members. Tsurutani observes the significance of the new leadership selection procedure and its importance. He also examines the character of its impact on the party's behavior and political future and its effects on Japanese politics.

316. ————. "A New Era of Japanese Politics: Tokyo's Gubernatorial Election." *Asian Survey* 12 (1972):429-443.

   Evaluates the 1971 Tokyo gubernatorial election, in which the incumbent was reelected by a coalition of Socialist and Communist parties. His opponent had been backed by the ruling Liberal Democratic Party. Tsurutani contends that this election symbolizes a new trend in Japanese politics that has recently emerged, in which voters want to bring about change through direct political participation.

317. Uchida, Mitsuru and Hans H. Baerwald. "The House of Councillors Election in Japan: The LDP Hangs in There." *Asian Survey* 18 (1978):301-308.

   Analyzes the results of the 1977 House of Councillors election, in which the Liberal Democratic Party managed to retain its control of the House. The issue of this election was the possibility that the LDP, which had governed Japan for over twenty years, might lose its majority status in the House.

2. LOCAL POLITICS AND GOVERNMENT

318. Brett, Cecil C. "The Komeito and Local Japanese Politics." *Asian Survey* 19 (1979):366-378.

   Surveys the potential for growth of the Komei Party in Japanese local government. The Komeito, or Clean Government Party, was founded in 1964 and has been a subject of interest for a number of reasons, particularly since its rapid rise to national prominence and its often stated goal of becoming the leading party in the national government. In addition, it is closely connected to the Soka Gakkai, or mass Buddhist lay organization, and many Japanese have reservations about the idea of religion in politics and of the prospects, even though remote, of a Japan under the political control of a religious organization. Uses nationwide local elections data as well as evidence obtained in a field study carried out in Okayama prefecture in April and May 1978.

319. Choi, Sung-il. "Public Policy in the Japanese Prefectures: The Impact of Environment, Politics, and Resources upon Policy Formation." *Asian Survey* 17 (1977): 839-856.

An empirical study of the extent to which the policy making process of the Japanese prefectures is determined by political structural characteristics, the environment, and the resource base. The findings are compared with those of American state politics.

320. Gotoda, Teruo. *The Local Politics of Kyoto*. Berkeley: Institute of East Asian Studies, University of California, 1985.

In an attempt to analyze the power structure and political process in Kyoto politics within the overall context of the national power structure, and to observe the links between local and national politics, Gotoda studies the twenty-eight years' tenure in office of the late Governor Ninagawa Torazo in Kyoto for almost three decades following the Allied Occupation of Japan. Gotoda addresses the following questions: what was the extent of Ninagawa's success, and who supported him; what kind of relationships did he have with national politicians, with the national bureaucracy, with both national and local business leaders, with intellectuals, and with other interest groups; and what was his power base? This study may suggest a pattern of coalition on the national level, should the LDP fail in the distant future.

321. Muramatsu, Michio. "The Impact of Economic Growth Policies on Local Politics in Japan." *Asian Survey* 15 (1975):799-816.

Looks at recent political developments at the local level as they relate to the economic growth of the 1960s.

Local politics are examined in the context of national politics, and focus is on the following four issues: (1) the institutional linkage between the national government and the local communities, (2) decision-making as it affects local communities, (3) national and local conflicts, and (4) the impact of local actions upon national politics.

322. Park, Yung Ho. "The Local Public Personnel System in Japan. *Asian Survey* 18 (1978):592-608.

   The contemporary Japanese prefectural personnel system is examined with reference to the following questions: (1) Has the prefectural administration developed into the kind of autonomous machinery that the SCAP (Supreme Commander for the Allied Powers) reformers attempted to create, and if not, to what extent do current bureaucratic practices adhere to the intentions of SCAP reform? (2) Are the personnel practices of the local government in conformity with the principles of the 1950 Local Public Service Law, or based more on pre-reform traditions of personnel management?

323. Rix, Alan G. "Tokyo's Governor Minobe and Progressive Local Politics in Japan." *Asian Survey* 15 (1975):530-542.

   In the 1960s and 1970s many fundamental changes at the local level of Japanese politics occurred. One aspect of change has been the increasing electoral support for progressive candidates and consequently the increasing number of progressive local assemblymen and local executives. Minobe Ryokichi, the Governor of Tokyo, is the first progressive governor, and he was elected and re-elected in 1967, 1971, and 1975. Rix examines Minobe's administration and its policies.

324. Samuels, Richard J. "Local Politics in Japan: The Changing of the Guard." *Asian Survey* 22 (1982):630-637.

   Samuels discusses partisan upheavals and political realignments of the late 1960s and 1970s in Japanese local politics. He also examines the structural changes within the progressive and conservative opposition parties and the shifts in power between them.

325. ―――. *The Politics of Regional Policy in Japan: Localities Incorporated?* Princeton, N.J.: Princeton University Press, 1983.

   The concept of how one can best examine the way Japanese or any other local government is embedded in broader political, social, economic, and administrative environments is probed. Regional policy is studied by using translocal coalitions as the primary focus.

3. POLITICAL PARTICIPATION

326. Krauss, Ellis S. *Japanese Radicals Revisited: Student Protest in Postwar Japan*. Berkeley: University of California Press, 1974.

   Considers the changes in political beliefs and activities of those former student activists ("Ampo Generation") who participated in the violent 1960 anti-U.S.-Japan Security Treaty demonstrations in Tokyo ("Ampo Crisis"), which was the most intense confrontation between Japan's left and right political communities to occur after World War II. The material is based on the results of research Krauss did in 1969 and 1970 in which "Ampo Generation" students were surveyed and interviewed. Krauss contends that this research is important as a case study of the process of political socialization and a study of the relationship between society and polity in Japan.

327. Kuroda, Yasumasa. "Protest Movements in Japan: A New Politics." *Asian Survey* 12 (1972):947-952.

   One of the new developments in contemporary Japanese politics is the emergence of citizens movements. These movements consist of individuals who are interested in certain issues to the extent that they have formed organizations in order to obtain what they want. Kuroda observes the nature of these movements and discusses their significance for the future of Japanese politics.

328. Richardson, Bradley M. "Urbanization and Political Participation: The Case of Japan." *American Political Science Review* 67 (1973):433-452.

   Richardson explains tendencies in urban-rural political participation in Japan. He makes use of unpublished findings from a large number of Japanese surveys. These findings indicate that rural people participate politically more than their urban counterparts. In addition, rural voters are strongly involved in local politics and more concerned than urban residents about having their political needs represented.

4. POLITICAL PARTIES

329. Baerwald, Hans H. *Party Politics in Japan*. Boston: Allen & Unwin, 1986.

    Presents a broad survey of Japanese national party politics, which covers the period from 1955 to 1985. Focus is on the following topics: political parties and factionalism, national elections, the Diet or National Assembly, and the changing relationship between the governing and opposition parties.

330. Benjamin, Roger W. and Kan Ori. *Tradition and Change in Postindustrial Japan: The Role of the Political Parties*. New York: Praeger, 1981.

    Examines the Japanese party system and internal features thought to relate to it. Describes and assesses post-World War II political party change. Also deals with factionalism and presents an empirical study of personal support organizations in two prefectural legislatures. Finally, presents a discussion of the party system in relation to the overall process of political change in Japan.

331. Emmerson, John K. "The Japanese Communist Party after Fifty Years." *Asian Survey* 12 (1972):564-579.

    Traces the history of the Japanese Communist Party (JCP) from its beginnings in 1922 to the postwar period. Also assesses the political situation and achievements of the present JCP and briefly discusses its future.

332. Foster, James J. "Ghost-Hunting: Local Party Organization in Japan." *Asian Survey* 22 (1982):843-857.

    Japanese parties have developed strong and exclusive ties with particular interest groups and as a result, they have not had to represent all voters in a geographic area. Their local organizations have acted to control the financial and other resources of interest groups most closely affiliated with them, as well as to bring group members to the polls. This situation is the consequence of Japanese election law and the competition encouraged by multi-member election districts in which local and national candidates stand for office. The author discusses the organization of the five major Japanese political parties in Hyogo prefecture and examines how their organization structures are related to the electoral challenges they have faced. He also contends that the local organizations of the political parties are not "ghosts," as has been stated by a former Minister of Education.

333. Fukai, Shigeko N. "Beliefs and Attitudes of the Japanese Left During the Early 1970s." *Asian Survey* 20 (1980): 1185-1209.

Fukai attempts to shed some light on the controversy of the "decline of ideology" thesis in order to ascertain if the Japanese experience conforms to or contradicts the hypothesis. He raises the following questions: Have the leftist leaders begun to favor liberal democratic values rather than those of Marxism? And has Marxism in Japan become domesticated as a result of economic growth and affluence? Fukai evaluates these questions with the objective of clarifying the sources of surviving radicalism of the Marxist parties in Japan.

334. ―――――. "Japanese Politics in Transition?" *Current History* 84 (1985):409-437.

Despite the fact that the Liberal Democratic Party continues to dominate the overall political scene, there have been some signs of change within the party. Fukai examines these signs and the reasons for their occurrence as well as how they are occurring. Also discussed are the potential effects of these changes on Japan's domestic and foreign policies.

335. Fukui, Haruhiro. "The Liberal Democratic Party Revisited: Continuity and Change in the Party's Structure and Performance." *Journal of Japanese Studies* 10 (1984):385-435.

Identifies broader and longer-term patterns of continuity and change in the Liberal Democratic Party's structure and behavior in non-electoral contexts as they have evolved over the nearly thirty years of its existence. Three specific structural variables are used in the analysis: the party's membership, intraparty factions, and leadership.

336. ―――――. *Party in Power: The Japanese Liberal-Democrats and Policy-Making.* Berkeley: University of California Press, 1970.

Describes and analyzes the various decision-making situations of the Liberal Democratic Party. Focus is on the processes involved in the formulation of policies over issues of a more or less controversial nature, as interpreted in terms of the organizational framework and the interaction of persons and groups. Divided into three parts. Part One consists of a historical introduction. Part Two deals with four factors in LDP policymaking (membership, party organization, intra-party factions, and connections with external groups). Part Three contains three case studies: compensating former landowners, constitutional revision, and relations with the People's Republic of China.

337. Hrebenar, Ronald J. *The Japanese Party System: From One-Party Rule to Coalition Government.* Boulder, Colo.: Westview Press, 1986.

   Provides a comprehensive look at all of Japan's current major and minor national level parties. Little has been written in English about the important new parties that have emerged since 1960. Includes chapters on the laws and political forces affecting Japanese politics. A major theme is the fact that Japan shares many political patterns with other highly industrialized democracies, and the data presented here facilitate cross-national comparative studies of party systems.

338. Kim, Hong N. "The Crisis of Japan's Liberal Democratic Party." *Current History* 68 (1975):158-182.

   Assesses the causes of the crisis, the first since 1955, among which were the steady decline of the LDP's support, especially in the urban areas, and the deteriorating economic situation since 1972. With the resignation of Prime Minister Tanaka in November 1974 and the election of Takeo Miki as Prime Minister in December 1974, the future of the party and Miki's government were tested with the parliamentary elections for the House of Representatives in 1975.

339. Langer, Paul F. *Communism in Japan: A Case of Political Naturalization.* Stanford, Calif.: Hoover Institution Press, 1972.

   Studies the Japanese Communist Party (JCP) in the postwar period. It was formed in 1922, and after the war it emerged as a legitimate political party. The work is divided into six principal parts. The first two parts concern the historical setting, concentrating on the emergence, evolution, and organizational strength of the JCP. The third part deals with its role and organization. The fourth and fifth parts discuss the JCP national environment. Part Five deals with the relationship between the JCP and the international environment. Finally, Part Six focuses on the principal determinants of the JCP's behavior.

340. Lee, Jooinn. "Komeito: Sokagakkai-ism in Japanese Politics." *Asian Survey* 10 (1970):501-518.

    Analyzes the role of Komeito (Clean Government Party) in the Japanese political scene. It is the political voice of the Sokagakkai (Value Creating Society) lay Buddhist sect, and it is for this reason that it has yet to secure the trust of the people; many are afraid that if Komeito comes to power, it would mean a return of authoritarianism in Japanese politics.

341. MacDougall, Terry Edward, ed. *Political Leadership in Contemporary Japan*. Ann Arbor: Center for Japanese Studies, University of Michigan, 1982.

    Essays written by American political scientists on particular Japanese political leaders as seen in the context of specific issues that stress a variety of leadership styles, goals, and skills. The following leaders are included: former Liberal Democratic Party prime ministers Fukuda Takeo and Tanaka Kakuei; Kono Yohei, a conservative leader who founded the New Liberal Club; Asukata Ichio, Chairman of the Japan Socialist Party; parliamentary leaders; mayoral leaders; and powerful leaders without official bureaucratic or political roles. MacDougall maintains that these various leadership styles in practice narrow seemingly unbridgeable gaps in partisan perspectives.

342. McKean, Margaret A. "Japan's Beleaguered Ruling Party." *Current History* 75 (1978):158-182.

    Japan is faced with international pressure to play a larger political role in world affairs appropriate to her economic stature, but for reasons McKean discusses here, this is not likely to happen. The Liberal Democratic Party (LDP) is faced with domestic problems that will keep the government from expanding into international affairs, according to McKean. Among the problems considered are a decline in the LDP's popular support, the Lockheed scandal of 1976, and opposition to nuclear power from the public.

343. Rohlen, Thomas P. "Violence at Yoka High School: The Implications for Japanese Coalition Politics of the Confrontation Between the Communist Party and the Buraku Liberation League." *Asian Survey* 16 (1976):682-699.

   Discusses the events that led Ryokichi Minobe, the left-oriented governor of Tokyo, to suddenly withdraw his candidacy for an almost certain third term in February 1975. At Yoka High School, which is a few hours from Osaka, an intense dispute had been going on throughout the summer and fall of 1974 between teachers, students, and parents concerning the formation of a club for the study of Burakumin problems. Some wanted to have the club sponsored by the Communist-led teachers, while others wanted it sponsored by a group outside the school, the Burakumin Liberation League. In November 1974 negotiations collapsed, and the Burakumin Liberation League began to exert pressure on the teachers. The teachers' opposition stiffened under this pressure, and they refused to negotiate until all outside pressure was removed from the school. This condition was not met and tension escalated. On November 22, 1974 extreme violence erupted between the League members and their supporters and the teachers. Rohlen explains that antagonism between the Communist Party and the Burakumin Liberation League, which had been growing since 1965, was responsible for this violence. He also examines the political significance of the incident in light of the state of contemporary local opposition politics.

C. FOREIGN RELATIONS

344. Emmerson, John K. *Arms, Yen & Power: The Japanese Dilemma*. New York: Dunellen, 1971.

   Describes Japanese national security policy within the framework of Asian and American relations. Briefly looks at Japan's present economic status and political situation and discusses priority interests for Japan in foreign affairs. Among these priority interests are the Japanese-American relationship, security, relations with Asian neighbors, and certain decisions for the 1970s which will affect the security of Japan and its relations with the countries of Asia and the United States.

345. Langdon, Frank. *Japan's Foreign Policy*. Vancouver: University of British Columbia Press, 1973.

   As signified by former President Nixon's visits to Peking and Moscow in 1972, the major countries are moving towards a balance of power in which the United States is not as vigorously opposed to China and the Soviet Union, nor as closely supportive of Japan and Taiwan. Langdon attempts to provide the basis for understanding the likely impact of these changes on Japan's foreign policy by examining the recent changes in Japan's international environment. The author has selected the most important objectives of the Japanese government leaders and has described the policies of Japan that are designed to achieve these objectives. Concentrates on the period since 1960, and most of the policy developments that are described occurred during the cabinets of Prime Ministers Ikeda and Sato. However, earlier policy decisions are included when relevant.

346. Minor, Michael. "Decision Models and Japanese Foreign Policy Decision Making." *Asian Survey* 25 (1985):1229-1241.

   Minor argues that there is a need for a framework for the comparative analysis of Japanese foreign policy decision-making, and here he attempts to establish such a framework. Three case studies are examined that lead to "decision models" that provide a preliminary typology of Japanese foreign policy decision processes. The typology is based on the assumption that the nature of the decision involved is an important factor in policy-making variation. Three types of decisions are studied: (1) the routine foreign policy decision, (2) the political decision, and (3) the critical decision.

347. Mochizuki, Mike. "Japan's Foreign Policy." *Current History* 84 (1985):401-435.

   Examines the foreign policy of the Nakasone government, which the author finds to have a new vitality, national confidence, and commitment to democratic principles, and which has reinforced the goals of American foreign policy.

348. Pyle, Kenneth B. "The Future of Japanese Nationality: An Essay in Contemporary History. *Journal of Japanese Studies* 8 (1982):223-263.

   A look at the ongoing national debate in Japan about

its postwar order and future role in the world in light of the tremendous changes it has undergone since the end of World War II.

1. TREATIES

349. Adams, L. Jerold. "Japanese Treaty Patterns." *Asian Survey* 12 (1972):242-258.

    Discusses postwar (1951-1965) trends and characteristics of Japanese bilateral treaty patterns. A quantitative analysis of Japanese treaties concluded during the above mentioned period that establishes the total volume of treaties and the distribution and trends of treaty practice. Includes only formal or original documents.

350. ———. *Theory, Law and Policy of Contemporary Japanese Treaties*. Dobbs Ferry, N.Y.: Oceana Publications, 1974.

    Presents a general and comprehensive study of Japanese treaties. Uses both quantitative and qualitative data in the analysis of three aspects of Japanese treaty-making and practice: theory, law, and policy. Concentrates on the twenty-year period since the signing of the Treaty of Peace in 1951. Includes a calendar of Japanese treaties from 1951 to 1970.

2. DEFENSES

351. Adelman, Kenneth L. "There *Is* Such a Thing as a Free Ride." *Across the Board* 18 (1981):36-40.

    Japan has been spending only 0.9 percent of its GNP on defense, and the United States has been bearing most of the expense. But as Adelman indicates, there has been prodding by the Japanese business sector and government officials as well as by the United States for Japan to do more for its own defense.

352. Gale, Roger W. "Nuclear Power and Japan's Proliferation Option." *Asian Survey* 18 (1978):1117-1133.

    In Japan, nuclear power is perceived as more a matter of vital national security than in most other countries. It would enable Japan to achieve energy independence, and would provide her with the capability to build nuclear weapons. However, there is no evidence that any change will occur in its non-nuclear policy at present. Gale examines the proliferation potential inherent in Japan's civil nuclear power industry and how it could be employed for military purposes as well as the internal and external constraints and safeguards on Japan's freedom of action.

353. Mendel, Douglas H., Jr. "Japanese Defense in the 1970s: The Public View." *Asian Survey* 10 (1970):1046-1069.

    An analysis of the results of the author's 1970 national survey on the views of the Japanese national public on various defense issues. Focuses on showing the depth and nature of Japanese public opposition to expanded defense forces, especially nuclear, and to either Japanese or United States defense of other Asian nations.

354. Morley, James William, ed. *Forecast for Japan: Security in the 1970s*. Princeton, N.J.: Princeton University Press, 1972.

    Essays by scholars on the major influences that will affect Japan's security policy and Japan's responses to them. Three specific influences are discussed here: the fiscal and strategic attitudes of officials, the balance of domestic political forces, and pressures in the international environment.

355. Pempel, T.J. "Japan's Nuclear Allergy." *Current History* 68 (1975):169-183.

    Discusses efforts made by the governments of both Japan and the United States to weaken the opposition of the Japanese public to nuclear weapons.

356. Shilling, David. "A Reassessment of Japan's Naval Defense Needs." *Asian Survey* 16 (1976):216-229.

    Shilling argues that it is possible for Japan to reduce its dependence on United States naval forces for economic survival in the context of a world-wide conflict, and thus reduce the United States defense burden in the Pacific without undertaking a large military buildup that would raise tensions in Japan and the rest of Asia.

3. MILITARY POLICY

357. Curtis, Gerald L. "Japanese Security Policies and the United States." *Foreign Affairs* 59 (1981):852-874.

    Looks closely at Japan's foreign policy toward the Soviet Union and China, and how Japanese leaders view American policy toward these countries, as well as the state of Japanese thinking concerning the country's defense position. Also examines the changing character of Japanese political leadership in the next decade, which has its own important implications for the conduct of Japan's foreign relations and for United States efforts to maintain and strengthen a relationship vital both to United States policy in East Asia and to broader American national interests.

358. Endicott, John E. *Japan's Nuclear Option: Political, Technical, and Strategic Factors*. New York: Praeger, 1975.

    Appraises Japan's future nuclear weapons policy by examining the international, domestic, technical, and strategic factors that relate to this issue.

359. Han, Sungjoo. "Japan's 'PXL' Decision: The Politics of Weapons Procurement." *Asian Survey* 18 (1978):769-784.

    In 1977 the National Defense Council of Japan approved a plan to receive 45 antisubmarine patrol airplanes, which would initially be imported from the United States and subsequently produced in Japan under license. This decision, known as the "PXL" (next-generation antisubmarine patrol aircraft) was the culmination of the nine year delay by the government in reaching a decision. A further cause for delay was the Lockheed bribery scandal in 1976. Han provides a case study of the decision, in which the process of decision-making in Japan on weapons procurement can be observed. It involves various aspects of Japanese politics such as the role and power of the Defense Agency, the nature of business influence in government decision-making, and the interrelationships among various government agencies.

360. Inoguchi, Takashi. "Japan's Images and Options: Not a Challenger, but a Supporter." *Journal of Japanese Studies* 12 (1986):95-119.

    Examines the changes Japan has made in security and economic policy in the past decade, and presents suggestions for some of Japan's future options.

361. Okimoto, Daniel I. "Japan's Non-Nuclear Policy: The Problem of the NPT." *Asian Survey* 15 (1975):313-327.

Examines the reasons for Japan's delay in ratifying the Nuclear Nonproliferation Treaty (NPT). The Japanese government signed the Treaty on February 3, 1970, more than eighteen months after it was drafted, and ratification was made contingent on a satisfactory resolution of some concerns. At the time of the writing of this article in 1975, the Diet had not yet ratified the Treaty. Okimoto looks at the kinds of reservations that were held about the Treaty and the factors that explain the prolonged delay in Diet approval.

362. Quester, George H. "Japan and the Nuclear Non-Proliferation Treaty." *Asian Survey* 10 (1970):765-778.

Analyzes the reasons for Japan's delay in ratifying the Nuclear Non-Proliferation Treaty, which it had signed in 1970.

363. Sorenson, Jay B. *Japanese Policy and Nuclear Arms*. New York: American-Asian Educational Exchange, 1975.

A brief discussion of the various problems involved in any Japanese decision concerning the adoption of a nuclear arms policy.

364. Weinstein, Martin E. *Japan's Postwar Defense Policy, 1947-1968*. New York: Columbia University Press, 1971.

Weinstein discusses Japan's postwar defense policy, which he considers to be prudent and effective. However, he contends that a new policy may be necessary in the future because of changes in the distribution of power in the Far East and in Japan itself.

V
GENERAL WORKS ON THE ECONOMY

A. ECONOMIC CONDITIONS

365. Abegglen, James C. "The Economic Growth of Japan." *Scientific American* 222 (1970):31-37.

    Abegglen examines certain factors that he considers to be conducive to Japan's economic growth, among which are debt financing, the government-business partnership, the employment system, government policies, and voluntary saving. He maintains that Japan's economic system appears to be the most efficient in the world for generating high productivity, and that it should continue to grow.

366. Allen, G.C. *The Japanese Economy*. New York: St. Martin's, 1981.

    A survey of Japan's economy that analyzes the operations of its various sectors since World War II and explains how it has achieved its success. It examines the financial system, agriculture, manufacturing industry, industrial relations, foreign trade and investment, as well as the government-business relationship. Emphasis is on the contribution of Japan's social and political institutions to its progress. Allen also speculates on probable economic changes of the 1980s.

367. ———. *A Short Economic History of Modern Japan*. 4th ed. New York: St. Martin's, 1981.

    Traces the economic history of Japan from 1867 to 1937, and from 1945 to 1979. Major emphasis is on industrial and financial development, economic policy, and the reasons for Japan's economic achievements.

368. Anderson, William S. "Meeting the Japanese Economic Challenge." *Business Horizons* 24 (1981):56-62.

   Looks at the reasons behind Japan's economic success, and for the decline of the United States economy. Suggestions are offered for the revitalization of the American economy, and the question of America's ability to meet Japan's economic challenge successfully is raised.

369. Barnhart, Michael A. *Japan Prepares for Total War: The Search for Economic Security, 1919-1941*. Ithaca, N.Y.: Cornell University Press, 1987.

   Examines the events leading up to World War II in the context of Japan's quest for economic security. Following the collapse of Germany in 1918, Japan realized that nations had to be able to supply themselves during wartime with adequate quantities of raw materials and manufactured goods rather than relying on other countries. As a consequence, the empire began to reorganize itself in a search for economic self-sufficiency. Barnhart focuses on the period from 1938 to 1941 and discusses Japan's drive for security and the ways in which this drive shaped its internal and external policies. He also explores American economic pressure on Tokyo and looks at its impact on Japan's foreign policy and domestic economy. Barnhart argues that Japan's need for security slowly became an impulse for empire and it led directly to the Pacific War.

370. Bieda, K. *The Structure and Operation of the Japanese Economy*. New York: John Wiley and Sons, 1970.

   Japan's high economic growth rate and the factors that have influenced it are analyzed. Included are the factors of the economic plans and fiscal and monetary policies of the government, postwar farmland reform, and the unique characteristics of Japan's monetary and industrial structures. Also presents a fairly detailed study of the Japanese tax system, agricultural situation, the capital market, and the "keiretsu" (multiple-firm oligopolies).

371. Blumenthal, Tuvia. "Exports and Economic Growth: The Case of Postwar Japan." *Quarterly Journal of Economics* 86 (1972):617-631.

   Considers the contributions of exports to the growth rate of the GNP, and the cyclical relation between exports and the GNP.

372. Boltho, Andrea. *Japan: An Economic Survey, 1953-1973.* London: Oxford University Press, 1975.

   Uses a macro-economic quantitative approach in describing the Japanese economy and the factors responsible for its growth from 1953 to 1973. Among the factors discussed are capital, labor, economic policies, foreign trade, and income distribution.

373. Bunke, Harvey C. "A Japanese Pilgrimage." *Business Horizons* 24 (1981):2-9.

   Compares American and Japanese economic performance and examines the reasons for Japan's economic success. Bunke discusses the factors he considers to be responsible for Japan's economic growth, and among these are its drive for increased productivity, higher levels of savings, a disciplined and well-educated work force, quality control circles, and the commitment by government and industry to promote economic growth.

374. Business Intercommunications, Inc. *White Paper on Japanese Economy.* Tokyo, Business Intercommunications, Inc.

   An annual review of the Japanese economy, published in Japan as a government White Paper by the Economic Planning Agency. The English edition is an abridged version.

375. Donnelly, Michael W. "Japan's Search for Food Security." *Current History* 75 (1978):164-183.

   Japan has often faced an uncertain food supply because of its limited food production and uncontrolled population growth. The problem has been exacerbated by rapid economic change, which has caused increased affluence and lowered birth rates, which have led to changes in food habits. Rice consumption has declined, and the consumption of meat, eggs, dairy products, and fruit and vegetables has increased. Consequently, Japan has become a major importer of many agricultural products, and this situation has spurred attempts to increase domestic production in order to become more self-sufficient.

376. *Economic Statistics Annual* (1967)- . Tokyo: Research and Statistics Dept., Bank of Tokyo.

   Contains financial statistics for money and banking, public finance, foreign trade, industry, labor, prices and household economy, and national accounts. In both Japanese and English.

377. The Economist. *Japan.* New York: Cambridge University Press, 1983.

   Briefs on Japan's political economy that have previously appeared in *The Economist.* They present a short, simple introduction for those unfamiliar with Japan. Among the topics discussed are balance of payments, trade, industry and industrial policy, finance, housing, politics, and defense and foreign policy.

378. Evans, Robert, Jr. *The Labor Economies of Japan and the United States.* New York: Praeger, 1971.

   Contrasts the differences and similarities of selected aspects of the labor economies of Japan and the United States. Includes the influence of non-economic aspects such as history, law, culture, and social structure as well as economic aspects. Among the issues discussed are institutional context of the labor market, employment and manpower, aggregate wage patterns and relationships, wage differentials, and low-wage industries.

379. Financial Times. *Japan: Miracle '70: A Business Guide to the World's Third Economic Power.* London: Longman, 1970.

   A special survey of Japan that was prepared in order to present an up-to-date picture of Japan's economy in time for EXPO '70, which was held in Japan. It examines the economic boom as well as the national and international problems and responsibilities it has brought. Also provides an introduction to the history and art of Japan and to the Japanese way of life. The final section includes a business person's guide to Japan.

380. "Focus on Japan: Nakasone's Post-Industrial Society." *Far Eastern Economic Review* 118 (1982):22-26, 45-92.

   Consists of various articles about the industrial and political situation of Japan in 1982. Among the topics included are Prime Minister Yasuhiro Nakasone's political victory, the computer software industry, database services, general trading companies, information network systems, retailing, heavy industry, and women at work.

381. Frank, Isaiah, ed. *The Japanese Economy in International Perspective.* Baltimore, Md.: Johns Hopkins University Press, 1975.

Illuminates a number of aspects of the Japanese economy that greatly affect its foreign relations. Among the aspects discussed are industrial policy, economic policy, distribution in Japan, the Japanese farmer and politics, foreign trade, exports, raw-materials policy, and foreign direct investment.

382. ———— and Ryokichi Hirono, eds. *How the United States and Japan See Each Other's Economy: An Exchange of Views between the American and Japanese Committees for Economic Development.* New York: Committee for Economic Development, 1974.

A companion volume to *Toward a New International Economic System: A Joint Japanese-American View* (1974). Represents the views of each of the participating groups toward economic and social development in the other country.

383. Gregory, Ann. *The Japanese Economy and Business System: Patterns and Influences upon Growth.* New York: Japanese-American Business Administration & Cultural Studies Program, Graduate School of Business Administration, New York University, 1982.

A brief review of the macro and micro explanations of Japanese economic performance and the role of government policy in meshing favorably with Japanese workers and management. Discusses the effects of economic policy on economic growth, the evolution and expansion of the Japanese firm, the organization structure, decision-making patterns and personnel policies of the large firm, and major internal and external forces affecting Japan's future economic performance.

384. Gregory, Gene. "Japanese Economic Growth: The Human Equation." *Asian Survey* 15 (1975):851-869.

Gregory discusses his thesis that economic growth has improved the quality of life in Japan, despite the environmental problems it has created. He contends that the infant mortality rate has decreased, the life expectancy rates have increased, the rate of savings is high, and there is more time and money for leisure activities and travel.

385. Grootaert, Christiaan. *The Relation between Final Demand and Income Distribution, with Application to Japan.* New York: Springer-Verlag, 1983.

   A mathematical economics approach to the study of the effects of changes in the structure of final demand, which occur with economic growth, on income distribution. An equilibrium model of income distribution is applied to Japan during the period from 1959 to 1969, a time of rapid economic growth.

386. Haitani, Kanji. *The Japanese Economic System: An Institutional Overview.* Lexington, Mass.: Lexington Books, 1976.

   Describes Japan's major economic institutions and their political, social, and cultural dynamics.

387. Hall, Robert B., Jr. *Japan: Industrial Power of Asia.* 2d ed. New York: D. Van Nostrand, 1976.

   A brief view of modern, urban-industrial Japan. Examines some aspects of its changing role in the world as a result of its industrial importance. Emphasis is on change. Among the aspects included are the agricultural revolution, the industrial miracle, urban-industrial society, social conditions, trade, and political relations.

388. Halliday, Jon. *A Political History of Japanese Capitalism.* New York: Pantheon Books, 1975.

   Halliday is concerned with the interpenetration of class structure and class conflict, mode of production, politics and ideology within the Japanese state, the relationship between this structure and Japan's global system of imperialism, and the changes within essential structural continuity that have characterized this dynamic configuration through both the prewar and postwar periods.

389. Hamada, Tomoko. "Corporation, Culture and Environment: The Japanese Model." *Asian Survey* 25 (1985):1214-1228.

   Discusses the Japanese model of social change, which is a model of a rationally planned economy and socioeconomic gradualism based on education, sex, and age. The latter factors determine a person's social status, which is related to his or her economic status, and they explain the basic structure of Japanese society. The Japanese model is contrasted with the market-oriented

General Works on the Economy 107

economy of Western society and the class conflict of the underdeveloped country.

390. Hirschmeier, Johannes. "The Japanese Spirit of Enterprise, 1867-1970." *Business History Review* 44 (1970): 13-38.

The author contends that the Japanese spirit of enterprise is influenced by two primary factors: harmony within and for the group, and a strong sense of economic nationalism. These factors have been responsible for Japan's rapid industrialization at the turn of the century and for the rapid postwar economic recovery.

391. Hollerman, Leon. "A Sampling of Japanese Economic Issues--A Review Article." *Journal of Asian Issues* 40 (1981):735-743.

A critique of works that are concerned with the following issues: Japan's economic growth; Japan's economic structure, behavior, and performance; and its relations with the United States. The works discussed here are Ohkawa, *Patterns of Japanese Economic Development* (1978); Ohkawa, *Japanese Economic Growth* (1973); Suzuki, *Money and Banking in Contemporary Japan* (1980); Sato, *Industry and Business in Japan* (1980); and Tasca, *U.S.-Japanese Economic Relations* (1980).

392. "How Japan Competes." *Dun's Review* 114 (1978):65-87.

A special report that concentrates on Japan's export success and import restrictions. Includes an article by Herman Kahn on Japan's role in the '80s, as well as articles on selling and foreign corporate financing in Japan, investing in the Tokyo stock market, and profiles of six powerful Japanese business leaders.

393. Hunsberger, Warren S. *Japan: New Industrial Giant.* New York: American-Asian Educational Exchange, 1972.

Examines the causes and consequences of Japan's postwar economic success, future problems and United States-Japan trade relations. Presents a background to recent economic growth and discusses growth and change in production and consumption. Also looks at domestic trends and issues and examines issues that are present in Japan's future (viz., international, economic, security, and political).

394. Ike, Nobutaka. *Japan: The New Superstate*. San Francisco: W.H. Freeman, 1974.

    An account of Japan's rapid economic growth rate, and of its negative environmental and social consequences, such as pollution and individual and social tensions. Delineates the historical, cultural, social, and economic factors responsible for the growth rate and shows how they are interrelated.

395. *Japan Economic Almanac* (1985)-   . Tokyo: Japan Economic Journal.

    Continues *Industrial Review of Japan: An Annual In-Depth Report on the State of the Japanese Economy* (1956-1984). An annual report of issues and problems affecting the economy, with breakdowns by industry. Includes economic indicators.

396. Japan. Economic Planning Agency. *Economic Survey of Japan* (1952/53)-   . Tokyo: Japan Times.

    Annual analysis of the performance of the Japanese economy.

397. Japan Economic Research Center. *The Future of World Economy and Japan*. Tokyo, 1975.

    A complete revision of the Center's previous report, *Japan's Economy in 1980 in the Global Context...* (1972). This report analyzes and projects future economic trends, with emphasis on the petroleum resource problem and on inflation.

398. Japan. Ministry of Foreign Affairs. *Japan's Economy at the Crossroads: 30 Years of Transition*. Tokyo, 1976.

    A review of Japan's economic development during the last thirty years (1945-1975). Includes a summary of the 1975 Economic Survey of Japan with a discussion of the economic prospects for 1976 and beyond, and a chronology of events in Japan's political and economic history.

399. *Japanese Economic Studies* 1 (1972)-   . Armonk, N.Y.: M.E. Sharpe.

    Contains translations of economics material from Japanese sources (primarily scholarly journals and books). The selections are intended to reflect developments in the Japanese economy and to be of interest to those professionally involved with the subject. Some issues are devoted to specific topics. Published quarterly.

400. "Japan's Strategy for the '80s." *Business Week* (Dec. 14, 1981):39-120.

    A special issue devoted to the following topics: changes in the economic and business structure, the semiconductor industry, information processing, future research activities, and social problems.

401. Jorgenson, Dale W. and Mieko Nishimizu. "U.S. and Japanese Economic Growth, 1952-1974: An International Comparison." *Economic Journal* 88 (1978):707-726.

    An international comparison of aggregate economic growth in the United States and Japan during the period from 1952 to 1974. Analyzes differences between American and Japanese levels of output and allocates these differences between differences in factor input and differences in levels of technology in the two countries. Also analyzes differences between levels of factor input between the two countries according to differences in capital and labor input.

402. Kahn, Herman. *The Emerging Japanese Superstate: Challenge and Response*. Englewood Cliffs, N.J.: Prentice-Hall, 1970.

    Predictions of Japan's economic, technological and military future in the 1970s and 1980s. Some attention is also paid to the quality of life aspects of Japan's future, such as aesthetic, artistic, and cultural issues. The author maintains that the phrase "challenge and response" in the title implies a challenge to the Japanese themselves, as well as to the United States and other countries.

403. ———— and Thomas Pepper. *The Japanese Challenge: The Success and Failure of Economic Success*. New York: Thomas Y. Crowell, 1979.

    Examines some current problems in the Japanese economy, and discusses solutions and alternative goals. The authors' objective is to contribute to a greater understanding in the United States and elsewhere of the nature of Japan's problems and their impact on international business. Analyzes problems that are cited as being associated with the following six areas: (1) the continu-

ing recession, (2) yen issues, (3) lack of infrastructure
and amenities, (4) long-term industrial restructuring,
(5) institutional issues, and (6) public and private
debate over the preceding issues.

404. Kanamori, Hisao. "What Accounts for Japan's High Rate
of Growth?" *Review of Income and Wealth* 18 (1972):155-
171.

Investigates the sources of economic growth in Japan
and compares them with those in the United States and
Europe. Focuses on the reasons why Japan's growth rate
is considerably higher than that of other countries.

405. Kaneko, Yoshio. "Employment and Wages." *Developing
Economies* 8 (1970):445-474.

A study of the impact of an educated, technically adept
labor force on Japan's postwar economic growth and the
balance between wages and productivity.

406. Kelley, Allen C. and Jeffrey G. Williamson. *Lessons
from Japanese Development: An Analytical Economic History*. Chicago: University of Chicago Press, 1974.

A history of Japan's economic development from 1887
to 1915 that uses the new economic history methodology.
This approach involves the following steps: formal model
building, the application of a general equilibrium model
to economic history, quantitative analysis and testing,
and an exhaustive use of the "counterfactual." The authors also make use of the more traditional descriptive
accounts of Japanese economic development.

407. Kornhauser, David. *Japan: Geographical Background to
Urban-Industrial Development*. 2d ed. New York: Longman, 1982.

An anthropo-geographical analysis of the transformation
of the Japanese landscape within a historical framework.
Reviews the history of agricultural development and
change and looks at the history of the city from the
eighth century to the present. Also examines the growth
and evolution of commerce and history, and considerable
attention is paid to the effects of external influences
such as war and economic disruptions in shaping Japan's
industrial successes and failures. Looks at the problems
facing Japan's contemporary urban-industrial scene.
Includes a selective, annotated bibliography.

408. Kosai, Yutaka. *The Era of High-Speed Growth: Notes on the Postwar Japanese Economy*. Tokyo: University of Tokyo Press, 1986.

   The author, an economist who participated in policy-making during Japan's period of rapid economic growth, presents a history of the contemporary Japanese economy that covers the period from 1945 to the early 1980s. He attributes economic growth to reliance on the market mechanism of classical capitalist theory rather than on the distinctive values, customs and behavioral style of Japanese society.

409. ——— and Yoshitaro Ogino. *The Contemporary Japanese Economy*. Armonk, N.Y.: M.E. Sharpe, 1984.

   Adapted from *Nihon Keizai Tembo*, published in Japanese in 1980. Looks at the interplay of market forces and of overall trends in the Japanese economy. Discusses macroeconomic trends in the economy since the end of World War II, the microeconomic foundations of the economy, and socio-political aspects of the contemporary Japanese economy.

410. Kurihara, Kenneth K. *The Growth Potential of the Japanese Economy*. Baltimore, Md.: Johns Hopkins Press, 1971.

   Fundamental factors responsible for Japan's economic growth at present and in the decades ahead are analyzed in a theoretical and empirical framework. Among the factors discussed here are demilitarization, consumption and saving, private investment, the fiscal-monetary milieu, technological progress and productivity gains, and the balance of payments.

411. Mahajan, V.S. *Development Planning: Lessons from Japanese Model*. Calcutta: Minerva Associates Publications, 1976.

   Mahajan suggests that the Japanese model is worth emulating and is suitable for incorporation into development planning. He presents a discussion of Japan's economic development as well as of the growth and distribution of its national income, and of the role played by savings, investment, and foreign capital in the economy. In addition, the "ie" system is examined, in which loyalty to the family and through it to the country has played an important role in the maintenance of the existing as well as the creation of new capital assets, and also the military policy of the government and its impact on Japanese industrialization.

412. Minami, Ryoshin. *The Economic Development of Japan: A Quantitative Study.* New York: St. Martin's, 1986.

   A comprehensive study of the last one hundred years of Japan's economic growth, from the Meiji period to the present day. The major part of the book concentrates on the factors responsible for Japan's economic success during the Meiji period, and the reasons why Japan achieved a more rapid rate of economic growth than other developed countries. The author also evaluates results of Japan's economic growth and makes predictions for its future. Contains long-term, structural, and quantitative analyses, as well as comparisons with other countries. Covers the following topics: overview of the economic history of Japan, modern economic growth and production and demand, causes and results of modern economic growth, and retrospect and prospects of modern economic growth.

413. ⸻. *The Turning Point in Economic Development: Japan's Experience.* Tokyo: Kinokuniya Bookstore Co., 1973.

   Only in recent years (early 1960s) has the surplus labor in Japan's economy disappeared, and now Japan can be considered to have passed the "turning point." Minami discusses the theory of the turning point and its presence in the Japanese economy.

414. Miyoshi, Shuichi. "Dollar Crisis." *Japan Quarterly* 19 (1972):28-35.

   The effects of President Nixon's announcement of August 15, 1971 concerning emergency economic measures, including a ten percent import surcharge and suspension of convertability of dollars into gold on Japan's economy are discussed.

415. Monroe, Wilbur F. "The Rise of Tokyo as an International Financial Center." *Journal of World Trade Law* 8 (1974):655-667.

   Concerned with recent developments in which Tokyo is becoming an international financial center. The issues of international monetary reform and the international oil crisis are appraised briefly for their possible impact upon Tokyo's development.

416. ———— and Eisuke Sakakibara. *The Japanese Industrial Society: Its Organizational, Cultural, and Economic Underpinnings*. Austin: Bureau of Business Research, University of Texas at Austin, 1977.

An analysis of the postwar economy that integrates social and cultural factors with the more traditional economic analysis. Discusses the following factors: mutual dependence, or "amae," verticalism in the Japanese organization, lifelong employment and the seniority system, the educational system, non-economic factors, economic considerations, industry and production patterns, the political-economic structure, and the dual structure of Japanese diplomacy.

417. Morishima, Michio. *Why Has Japan "Succeeded"? Western Technology and the Japanese Ethos*. Cambridge: Cambridge University Press, 1984.

Morishima attributes Japan's economic success and technological development to the influences of Confucianism, Shintoism, and Buddhism.

418. Nagasu, Kazuji. "Japanese Economy in the Seventies." *Japan Quarterly* 19 (1972):140–147.

An amplification and explanation of the main points of the "manifesto" written in October 1971 by a group of Japanese economists on the currency problem that was precipitated by President Nixon's economic announcement of August 15. Nagasu was a member of the group and one of the drafters of the announcement, which was entitled: "Now Is the Time for Realignment of the Economy at Home and Abroad."

419. Nakamura, Takafusa. *Economic Development of Modern Japan*. Tokyo: Ministry of Foreign Affairs, 1985.

A brief analysis of the salient points of Japan's economic development from 1868 to the 1980s.

420. ————. *The Postwar Japanese Economy: Its Development and Structure*. Tokyo: University of Tokyo Press, 1981.

Summarizes the progress of the economy from its postwar devastation to its present high growth rate. Part One presents an historical account of the Japanese economy during the wartime, postwar, and rapid growth periods. Part Two discusses the problems that arose during the course of growth, among which are fiscal, monetary, labor, agricultural, and small business. Part Three examines Japan in the 1970s.

421. Nanto, Dick K. "Japan's Economy." *Current History* 84 (1985):414-434.

    As the result of changes in the conditions that had supported its rapid economic development, Japan is now at a major turning point in its economic history. Nanto examines the features of Japan's new economic age and its prospects for the future.

422. Nishikawa, Shunsaku, ed. *The Labor Market in Japan: Selected Readings.* Tokyo: Japan Foundation, 1980.

    Collected essays that originally appeared in a variety of periodicals and journals. The chapters have been organized around two major themes: the labor market, and wage determination. Most of the essays are behavioral in approach and many utilize quantitative analysis. In addition, many place the labor market in a socioeconomic framework.

423. Nishimizu, Mieko and Charles R. Hulten. "The Sources of Japanese Economic Growth: 1955-71." *Review of Economics and Statistics* 60 (1978):351-361.

    An empirical analysis of the sources of Japan's postwar economic growth. Separates the Japanese private domestic economy into ten sectors, and for each sector the growth of real gross output is allocated among the growth rates of (a) real intermediate input, (b) real capital services, (c) the quantity and quality of real labor services, and (d) a residual associated with the growth of total factor productivity. The sectors are then aggregated to obtain an estimate of the sources of growth for the private domestic economy as a whole. The principle conclusion is that produced factors of production-capital and intermediate goods were the predominant source of sectoral economic growth in Japan for the period from 1955 to 1971.

424. Ohkawa, Kazushi and Henry Rosovsky. *Japanese Economic Growth: Trend Acceleration in the Twentieth Century.* Stanford, Calif.: Stanford University Press, 1973.

    Explains the rapid growth of the Japanese economy during the twentieth century, with special emphasis on the years following World War II. The approach is quantitative and macroeconomic, and focus is on private investment spurts, technological progress, and trend acceleration in a national income framework.

425. ——— and Miyohei Shinohara. *Patterns of Japanese Economic Development: A Quantitative Appraisal*. New Haven, Conn.: Yale University Press, 1979.

　　Presents and analyzes statistical data from the *Estimates of Long-Term Economic Statistics of Japan Since 1868 (LTES)* project. The book is divided into four parts. Part One discusses overall patterns; Part Two is concerned with production and trade; Part Three deals with product allocation; and Part Four discusses factor shares, prices, and population.

426. Ohmae, Kenichi. *Beyond National Borders: Reflections on Japan and the World*. Homewood, Ill.: Dow Jones-Irwin, 1987.

　　Originally published in Japanese in 1986 under the title: *Now That I Have Seen the World, I Can See Japan Better*. Ohmae challenges the Japanese to reassess how they see themselves and their responsibilities to the people of other countries. He argues that Japan must stop thinking of itself as an isolated island and join the global community. He also discusses the issues of United States-Japan trade and the economics of international competition.

427. Olsen, Edward A. *Japan: Economic Growth, Resource Scarcity, and Environmental Constraints*. Boulder, Colo.: Westview Press, 1978.

　　A study, from a neo-Malthusian perspective, on Japan's economic vulnerability, which has been created by a scarcity of natural resources, and its consequences for Japan's position in international relations. Olsen contends that Japan's situation is potentially more serious than the circumstances of other advanced industrialized countries, and therefore it may provide an instructive example.

428. Organisation for Economic Co-operation and Development. *Economic Surveys: Japan*. 1964-   . Paris.

　　Annual survey of Japan's economic developments and prospects.

429. Ozawa, Terutomo. "Japan's Technological Challenge to the West: At a New Crossroads." *Asian Survey* 14 (1974):578-587.

   Looks at Japan's postwar economic drive in historical perspective. Also discusses some of the domestic problems that have resulted from economic expansion, among which are environmental pollution and urban congestion. Ozawa maintains that Japan is now confronted with new challenges to give greater attention to improvements in the social infrastructure, and to solve environmental problems. In addition, Japan must now compete at home against Western firms for the rising incomes of Japanese consumers, and also continue to upgrade its technological capacity to create new industries.

430. Pepper, Thomas, Merit E. Janow and Jimmy W. Wheeler. *The Competition: Dealing with Japan.* New York: Praeger, 1985.

   Describes recent and probable future changes in Japan's economy, and shows how the United States and Japanese economies are becoming increasingly similar because of domestic and international factors.

431. Pezeu-Massabuau, Jacques. *The Japanese Islands: A Physical and Social Geography.* Rutland, Vt.: Charles E. Tuttle, 1978.

   The author discusses what he considers to be a major force behind Japan's economic development, namely, the handicap of overpopulation and the firm determination to provide a standard of living that would permit the population to subsist. He also contends that successful economic development has persisted despite the naturally unfavorable environment, which includes a limited amount of land suitable for farming and unstable weather conditions.

432. Rebischung, James. *Japan: The Facts of Modern Business and Social Life.* Rutland, Vt.: Charles E. Tuttle, 1975.

   Rebischung's intention is to report as objectively as possible on the current Japanese scene and to provide a more balanced view of Japan than he feels is given in travel folders, official publications, and magazines. The information is based on trips to Japan the author made during the period from 1970 to 1972. He is a former member of the United States Army Occupation of Japan.

General Works on the Economy 117

Among the topics discussed here are population density, industrialization, work force, industry, wages and income, education, quality of life, and industrial pollution.

433. *Recent Economic Trends in Japan in 1977.* Tokyo: Economic Research Dept., Bank of Japan, 1978.

    A descriptive account of the state of the economy and finance. There is also a 1978 addition.

434. Rehder, Robert R. "Japan's Synergistic Society: How It Works and Its Implications for the U.S." *Management Review* 70 (1981):64-66.

    Rehder contends that the main power source for Japan's socioeconomic system lies in the cooperative action, or synergism, of all its interrelated parts, rather than in any one or several of its many elements. Rehder further maintains that if the United States were to accept the synergistic model of Japanese productivity and economic performance, the implications for American business and government leaders would be extensive and productive.

435. Richardson, Bradley M. and Taizo Ueda, eds. *Business and Society in Japan: Fundamentals for Businessmen.* New York: Praeger, 1981.

    Chapters written by American scholars on Japan that explain Japanese business and its overall environment within the context of sociocultural, political, economic, and historical factors. Organized into major sections that deal with business and labor, the Japanese economy, the overall social and political environment both past and present, and practical considerations regarding entrance into the Japanese market and other aspects of social and business relationships with Japanese business colleagues.

436. Rosovsky, Henry. "Japan's Economic Future." *Challenge* 16 (1973):6-17.

    Rosovsky discusses his predictions that Japan's rapid economic growth rate of the 1950s and 1970s will start slowing down by the late 1970s, and will continue to do so through the 1990s, partly for reasons beyond Japan's internal control, and partly due to possible future government financed improvements in the quality of life.

437. Saso, Mary and Stuart Kirby. *Japanese Industrial Competition to 1990*. Cambridge, Mass.: Abt Books, 1982.

   An assessment of the competitive aspects of Japanese industry and of social, political, and economic conditions and trends in the 1980s. Divided into two parts. Part One discusses how to compete and how to cooperate with Japanese industry, and includes information on the structure of a typical Japanese manufacturing company, and on Japan's industrial performance from 1960 to 1980. Part Two encompasses Japan's role in the 1980s and includes discussions on the energy scene, the Japanese base for development, trends in trade, and beyond 1980.

438. Shimokobe, Atsushi. "Concepts and Methodology of Regional Development." *Developing Economies* 8 (1970): 497-511.

   Focuses on regional development in Japan during the 1950s and 1960s. The 1969 comprehensive national development plan is explained, and problems of regional development resulting from drastic environmental changes are discussed.

439. Shinohara, Miyohei. "Causes and Patterns in the Postwar Growth.: *Developing Economies* 8 (1970):349-368.

   A selective analysis of some of the key factors in Japan's high postwar economic growth and of growth patterns.

440. ―――. *Industrial Growth, Trade, and Dynamic Patterns in the Japanese Economy*. Tokyo: University of Tokyo Press, 1982.

   A collection of articles, most of which were originally published ten to twenty years ago, in which the author strives to provide new information on the subject, rather than praising Japan's economic success since the postwar period.

441. ―――. *Structural Changes in Japan's Economic Development*. Tokyo: Kinokuniya Bookstore Co., 1970.

   Companion volume to the author's earlier work, *Growth and Cycles: The Japanese Economy* (1962). In this work, Shinohara presents a qualitative analysis of Japan's rapid economic growth during the pre- and post-World War II periods, and of the structural changes that accompanied it.

442. Simonis, Heide and Udo Ernst Simonis, eds. *Japan: Economic and Social Studies in Development*. Wiesbaden: Otto Harrassowitz, 1974.

Consists of a selective collection of contemporary economic and social studies related to the general theme of development. They provide an account of different sectors of the Japanese economy and society and of different scientific approaches in dealing with them. They also give due consideration to the economic, social, and political interdependencies and the unique features of the Japanese system.

443. Smith, Charles. "Focus: Industrial Japan '84." *Far Eastern Economic Review* 126 (1984):45-84.

A synopsis of developments in the Japanese economy during 1984. Emphasis is on the small company sector and the system of venture-capital financing providing high-risk funds. Among the topics discussed are venture-capital industry, venture promotion, and venture business. Also presents case studies of young venture-business companies.

444. Taira, Koji. "Japan after the 'Oil Shock': An International Resource Pauper." *Current History* 68 (1975): 145-184.

Describes the effects of the 1973 Arab oil embargo on Japan's economy and on its trade relations with the United States and Europe.

445. ──────. "The 1973-1978 Stagflation in Japan: A Watershed?" *Current History* 75 (1978):170-184.

Observes Japan's capacity to survive and its ability to adapt to change by studying the economic crisis of 1973-1978.

446. Thrush, John C. and Philip R. Smith. *Japan's Economic Growth and Educational Change, 1950-1970*. Lincoln, Neb.: EBHA Press, 1980.

A study of the effects of Japan's rapid economic growth during 1950 to 1970 on the structure, function, and internal interactions of its educational system.

447. Tsurumi, Yoshihiro. "Critical Choice for Japan: Cooperation or Conflict with the United States." *Columbia Journal of World Business* 12 (1977):14-20.

A discussion of the changes that have occurred both

in Japan's economy and the world economy since Japan's rapid economic recovery of the 1950s and 1960s. Some of these changes are (1) the politics of interdependency between Japan and the rest of the world have become more complex, (2) it has become necessary to change the government-business relationship in Japan in order to be more in touch with the present economic situation, and (3) there is no longer a visible economic model for Japan to follow (in the past the United States and Europe served this function); now it will have to go it alone. Tsurumi also assesses the impact of these and other changes on Japan's future economic growth and on the future of United States-Japan relations.

448. Uchino, Tatsuro. *Japan's Postwar Economy: An Insider's View of Its History and Its Future.* Tokyo: Kodansha International, 1983.

Economic policies that were adopted during the postwar period as well as those that were not, and those that were abandoned, are discussed by a former member of the Japan Economic Stabilization Board and of the Economic Planning Agency.

449. Van Zandt, Howard F. "Japanese Culture and the Business Boom." *Foreign Affairs* 48 (1970):344-357.

Examines the methods employed by the Japanese to achieve their postwar economic recovery, which the author contends were influenced by cultural factors. Also traces these influences back to their origin so that they can be understood within the economic framework.

450. Woronoff, Jon. *The Japan Syndrome: Symptoms, Ailments, and Remedies.* New Brunswick, N.J.: Transaction Books, 1986.

The author presents his assessment of the contemporary problems of the Japanese economy and society. Woronoff contends that while the economic system is extremely productive, it is not very fruitful for the workers; they get very little out of the large effort they put in. In addition, the strong points and merits, which are basically related to modern exporting sectors, are somewhat pointless today when Japan's exports are so often rejected abroad. He makes suggestions for improvement and discusses other sectors that might be developed to stimulate growth. Woronoff also discusses how Japan could better adapt to the inevitable economic slowdown and meet emerging social problems.

451. ———. *Japan: The Coming Economic Crisis*. 6th ed. Tokyo: Lotus Press, 1982.

Woronoff presents his view that Japan's economic success will not continue, as evidenced by signs such as the drop in growth rate and the appearance of bankruptcies and unemployment. He also examines some of the negative aspects of Japan's economy.

452. Wright-Boulton, J. and B.W. Jenney. "Secrets of Japanese Success." *Management Today* (Jan. 1981):64-67, 120.

Considers the reasons behind Japan's economic success. The authors maintain that the economy may have grown rapidly only since the end of World War II, but the foundation for its successful economic strategy has long been laid. This foundation was the "house system," which had been firmly established in Japan's feudal society by the middle of the nineteenth century. The successful manufacturing strategy that has developed since the end of World War II, and which has emphasized the production of goods with a high added value, and the facing up to the transportation problems resulting from the country's geographical location in relation to its markets are examined. This strategy takes into account the precepts of Confucianism, which recognizes that the unity of economics and politics are based on the importance of economic activities, provided they contribute to the social harmony. Also looks at some of the problems facing Japan's economy and society.

453. Yoshihara, Kunio. *Japanese Economic Development: A Short Introduction*. Tokyo: Oxford University Press, 1979.

Describes the development of the economy and its characteristics, with emphasis on industrialization and international trade. Considers the influence of early social and political conditions as well as the undesirable social consequences of economic development.

454. Yoshitomi, Masaru. "Supply Management: The Economic Key to Survival in the 1980s." *Asian Survey* 20 (1980):683-693.

As are many other countries, Japan is faced with two major economic problems for the 1980s: the constant real increase in the price of oil, and the decline of the value of the dollar and the collapse of the dollar-backed international monetary system. Yoshitomi discusses the effects of these problems on Japan as well as the ability of the Japanese economy to handle them by adopting supply management.

B. SOCIAL EFFECTS OF ECONOMIC GROWTH

455. Dore, Ronald P. *Shinohata: A Portrait of a Japanese Village.* New York: Pantheon Books, 1978.

    Dore presents a first-hand account of the social history of Shinohata, a village about ninety-five miles outside of Tokyo. It begins with early Japan and continues up to the postwar era. He discusses the changes in the way of life of the villagers that have resulted from Japan's economic progress and industrialization. Among the changes he examines are the local economy, tradition and relationships between family members, superiors and inferiors, neighbors, and man and nature.

456. Drucker, Peter F. "Japan: The Problem of Success." *Foreign Affairs* 56 (1978):564-578.

    Discusses the changes in social structure and values which have resulted from Japan's economic success. Also takes into account the aging of the population and its effects on lifetime employment and the seniority wage system.

457. ————. "The Price of Success: Japan Revisited." *Across the Board* 15 (1978):28-35.

    Drucker contends that the basic policies on which Japan's society is based presume yesterday's rural society and consumption, and as a consequence the results of economic progress have had a great impact on Japan's social structure and social values and on her ability to compete economically. He discusses the following consequences of economic progress: increased life span, making education more accessible to more of the population, and the shift of a near-majority of the labor force employed in farming into the industrial sector in a relatively short time.

458. Hidaka, Rokuro. *The Price of Affluence: Dilemmas of Contemporary Japan.* Tokyo: Kodansha International, 1984.

    Hidaka expresses his view on the problems he believes

have been created by Japan's economic prosperity. Foremost among these problems is Japan's "controlled society" that is under extremely tight constraints. It is characterized by induced integration rather than oppressive control. Life is becoming more standardized and passive, and it is lacking opportunities for self-expression and self-fulfillment. Individuals seek only to secure a position on the path to a good, comfortable life that has been laid out for them in society.

459. Ike, Nobutaka. "Economic Growth and Intergenerational Change in Japan." *American Political Science Review* 67 (1973):1194-1203.

    Analyzes the results of a quantitative study of the effects of economic growth on changes in intergenerational value priorities. The information is based on surveys of national character carried out by the Japanese Institute of Mathematical Statistics in 1953, 1958, 1963, and 1968.

460. Levine, Solomon B. "Japan's Economy: End of the Miracle?" *Current History* 68 (1975):149-181.

    Focus is on Japan's domestic problems that have resulted from high economic growth, among which are urban congestion, air and water pollution, inadequate housing, low levels of social security, and inappropriate educational opportunities.

461. ―――. "Japan's Growth Economy: Joy and Anguish." *Current History* 60 (1971):218-224, 243.

    Japan's rapid economic growth has ushered in a multitude of economic as well as social and environmental problems, and Levine discusses them here. Among the problems he examines are substandard and overcrowded housing conditions, pollution, and hazardous transportation. He also contends that the social costs of growth will continue to outweigh the benefits.

462. Norbeck, Edward. *Country to City: The Urbanization of a Japanese Hamlet.* Salt Lake City: University of Utah Press, 1978.

    A study of Takashima, a small island community within the boundaries of Okayama prefecture that consists of two related studies conducted by Norbeck. The first study is a detailed ethnographic description of Takashima as it existed in 1950 to 1951, as an isolated, impoverished fishing community, and which was originally published in 1954 under the title: *Takashima: A Japanese Fishing Community*. The second study describes and discusses the same community as it existed late in 1974, giving special attention to changes that had occurred since the original study was conducted. During this time, Takashima underwent many changes of Westernization and industrialization, and by 1975, familial and community organization and relationships had changed as the result of adapting to economic and other changes, and other aspects of life had become similarly altered.

463. Passin, Herbert. "Changing Values: Work and Growth in Japan." *Asian Survey* 15 (1975):821-850.

    Discusses changes in the domestic environment that have resulted from postwar economic developments and the changes in values concerning economic growth and work. Among the domestic changes considered here are the steady rise in the educational level of the workforce; the spread of new values of democratization, equality, and individualism; affluence; and the awareness by Japanese youth of the new life styles and attitudes of their counterparts in other advanced industrial countries.

464. Sethi, S. Prakash. "Why Japanese Business Is Losing Its Halo." *Business and Society Review* 12 (1974-75): 35-43.

    Examines the social problems that are facing Japan as the result of its high economic growth. Focus is on two major areas of public concern: consumer dissatisfaction and environmental problems; questions are being raised as to the degree to which companies are degrading the quality of life; and the companies are being asked about the actions they are taking to reverse this trend to restore public confidence.

465. Shimpo, Mitsuru. *Three Decades in Shiwa: Economic Development and Social Change in a Japanese Farming Community*. Vancouver: University of British Columbia Press, 1976.

    Describes the process of social change in the postwar period in a rural Japanese community that has resulted from industrialization. Shimpo defines industrialization here as the growing use of mechanized machinery in a production process and the growing role of money as an incentive to action within a market economy. Social change, as used here, refers to the change in rules positioning individuals with the social system and the rules that govern the authority associated with each position within the system. Ultimately, it refers to a change in these rules as they operate within and between a series of particular rural Japanese institutions, such as the village, the hamlet, the household, and the irrigation system.

466. Wimberley, Howard. "On Living with Your Past: Style and Structure among Contemporary Japanese Merchant Families." *Economic Development and Cultural Changes* 21 (1973):423-428.

Raises the question of the continuation of present-day urban life styles, which are largely shaped by traditions of the preindustrial past, into the future. Analyzes a comparative study conducted in Japan in 1971 of merchant families and white-collar families in the city of Kanazawa.

467. Yamamoto, George K. and Tsuyoshi Ishida, eds. *Selected Readings on Modern Japanese Society*. Berkeley, Calif.: McCutchan Pub. Corp., 1971.

Collected articles on the social consequences of Japan's economic modernization process. The selections focus on the following topics: the family, the small group, interpersonal relations and the psychological effects of traditional culture on individuals; social class relations in rural settings; urban centers and their associated class structures; aspects of contemporary educational, political, and religious institutions; cultural and technical change; and Japan as a model of economic development.

VI
ECONOMIC PLANNING

A. ECONOMIC POLICY

468. Allen, G.C. *Japan's Economic Policy*. New York: Holmes & Meier, 1980.

    A collection of papers previously written by the author on Japan's economic growth and development from the prewar to the postwar era. Emphasizes the role of the government. Includes discussions of the problems of economic growth; social institutions and economic purpose; and education, science, and economic development.

469. Birmingham, Hobart McK. "Japanese Postwar Attitudes towards International Trade and Investment." *Hastings International and Comparative Law Review* 2 (1979):1-20.

    Explains why the Japanese economy had for so long remained virtually closed not only to trade and investment of the United States, but also to that of the entire industrialized world. The author examines the nationalistic orientation of the business-government alliance established during the Meiji Era, the government validation process, and the five steps of the post-war capital liberalization program.

470. Codrea, John E. "The Fifth Liberalization of Capital Movements into Japan." *Case Western Reserve Journal of International Law* 6 (1974):279-291.

    In 1967, the Japanese government, in response to pressure by the OECD countries and the United States, began a program of liberalization of foreign investment in Japan. Under this program, five rounds of liberalization have taken place. Codrea briefly examines some of the highlights of the 1967 to 1973 liberalization program.

471. *Economic Views from Japan: Selections from Economic Eye.*
Tokyo: Keizai Koho Center, 1986.

A compilation of articles that have appeared in the Japanese journal *Economic Eye* (which consists of articles selected and translated from Japanese magazines for the insights they offer into Japanese views of the economy and business) primarily within the past three years. The articles cover the following topics: trade, international economic policy, industry and technology, management and labor, and finance.

472. Furuhashi, Yusaku. "Foreign Capital in Japan." *Columbia Journal of World Business* 7 (1972):50-56.

Although Japan has adopted a more liberal policy on foreign direct investment in recent years, a considerable array of restrictive measures are still maintained. Furuhashi discusses the underlying reasons for this slow, very careful approach to full capital liberalization. He examines the economic and industrial factors involved, as well as the social, cultural, and psychological attitudes that have led to the ambivalent, ethnocentric Japanese policy toward foreign capital and investment.

473. Japan. Economic Planning Agency. *Basic Economic and Social Plan: Toward a Vigorous Welfare Society 1973-1977.* Tokyo, 1973.

Since the Japanese Cabinet adopted the New Economic and Social Development Plan 1970-1975 in 1970, the situation both at home and internationally changed so radically that it was necessary to replace that plan with an entirely new one, the Basic Economic and Social Plan 1973-1977. This plan is presented here, and its goals are delineated and discussed. The goals are as follows: (1) the prevention of inflation, (2) the promotion of economic international collaboration, (3) a shift to a non-wasteful consumer life and to the reduction of environmental pollution, and (4) the promotion of national welfare, including social security.

474. ———. *New Economic and Social Development Plan 1970-1975.* Tokyo, 1970.

This Plan was designed to be the guiding principle for economic policies during the period from 1970 to 1975. In manipulating the policy measures, the government was to take appropriate measures corresponding to the external and international changes such as the progress of the internationalization of the economy and of the society, and the intensification of the labor shortage. In addition, the government was to make a special effort to obtain stabilization of prices and to improve the quality of life.

475. ——————. *New Economic and Social Seven-Year Plan.* Tokyo, 1979.

    Presents the Plan and discusses its goals. It was designed to be a guideline for economic management during the period from 1979 to 1985. It contains three basic directions as the basis for management of the economy. These directions are (1) rectifying imbalances among the various sectors of the economy, (2) promoting industrial restructuring and overcoming energy constraints, and (3) working for the realization of a new Japanese-type welfare society.

476. *Japan in the Year 2000: Preparing Japan for an Age of Internationalization, the Aging Society and Maturity.* English version. Tokyo: Japan Times, 1983.

    Analyzes the results of a study by the Long-Term Outlook Committee of Japan's Economic Council, on the future of Japan's economy and society.

477. Japan-U.S. Study Group, ed. *Japan's Economy and Japan-U.S. Trade 1982: 100 Questions and Answers.* Tokyo: Japan Times, 1982.

    Provides basic information to assist Japanese public relations activities in the United States by dispelling American misunderstanding and supplementing insufficient knowledge of Japan. Among the topics covered are Japan's policy on foreign aid and defense, Japan's external economic policy, Japan-U.S. economic and trade relations, Japan's investments in the U.S., and U.S. investments in Japan.

478. Johnson, Chalmers. "The 'Internationalization' of the Japanese Economy." *California Management Review* 25 (1983):5-26.

    Explores why and how Japan had a closed economy, and the efforts made in recent years to open it. Johnson maintains that Japanese government policy has been the main barrier rather than Japanese culture.

479. Kitamura, Hiroshi. *Choices for the Japanese Economy.* London: Royal Institute of International Affairs, 1976.

    Illuminates the basic issues the Japanese economy is confronted with in the 1970s in a broad historical perspective. Raises the question of what has gone wrong with Japan's legitimate pursuit of increasing its economic capacity that has created a social impasse (viz., social welfare has not increased commensurately). Examines the problems of whether the signs of strain and imbalance can be adequately dealt with by small adjustments or whether the whole framework of economic and social management is necessary. The author looks closely at some characteristics of the mechanics, structure and pattern of Japanese economic growth in the recent past. Includes the international aspects of rapid Japanese economic growth as well as the domestic.

480. Kojima, Kiyoshi. *Japan and a New World Economic Order.* Boulder, Colo.: Westview Press, 1977.

    Consists of essays from an updated collection produced over the past three years. They present discussion and suggestions for a new world and regional economic order from the perspective of the Japanese economy. Covers such topics as Japan in the world economy, Japan and the multilateral trade negotiations, a competitive bipolar key currency, foreign direct investment, the future of the Japanese economy, the reorganization of North-South trade, and economic integration in the Asian-Pacific region.

481. Kotabe, Masaaki, "The Roles of Japanese Industrial Policy for Export Success: A Theoretical Perspective." *Columbia Journal of World Business* 20 (1985):59-64.

    Presents a theoretical framework for Japanese industrial policy, drawing from international trade and commercial policy theories. Also singles out a number of key variables necessary for developing a sound theory of industrial policy. A response to R.P. Nielsen's argument, "Should a Country Move toward International Strategic Planning?" (*California Management Review*, Jan. 1983).

482. Magaziner, Ira C. and Thomas M. Hout. *Japanese Industrial Policy.* Berkeley: Institute of International Studies, University of California, 1980.

    An analysis of Japan's industrial policy, illustrated

Economic Planning

by case studies of policy in particular industries.

483. Matsushita, Konosuke. *Japan at the Brink*. Tokyo: Kodansha International, 1976.

    The author discusses his thoughts on the dangers he believes face the Japanese government, economy, and national spirit, and offers suggestions to prevent a catastrophe, which he considers to be imminent. He attributes these problems to the confused state of the government, and widespread unrest and uncertainty on the part of the people, and he considers this situation to be more serious than the economic slump.

484. Miyazaki, Isamu. "Economic Planning in Postwar Japan." *Developing Economies* 8 (1970):369-385.

    Discusses the features of specific government economic plans that were formulated from 1956-60 to 1970-75.

485. Morse, Ronald A., ed. *The Politics of Japan's Energy Strategy: Resources, Diplomacy, Security*. Berkeley: Institute of East Asian Studies, University of California, 1981.

    Essays that explore Japan's energy strategy, assess the domestic economic and political costs of these decisions, and examine the implications of Japan's policies for the world in economic and strategic terms. All of the contributors are experts with a special knowledge of and interest in Japan. Each essay attempts to link the domestic Japanese policy process to the broader international energy concept, and Japan's domestic public policy process is examined in detail.

486. Okimoto, Daniel I., ed. *Japan's Economy: Coping with Change in the International Environment*. Boulder, Colo.: Westview Press, 1982.

    Addresses the issue of Japan's need to adjust its economic policies due to such changes in the international environment as the decline of United States economic and military power and Japan's increased international economic influence, the onset of the energy crisis, and a general slowdown of growth rates.

487. Organisation for Economic Co-operation and Development. *The Industrial Policy of Japan*. Paris, 1972.

    Provides basic information on industrial policy instruments and issues as seen from the perspective of the government. While the main objective of this study is the mechanism of dynamic industrial expansion, it includes some policy problems that have been accentuated because of rapid industrial growth as well as problems of an internal nature that mainly relate to environmental protection and to the economic and social infrastructure, and also of an international nature, which are primarily concerned with capital and import liberalization.

488. Patrick, Hugh and Henry Rosovsky, eds. *Asia's New Giant: How the Japanese Economy Works.* Washington, D.C.: Brookings Institution, 1976.

The main purpose of this work is to contribute to better informed policymaking toward Japan in both the public and private sectors. It consists of essays by leading American social analysts that explain how the Japanese have managed their economy during the last twenty years, and that assess Japan's present and future economic prospects. The essays are concerned with such topics as the sources of economic growth; fiscal, monetary, and related policies; banking and finance; taxation; Japan and the world economy; technology; urbanization and urban problems; and social and cultural factors in Japan's economic growth.

489. Pempel, T.J. "Japanese Foreign Economic Policy; the Domestic Bases for International Behavior." *International Organization* 31 (1977):723-774.

A consideration of the view that Japan's strong foreign economic policy is essentially determined by its domestic political structures.

490. ──────. *Policy and Politics in Japan: Creative Conservatism.* Philadelphia, Pa.: Temple University Press, 1982.

Pempel contends that the historic combination of creativity and conservatism are the two most important features in modern Japanese politics. He seeks to explain the unique mix of consensus and conflict in Japanese policymaking processes, as well as the successes and failures in economic and social policy outcomes. Among the topics discussed are labor-management relations, social welfare, higher education, environmental protection, and administrative reform.

491. Pugel, Thomas A. "Japan's Industrial Policy: Instruments, Trends, and Effects." *Journal of Comparative Economics* 8 (1984):420-435.

    A discussion of the evolution of Japan's industrial policy in relation to changing economic conditions in Japan. Describes the specific instruments of the policy and the shifts in the extent of use and effectiveness of its instruments. Analyzes current efforts to promote high-technology industries and to assist the adjustment of structurally declining industries.

492. Rapp, William V. "Japan: Its Industrial Policies and Corporate Behavior." *Columbia Journal of World Business* 12 (1977):38-48.

    The evolution of industrial policies in Japan is examined, especially in relation to "supply management." Certain aspects of corporate behavior are discussed, and the author sees the cooperation between business and government as being one of the keys to the success of the past and the future.

493. Schmiegelow, Michele, ed. *Japan's Response to Crisis and Change in the World Economy*. Armonk, N.Y.: M.E. Sharpe, 1986.

    Emphasis is on problem areas where policies and structures, adaptive system change, and structural preservation are so inextricably associated that they cannot be overlooked. All of the contributors here deal with the interaction between the external economy and the domestic economy, and each more or less directly relates to one or both of the two basic categories of international economics: trade, and capital movements. Within each of the categories, the chapters are concerned with autonomous social structures or government policies.

494. Shishido, Toshio and Ryuzo Sato, eds. *Economic Policy and Development: New Perspectives*. Dover, Mass.: Auburn House Pub. Co., 1985.

    A collection of essays in honor of Dr. Saburo Okita, on his seventieth birthday on the following topics: general trade issues, economic development, industrial policy and technological change, and the Japanese economy.

495. Sinha, Radha. *Japan's Options for the 1980s*. New York: St. Martin's, 1982.

    Analyzes the nature of economic pressures from the

West on Japan and its economic, social, and political consequences. Also discusses the foreign pressures on Japan's pacifistic national security policy.

496. Snyder, Wayne and Tsutomu Tanaka. "Budget Policy and Economic Stability in Postwar Japan." *International Economic Review* 13 (1972):85-110.

   Measures the effects of various types of budget policy changes and evaluates their impact on the achievement of economic stability and balanced growth during the period from 1952 to 1967. Economic stability is seen here from two different perspectives: the total impact of all government budgets on short-term fluctuations in demand, and their impact on the long-term achievement of full utilization of Japan's potential output.

497. Tanaka, H. William and B. Jenkins Middleton. "Injured Industries, Imports and Industrial Policy: A Comparison of United States and Japanese Practices." *Case Western Reserve Journal of International Law* 15 (1983):419-443.

   Compares the nature and effectiveness of the approaches employed by the United States and Japan concerning declining industries, import competition and industrial policy. Also suggests how the American approach can be improved, particularly with regard to escape-clause relief from increased imports.

498. Tanaka, Kakuei. *Building a New Japan: A Plan for Remodeling the Japanese Archipelago*. Tokyo: Simul Press, 1973.

   Discusses plans to alleviate the urban overcrowding and industrial concentration along Japan's Pacific Coast. Among the programs proposed by former Prime Minister Tanaka are industrial relocation, and the formation of national information and communication networks.

499. Toyama, Kozo, Norifumi Tateishi and John Palenberg. "Trade Friction, Administrative Guidance and Antimonopoly Law in Japan." *Case Western Reserve Journal of International Law* 15 (1983):601-610.

   Recently, the Tokyo High Court issued two prominent decisions that focus on the conflict between the Ministry of International Trade and Industry's (MITI) use of administrative guidance to regulate the unification of prices, the limitation of production, and in some cases, outright cartelization, and the free market principles

that are present in the Japanese Antimonopoly Law. The
authors focus here on these decisions, popularly known
as the Oil Cartel Cases (1980), and their relationship
to international trade issues.

500. U.S. Congress. Joint Economic Committee. Subcommittee
on Monetary and Fiscal Policy. *Japanese and American
Economic Policies and U.S. Productivity: Hearings.*
97th Cong., 1st sess., 1981. Washington, D.C.: GPO,
1981.

Hearings held to discuss the development of United
States economic policy that would stimulate long-term
economic growth. Emphasis is on those aspects of Japanese economic policy that could possibly be applied in
the United States.

501. U.S. General Accounting Office. *Industrial Policy: Japan's Flexible Approach.* Washington, D.C., 1982.

The ability of Japan's industrial policy to adapt to
changes in the domestic and international economies is
examined. Five industrial sectors are analyzed as examples of policies for new or declining industries: computers, robotics, aircraft, shipbuilding, and textiles.

502. ————. *Industrial Policy: Case Studies in the Japanese Experience.* Washington, D.C., 1982.

A companion volume to the GAO's June 23, 1982 report
Industrial Policy: Japan's Flexible Approach. Presents
case studies that explain the assistance provided by
the Japanese government to five key industries, three
of which are high technology growth industries, namely,
computers, aircraft, and robotics, and two of which are
faced with unfavorable world market prospects: shipbuilding and textiles.

503. Wu, Yuan-li. *Japan's Search for Oil: A Case Study on
Economic Nationalism and International Security.* Stanford, Calif.: Hoover Institution Press, 1977.

Focuses on Japan's experience during the 1973-74 oil
crisis, which was brought on by an Arab threat of total
boycott and a sudden increase in the price of oil. Attention is centered on the nature and manner of Japan's
response to this economic threat and on some of the possibly serious implications for the rest of the world,
especially the United States. Treatment is limited to
the Japanese effort to achieve diversification and a

higher degree of national control of the nation's oil supply, to some of the constraints of Japan's future policy, and to future U.S.-Japan relations.

504. Yamamura, Kozo. *Policy and Trade Issues of the Japanese Economy: American and Japanese Perspectives.* Seattle: University of Washington Press, 1982.

Essays by Japanese and American economists on the Japanese economy and bilateral trade issues. Emphasis is on two topics: the examination of Japanese economic policies and the changing behavior of Japanese firms and individuals, with analyses of their significance in bilateral economic relations. The second topic is concerned with the economic policies of Japan and the United States.

505. Yao, Jiro, ed. *Monetary Factors in Japanese Economic Growth.* Kobe, Japan: Research Institute for Economics & Business Administration, Kobe University, 1970.

Consists of articles written by professors on monetary economics at several leading universities in the Kobe area. Investigates the monetary-fiscal aspects of Japan's economic growth process, and seeks to find the interactions between the monetary and the real factors, if any.

506. Yoshikawa, Akihiro and Brian Woodall. "The 'Venture Boom' and Japanese Industrial Policy." *Asian Survey* 15 (1985):692-714.

Examines Japanese industrial policy toward smaller enterprises and venture business in order to get a sense of the changes, both past and present, affecting the essential nature of Japanese industrial policy, because there is now increased policy emphasis on smaller enterprises as vital and important contributors to the economic well-being of the country. In addition, the authors point out the flaws in Japan's high growth industrial policy in the context of the changed economic conditions of a post-oil-crisis environment.

507. Yoshikawa, Seichi. "Fair Trade Commission vs. MITI: History of the Conflicts Between the Antimonopoly Policy and the Industrial Policy in the Post War Period of Japan." *Case Western Reserve Journal of International Law* 15 (1983):489-504.

On many occasions, conflicts between the Japanese Fair

Trade Commission (FTC) and Ministry of International Trade and Industry (MITI) have occurred over disagreements between the FTC's antimonopoly policy and MITI's industrial policy, and in the majority of situations MITI has won. However, Yoshikawa maintains that certain new trends in Japanese antimonopoly policy have happened because of the relaxation of cartels that took place during the postwar period and because of the present status of the restrictions on cartels, and he looks at these issues here.

B. INDUSTRY AND STATE

508. Drucker, Peter F. "Behind Japan's Success." *Harvard Business Review* 59 (1981):83-90.

    Drucker argues that Japan's economic success is not the result of a powerful government-business alliance, but rather it stems from an accurate perception of what modern business organizations require to function effectively and from astute assessments of the conduct that satisfies these requirements, such as taking competitiveness seriously, and considering the national interest first. He also maintains that "Japan, Inc." (exclusive government-business cooperation) is a myth, and that the Japanese have a variety of interest groups that compete strongly, and that government departments are not consistent in imposing government policy on the private sector.

509. Fukui, Haruhiro. "Economic Planning in Postwar Japan: A Case Study in Policy Making." *Asian Survey* 12 (1972):327-348.

    An analysis of the development of postwar governmental economic planning and policymaking, which Fukui considers as being the responsibility of a tripartite coalition of high ranking central government bureaucrats, members of the National Diet affiliated with the ruling Liberal Democratic Party, and leaders of organized big business, which is not open to opposition groups.

510. Hadley, Eleanor M. "The Secret of Japan's Success." *Challenge* 26 (1983):4-10.

    The author contends that Japan's postwar success is the result of the government-business relationship and industrial policy.

511. Horvath, Dezso and Charles J. McMillan. "Industrial Planning in Japan." *California Management Review* 23 (1980):11-21.

Examines industrial planning as it relates to industrial strategy and economic performance.

512. Ike, Brian. "The Japanese Textile Industry: Structural Adjustment and Government Policy." *Asian Survey* 20 (1980):532-551.

The author draws on examples from the textile industry in order to dispel some of what he considers to be widely held misconceptions regarding the efficiency of Japanese economic policy. The textile industry is being faced with increased international competition, and although government officials have acknowledged that textile production must be scaled down, the actual pattern of government assistance to the industry has been protective. Ike sees this situation as being indicative of pressure groups being accorded special government treatment unwarranted on the grounds of economic efficiency.

513. Johnson, Chalmers. *Japan's Public Policy Companies*. Washington, D.C.: American Enterprise Institute for Public Policy Research, 1978.

A survey of an important but relatively unknown sector of Japan's official economic bureaucracy, the public corporations and mixed public-private enterprises that serve as the operating arms of the official economic policy makers. Covers such topics as the types of public corporations, their origins, financing, operating problems, and their activities as extensions of the economic bureaucracy. Includes a detailed survey of the corporations in the energy sector.

514. ————. *MITI and the Japanese Miracle: The Growth of Industrial Policy, 1925-1975*. Stanford, Calif.: Stanford University Press, 1982.

A study of the Japanese economic bureaucracy, particularly of the Ministry of International Trade and Industry (MITI), the leading government collaborator with big business, which has been the defining characteristic of the economic system. Covers the following topics: the creation of the official industrial policy bureaucracy, the discovery and debate of the main issues of industrial policy, and the continuity between the prewar and postwar periods in terms of personnel and organizations.

515. ———. "The Reemployment of Retired Government Bureaucrats in Japanese Big Business." *Asian Survey* 14 (1974):953-965.

    Johnson explores the extent, causes, and effects of the hiring of retired government officials by business firms, and the attitudes of bureaucrats, businessmen and the public toward such practice.

516. Kaplan, Eugene J. *Japan, the Government-Business Relationship: A Guide for the American Businessman.* Washington, D.C.: Bureau of International Commerce, U.S. Dept. of Commerce, 1972.

    An explanation of the government-business relationship, particularly for those doing business with Japan. Includes case studies of three major industries: computers, automobiles, and steel.

517. Kotabe, Masaaki. "Changing Roles of the Sogo Shoshas, the Manufacturing Firms, and the MITI in the Context of the Japanese 'Trade or Die' Mentality." *Columbia Journal of World Business* 19 (1984):33-42.
    Examines the relationship between the Japanese government, the sogo shoshas (general trading companies), and the manufacturing companies within the Japanese "trade-oriented" economy. Central to the discussion is the distinction between "trade-oriented" and "anti-trade-oriented" policy by Professor Kojima, one of the most influential economists in international policy making in Japan. Also examines the changing role of MITI in relation to the issues of protectionism and Japanese multinational business transactions.

518. Lobb, John C. "'Japan, Inc.'--The Total Conglomerate." *Columbia Journal of World Business* 6 (1971):39-45.

    Lobb attributes Japan's economic success to its unique form of capitalism, in which the government, organized labor, and capital all work together ("Japan, Inc."). He points out certain industries as examples of Japan's economic success, and briefly discusses the zaibatsu (or "group") system as well as the role of the government. Lobb contends that for the United States to regain its competitiveness, it must rewrite obsolete antitrust laws and create a U.S.-type MITI, and make the labor unions subject to the new antitrust laws. In addition, the United States should adopt and modify Japanese trade practices.

519. McCraw, Thomas K., ed. *America versus Japan*. Boston: Harvard Business School Press, 1986.

   A comparative study of business-government relations in the United States and Japan conducted at the Harvard Business School that addresses the economic crisis between the two countries. The comparisons focus on trade, investment, production and distribution, agriculture, energy, the environment, financial institutions, tax, and disinvestment.

520. Taira, Koji. "Industrial Policy and Employment in Japan." *Current History* 82 (1983):362-393.

   The relationship between government-business determined industrial policy and Japan's productive economy is explored.

521. Uenohara, Michiyuki. "National Policy and Company R&D in Japan." *Research Management* 17 (1974):27-33.

   Describes the research and development (R&D) management and problems of the Nippon Electric Company, in Kawasaki, of which the author is General Manager of Central Research Laboratories. Also presents a detailed account of the interrelated roles of the private and government sectors in Japan's R&D activities and programs.

522. U.S. Congress. Joint Economic Committee. *Japanese Industrial and Labor Policy: Hearing*. 97th Cong., 2nd sess., 1982. Washington: GPO, 1982.

   Concerned with the methods of the Japanese government in promoting industrial development and achieving high rates of economic growth.

523. Van Zandt, Howard F. "Learning to Do Business with 'Japan, Inc.'" *Harvard Business Review* 50 (1972):83-92.

   Van Zandt discusses the interaction between government and business in Japan. He explains the governmental structure and government involvement with business, the role of trade associations as intermediaries in facilitating government-industry cooperation, and their influence on government. Van Zandt also shows how Japan's huge export surplus is forcing the government to eliminate some export promotion devices and to remove many import restrictions, despite resistance from Japanese companies and trade associations. Finally, advice is given for foreigners in dealing with government department and trade groups.

524. Vogel, Ezra F. *Comeback: Case by Case: Building the Resurgence of American Business*. New York: Simon and Schuster, 1985.

    A study of four Japanese industries that became highly competitive primarily as the result of cooperation between business and government. These industries are ship-building, machine tools and robots, coal mining, and information, and they are used here as examples from which American business can learn. The author also discusses some American business enterprises that have been successful because of business-government cooperation.

525. ─────. "Guided Free Enterprise in Japan." *Harvard Business Review* 56 (1978):161-170.

    Vogel contends that in addition to other factors, a web of relationships among business, government, and quasi-government organizations has also contributed to Japan's economic success. He presents an account of the role of the key participants: the Ministry of Finance, the Ministry of International Trade and Industry (MITI), the office of the Prime Minister, the Cabinet, the Diet, Keidanren (the Federation of Economic Organizations), trade sector organizations, union leaders, and company management.

VII
FINANCE

A. BANKS AND BANKING

526. Blumenthal, Tuvia. *Saving in Postwar Japan*. Cambridge, Mass.: East Asian Research Center, Harvard University, 1970.

   A brief analysis of some of the factors that are responsible for the high rate of saving in postwar Japan.

527. Japan Business History Institute, ed. *The Mitsui Bank: A History of the First 100 Years*. Tokyo: Mitsui Bank, 1976.

   Published to commemorate the centennial anniversary of Japan's first private bank. The history of Mitsui Bank is traced from its origins in 1683 up to 1975.

528. Kawaguchi, Hiroshi. "'Over-loan' and the Investment Behavior of Firms." *Developing Economies* 8 (1970):386-406.

   An analysis of the investment mechanism that is based upon the close connections between city banks and large firms in Japan and which has contributed greatly to its high economic growth rate.

529. Mizoguchi, Toshiyuki. "High Personal Saving Rate and Changes in the Consumption in Postwar Japan." *Developing Economies* 8 (1970):407-426.

   An explanation of the reasons for the high personal saving rate and for its upward trend. Also looks at the factors responsible for the rise in real per capita consumption expenditure as well as consumption patterns.

530. Prindl, Andreas R. *Japanese Finance: A Guide to Banking in Japan*. New York: John Wiley & Sons, 1981.

The author was general manager of a large foreign bank in Tokyo for four years, and this work reflects his experience. It is specifically written for corporate finance managers assigned to Japan and for companies with subsidiaries or joint ventures there or about to create such entities. It is a guide to the present structure of Japanese financial markets and how to deal with them. Prindl also questions why the system is so rigid and the banking structure still fragmented in the 1980s.

B. FINANCE

531. Bronte, Stephen. "Inside the Tokyo Ministry of Finance: The Most Powerful Men in Japan." *Euromoney* (June 1979):24-39.

Examines who the Tokyo Ministry of Finance bureaucrats are, what they are like, and what their thoughts are on their banks and the capital markets. Also looks at the self-perpetuating system of the Ministry of Finance, which moulds finance ministry bureaucrats and which foreign bankers find confusing.

532. ―――――. *Japanese Finance: Markets and Institutions*. London: Euromoney Publications, 1982.

Various aspects of the contemporary Japanese financial scene are discussed here, including fundamental changes taking place, analysis of financial institutions and markets, and predictions for its future.

533. Campbell, John Creighton. *Contemporary Japanese Budget Politics*. Berkeley: University of California Press, 1977.

An analysis of how the General Account budget was compiled from 1954 to 1974, and of the distinctive characteristics of Japanese budgeting, which according to Campbell are the role of the Liberal Democratic Party, primacy of the budget, high growth rate of the budget, equitable balancing, and stability of governmental priorities. Emphasis is on the behavior of complex organizations within the budgetary system.

534. Emery, Robert F. *The Japanese Money Market*. Lexington, Mass.: Lexington Books, 1984.

   An analysis of the major components of the Japanese money market. Emphasis is on the organization of the money market, its main participants, the types of instruments used, and important developments during the postwar period. The following topics are examined: an overview of the market, important money-market developments since 1945, the bill-discount market, the yen call-money market, the "Gensaki" market, the Tokyo dollar call market, official controls, interest-rate structure and trends, and an assessment of the market.

535. Goldsmith, Raymond W. *The Financial Development of Japan, 1868-1977*. New Haven, Conn.: Yale University Press, 1983.

   A quantitative approach to the financial structure and development in Japan. Explores the relationship between the capital formation ratio and the growth rate of capital stock. This relationship is indicative of the absolute and relative size of the funds that had to be provided to the sectors and units making capital expenditures, either internally out of their own savings or externally, either directly by domestic and foreign savers through the sale of financial instruments, or indirectly through domestic financial institutions.

536. Horne, James. *Japan's Financial Markets: Conflict and Consensus in Policymaking*. Boston: G. Allen & Unwin, 1985.

   An account of the formulation and implementation of regulatory policymaking in Japan's financial markets in the 1970s and early 1980s by the Liberal Democratic Party, the Ministry of Finance, financial institutions, and other corporate and non-corporate interests, and of their interactions with each other.

537. *The Japanese Financial System in Comparative Perspective: A Study*. Washington: GPO, 1982.

   Focus is on the contributions that Japanese financial institutions have made to Japan's high rates of investment, savings, and growth in the postwar era.

538. Lin, Ching-yuan. *Japanese and U.S. Inflation: A Comparative Analysis.* Lexington, Mass.: Lexington Books, 1984.

   A comparison of inflation and price stabilization in both countries before and after the 1973-1974 oil price shock. Emphasis is on the interaction between government policy and the development of the economy.

539. *Monthly Finance Review* 1 (1973)-   . Tokyo: Ministry of Finance.

   Contains information on current business conditions, economic and financial events of the month, speeches and statements, and main economic indicators of Japan.

540. Organisation for Economic Co-operation and Development. *Monetary Policy in Japan.* Paris, 1972.

   Elucidates how Japanese economic cycles from 1960 to 1971 were influenced by monetary policy and the reasons why the Japanese experience in this situation appears to differ from that of other countries. The following topics are discussed: financial structure, instruments, and techniques of monetary policy; impact of monetary policy; chronology of major changes in Japanese monetary policy; and econometric analysis of the impact of monetary policy.

541. Ozeki, Toshio. "An International 'Wall Street' Sprouts in Tokyo." *Columbia Journal of World Business* 7 (1972):53-57.

   Discusses the financial dynamics of the entry of shares of foreign companies on the Tokyo Stock Exchange.

542. Quirk, Peter J. "Exchange Rate Policy in Japan: Leaning against the Wind." *International Monetary Fund Staff Papers* 24 (1977):642-664.

   A quantitative analysis of the nature of foreign exchange market intervention in Japan since the introduction of a floating exchange rate for the yen in 1973. Covers the period from March 1973 to October 1976.

543. Shibata, Tokue, ed. *Public Finance in Japan.* Tokyo: University of Tokyo Press, 1986.

   Presents an overview of Japan's public finance system. Chapters written by scholars and government officials provide a framework of the system's basic features, from financial administration and budget formulation to taxation and revenue disbursement. Among the current issues discussed are expanding social welfare expenditures, growing dependence on government bonds for financing deficits, and the fiscal relation between the national and local government.

544. Shioda, Nagahide. "Changes in the Yen Valuation and Japan's Distributive Mechanism." *Japanese Economic Studies* 9 (1980):45-67.

    Examines the charges that the high Japanese domestic market prices of imported goods have not come down, despite the yen appreciation, because of Japan's peculiar distributive mechanism. Concentrates on imports of consumer goods.

545. Suzuki, Yoshio. *Money and Banking in Contemporary Japan: Its Theoretical Setting and Its Application.* New Haven, Conn.: Yale University Press, 1980.

    Essays by an eminent economist that analyze Japan's monetary mechanism within a quantitative, theoretical framework. The book is divided into five parts: part (1) Japan's financial structure, part (2) Japan's monetary mechanism, part (3) Japan's monetary instruments, part (4) the effectiveness of Japan's monetary policy, and part (5) prospects for the future.

546. ————. *Money, Finance, and Macroeconomic Performance in Japan.* New Haven, Conn.: Yale University Press, 1986.

    An analysis of changes in Japan's monetary and financial system and monetary macroeconomic performance since 1973, when the transition to floating exchange rates and the first oil crisis drastically affected Japan's economy.

547. Yoshitomi, Masaru. "An Appraisal of Japanese Financial Policies." *World Economy* 6 (1983):27-38.

    Evaluates macroeconomic policies undertaken in Japan after the second oil price hike between the spring of 1979 and the spring of 1980. Emphasis is on the relationship between the macroeconomic policies undertaken and the growth of the country's export surplus.

548. ———. *Japan as Capital Exporter and the World Economy*. New York: Group of Thirty, 1985.

   Briefly examines the development of Japan's role as an international creditor through the evolution of its balance of payments.

C. TAXATION

549. Brockman, Rosser H. "Japanese Taxation of the Foreign Income of Japanese Corporations." *Hastings International and Comparative Law Review* 2 (1979):73-104.

   Describes in general terms the Japanese domestic tax treatment of the foreign income of Japanese corporations. Brockman discusses the source rules, taxation of undistributed profits of designated tax haven subsidiaries, and the foreign tax credit and domestic provisions affecting foreign income. The author also evaluates whether such taxation treatment tends to encourage or discourage overseas business activities by Japanese corporations.

550. Pepper, H.W.T. "Corporate Taxation in Japan." *Case Western Reserve Journal of International Law* 6 (1974): 237-249.

   Examines the corporate tax system in Japan, and delineates its major features. Some of the features discussed here are its moderate rates, the variety of "special" reliefs, the stability of the corporate tax system, and the use of an "imputation" system in which a shareholder receives a credit for the corporate tax on the income out of which dividends were paid.

551. U.S. Congress. Joint Economic Committee. *Japanese Tax Policy: Hearing, 98th Cong., 2nd sess., 1984*. Washington, D.C.: GPO, 1985.

   Concentrates on the major features of the Japanese tax system and its incentives for saving and investment. Also examines the impact of the postwar tax system on the economy.

VIII
COMMERCE, BUSINESS, AND INDUSTRY

A. COMMERCE AND BUSINESS

1. COMMERCE

552. Akao, Nobutoshi, ed. *Japan's Economic Security.* New York: St. Martin's, 1983.

    Examines Japan's natural resource concerns and its foreign policy regarding resource issues and the impact of this policy on the economy and the manner in which these policies influence, and are influenced by, its foreign policy. Also studies the political problems, contemporary and historical, resulting from Japan's overall strategic and security concerns in this area.

553. Haitani, Kanji. "Japan's Trade Problem and the Yen." *Asian Survey* 13 (1973):723-739.

    Discusses Japan's trade surplus problem and the failure of the yen revaluation of December 1971 to reduce it. The trade imbalance is examined from the following perspectives: its relationships with the structures of Japan's trade and industry, the role of yen revaluations as a solution to the trade problem, and alternative solutions.

554. Hirschmeier, Johannes and Tsunehiko Yui. *The Development of Japanese Business, 1600-1980.* 2d ed. Boston: G. Allen & Unwin, 1981.

    A systematic treatment of the rise of Japanese business, against the background of contemporary social and political conditions. The chapters are divided into four sections: (1) the merchants of Tokugawa Japan, 1600-1867, (2) the Meiji entrepreneurs, 1868-95, (3) college graduates as business leaders, 1896-1945, and (4) the organizers of Japan's economic development. Each of the chapters has the same structure, in which the socioeconomic conditions, leadership and business elites, internal and external structures, and the impact of values are discussed. This second edition has been revised and updated to include the war years and developments of the 1970s. The first edition was published under the title: *The Development of Japanese Business, 1600-1973*, and was published in 1975.

555. Hollerman, Leon. "Liberalization and Japanese Trade in the 1970s." *Asian Survey* 10 (1970):427-437.

    Hollerman discusses Japan's successful trade situation and presents reasons as to why its future economic growth will be impaired unless economic liberalization takes place.

556. Imai, Masaaki. *Never Take Yes for an Answer: An Inside Look at Japanese Business for Foreign Businessmen.* Tokyo: Simul Press, 1975.

    The author, president of an international management consulting and executive recruiting firm, draws on his experience to describe for foreign business persons unique features of Japanese business and key points in dealing with the Japanese. Included are sections pertaining to Japanese management, managing foreign companies in Japan, and Japanese multinational business.

557. Matsukawa, Michiya. *The Japanese Trade Surplus and Capital Outflow*. New York: Group of Thirty, 1987.

    A brief sketch of the present state of Japanese foreign trade and surplus, the main features of change in recent years, and its future. Also discussed are the changes in Japan's capital transactions, with emphasis on its capital outflow in recent years and prospects for the next few years.

558. Namiki, Nobuyoshi. "Growth of Japanese Exports." *Developing Economies* 8 (1970):475-496.

    Looks at the changes in the Japanese balance of trade after 1955 and the reasons for the high growth rate of exports, the increase in growth-competitive power, and the choices in international economic policies.

559. Norbury, Paul and Geoffrey Bownas, eds. *Business in Japan: A Guide to Japanese Business Practice and Procedure.* Rev. ed. Boulder, Colo.: Westview Press, 1980.

A pragmatic socioeconomic approach to Japan's business environment of the 1980s, written for those wanting to do business in Japan. The following topics are included: understanding the Japanese, Japan's new industrial policies, approaches to Japan's market, finance and the banks, business strategy and management, and adjusting to Japan.

560. Rose, Sanford. "The Secret of Japan's Export Prowess." *Fortune* (Jan. 30, 1978):56-62.

Rose contends that Japanese manufacturers have a clearer understanding of the dynamics of international competitiveness than American manufacturers. Japan's success in external trade depends to a great extent on the rapid growth of its internal economy, and in turn, the growth of export markets helps to increase domestic productivity, something which, according to Rose, has never been adequately understood by American producers. In addition, Rose maintains, the Japanese have grasped the implications of and have acted with thoroughness upon the principle that unit costs tend to decline as more units are produced, so that in the early stages of market development the Japanese producer offers a limited number of models. Finally, and even more important, Japanese manufacturers clearly understand the competitive payoff from rapid growth.

561. *Standard Trade Index of Japan* (1957)- . Tokyo: Japan Chamber of Commerce and Industry.

An annual, comprehensive directory of Japanese companies and products involved in foreign trade. The appendix includes a list of Japanese government agencies, and industrial and commercial organizations.

562. Tsurumi, Yoshihiro. *Technology Transfer and Foreign Trade: The Case of Japan, 1950-1966.* New York: Arno Press, 1980.

Published edition of the author's dissertation submitted to the Graduate School of Business administration, Harvard University, in 1968. It examines Japan's absorption of foreign technologies and the subsequent development of its own industries, and the impact of technology transfer on its foreign trade.

2. COMMERCIAL POLICY

563. Higashi, Chikara. *Japanese Trade Policy Formulation*. New York: Praeger, 1983.

Written by a former Ministry of Finance career official. Emphasis is on Japanese international trade policy formulation towards the United States. The approach is multidisciplinary, and the work integrates the ideas of economists and political scientists with those of behavioral scientists. Includes the following topics: international domestic economic environment of trade policy formulation, institutional aspects of trade policy formulation, and selected incidents of trade policy formulation.

564. Ho, Alfred K. *Japan's Trade Liberalization in the 1960s*. White Plains, N.Y.: International Arts and Sciences Press, 1973.

A study of the relationship between trade liberalization and economic development. Compares Japanese economic performance in the period of trade controls prior to 1960 with that in the period of trade liberalization after 1960. Discusses trade liberalization in practice and theory, and analyzes Japan's trade liberalization.

3. CULTURAL ASPECTS OF BUSINESS

565. Bartels, R. "National Culture-Business Relations: United States and Japan Contrasted." *Management International Review* 22 (1982):4-12.

Comparisons are made between United States and Japanese business, with emphasis on the influence of cultural factors. Bartels argues that rather than attempting to imitate successful Japanese practices, which might not yield the same results in the United States, the United States should recover the cultural values it once had.

566. Ross, Steven. "What Is Japan, and What Is Not Japan?" *Business and Society Review* 37 (1980-81):31-36.

Ross attempts to clear up some American-held misunderstandings about Japanese business. He discusses some

of the more widespread myths and then counterbalances
them with what he considers to be the real or actual
situation.

4. CORPORATIONS

567. Barrett, M. Edgar and Judith Ann Gehrke. "Significant
Differences between Japanese and American Businesses."
MSU Business Topics 22 (1974):41-50.

Contrasts Japanese and American businesses with reference to seven key areas: debt, monetary control by government, tax incentives, concentrated ownership, economic groupings of companies, trading companies, and principal banks.

568. Fruin, W. Mark. "The Family as a Firm and the Firm as a Family in Japan: The Case of Kikkoman Shoyu Company Limited." *Journal of Family History* 5 (1980):432-449.

An examination of the firm-family analogy within the context of the history of the Kikkoman Shoyu Company Limited. Fruin contends that this analogy has been inappropriate in most instances when applied to Kikkoman. In prewar Japan, managers used the concepts of the patriarchal state with the emperor as father, and the identity of the state with the household, in order to obtain the loyalty and labor of employees. Fruin maintains that the firm-family analogy is prevalent in large contemporary Japanese firms.

569. ―――. *Kikkoman: Company, Clan and Community.* Cambridge, Mass.: Harvard University Press, 1983.

The Kikkoman Corporation is the oldest continuous enterprise among the two hundred largest industrial firms in Japan. Fruin traces its history and development from the seventeenth century to the present. He shows how the company came to dominate a town (Noda) and a clan (the Mogi-Takanashi families), and how in more recent times, changes in the composition of the community and in the conception of the family have resulted in an extensive transformation of its business practices. The evolution of Kikkoman from a traditional small family business into the giant managerial, diversified multinational corporation that it is today is analyzed in a very detailed manner.

570. Goto, Akira. "Statistical Evidence on the Diversification of Japanese Large Firms." *Journal of Industrial Economics* 29 (1981):271-278.

    Studies the degree of diversification of 124 large Japanese firms between 1963 and 1975. The results indicate that diversification is increasing steadily among the firms studied, and that they are re-diversifying more into unrelated commodities.

571. Mannari, Hiroshi. *The Japanese Business Leaders*. Tokyo: University of Tokyo Press, 1974.

    A sociological analysis of Japan's business elite in 1960, 1920, and 1880, which is based on a research project. The appendix includes the results of a 1970 followup questionnaire on Japanese business leaders in 1970.

572. Murakami, Teruyasu. "Recent Changes in Long Range Corporate Planning in Japan." *Long Range Planning* 11 (1978):2-5.

    Discusses an emerging new stage in Japanese long range corporate planning, which reflects the struggles of Japanese companies against the new economic situation in which it is very difficult to enjoy a high economic growth rate. Hitachi is used as an illustration of the main features of the struggles, and also as an example of the various new aspects manifested in Stage IV of Japanese long range corporate planning, which are described with reference to their economic and social backgrounds and their implications for Japanese companies.

573. Pascale, Richard Tanner and Thomas P. Rohlen. "The Mazda Turnaround." *Journal of Japanese Studies* 9 (1983):219-263.

    A description of the successful recovery of Toyo Kogyo, the maker of Mazda automobiles, from the brink of bankruptcy. Presents a detailed portrait of the interplay between economically significant events and institutional and cultural factors.

574. Sueno, Akira. *Entrepreneur and Gentleman: A Case History of a Japanese Company*. Rutland, Vt.: Charles E. Tuttle, 1977.

    An autobiographical account by the author, founder of Showa Boeki, an important medium-sized packaging company that does business around the world. Sueno discusses

Commerce, Business, and Industry 155

his business philosophy and practices as well as his philosophy of life and experiences.

a. Foreign Business Enterprises

575. *Breaking the Barriers*. Tokyo: Survey Japan, 1982.

Case studies of twenty-two successful foreign firms in Japan. The appendix includes a list of foreign-affiliated corporations in Japan having investments of 50% or more, with their addresses and nature of business.

576. Henderson, Dan Fenno. *Foreign Enterprise in Japan: Laws and Policies*. Chapel Hill: University of North Carolina Press, 1973.

Deals with the contemporary situation and legal and business problems of foreign enterprise in Japan against the broader background of economic internationalism. Among the areas discussed here are the scale of foreign investments, the general environment for foreign enterprise, and legal problems of foreign enterprises.

577. Kraar, Louis. "Japan Is Opening Up for 'Gaijin' Who Know How." *Fortune* 89 (1974):146-149, 153-157.

Kraar discusses the successes and failures of various United States companies in Japan, and he contends that the only way to operate there is to accept the country's ways and adapt to them.

578. McKinsey & Company, Inc. *Japan Business: Obstacles and Opportunities*. N.p.: President Inc., 1983.

An analysis of the key factors for United States firms for doing business in Japan. Addresses the issues of the reality of doing business in Japan; the real or perceived obstacles; and opportunities that exist for United States firms, specifically in the fields of financial services, computer software services, medical management services, video tape rentals, and truck leasing. Also includes lessons to be learned from successful and not-so-successful companies.

b. General Trading Companies

579. Anthony, D.F. "The Japanese General Trading Company: Model for the United States." *Asian Forum* (1979):61-66.

Describes the historical development, organization, and services of Japanese general trading companies, whose goal is to increase growth and secure a larger share of world markets rather than to achieve immediate profit. The author suggests that since these companies are so successful, Americans should use their services and also use them as a model for developing better foreign trade organizations in the United States.

580. Helou, Angelina. "Sogo Shoshas and Japan's Foreign Economic Relations." *Journal of World Trade Law* 13 (1979):257-263.

    An examination of the role of the sogo shoshas (general trading companies) in three main areas of Japan's international economic relations: (1) the imports of raw materials, (2) the exporting problem, and (3) the country's recent overseas investment activities.

581. *The Japanese Edge: The Real Stories Behind a Sogo Shosha --One of Japan's Unique New Class of Global Corporations.* Tokyo: Marubeni Corp., 1981.

    Written to illustrate the tenet of Marubeni sogo shosha that the staff members of a sogo shosha are important contributors to Japan's economic success. Here they are introduced and their aims and accomplishments are used to show how they make a great international Japanese corporation work. They are employees of Marubeni, and their stories of their problem solving, meeting of challenges, removal of barriers, and the furthering of trade and communication are true.

582. Kojima, Kiyoshi and Terutomo Ozawa. *Japan's General Trading Companies: Merchants of Economic Development.* Paris: Development Centre, Organisation for Economic Co-operation and Development, 1984.

    Observes the overseas investment activities of Japan's top nine general trading companies in developing countries and pinpoints their major characteristics. The investment activities have been divided into three major areas: trading networks, manufacturing resource development, and non-trade service ventures.

583. Pucik, Vladimir. "Promotion Patterns in a Japanese Trading Company." *Columbia Journal of World Business* 20 (1985):73-79.

    Analyzes promotion patterns among middle managers in one of the largest Japanese trading firms. Its objective is to illustrate the basic patterns of promotion timetables through a longitudinal analysis of promotion data. The results are compared with those of studies of organizations in Japan about the career progression of Japanese managers. Most observers agree that the key role in carrying out the activities of a typical Japanese firm is played by middle managers.

584. Tsurumi, Yoshihiro. *Sogoshosha: Engines of Export-Based Growth*. Montreal: Institute for Research on Public Policy, 1980.

    The development of the large Japanese sogo shoshas, or general trading companies, is analyzed as well as their adaptation to changes in the business environment.

585. Yoshihara, Kunio. *Sogo Shosha: The Vanguard of the Japanese Economy*. New York: Oxford University Press, 1982.

    A history of the large Japanese trading companies and of their role in the economy.

586. Yoshino, M.Y. and Thomas B. Lifson. *The Invisible Link: Japan's Sogo Shosha and the Organization of Trade*. Cambridge, Mass.: MIT Press, 1986.

    A study of the sogo shosha (general trading company) as a business institution and of its role as coordinator of its client firms. Focuses on the six largest firms in this sector: Mitsubishi Corporation, Mitsui & Company, C. Itoh, Marubeni Corporation, Sumitomo Corporation, and Nissho-Iwai.

587. Young, Alexander K. "Internationalization of the Japanese General Trading Companies." *Columbia Journal of World Business* 9 (1974):78-86.

    Examines the strategic responses to the changing world economy by the ten largest general trading companies (sogo shosha) in the period from 1955 to 1973.

588. ————. *The Sogo Shosha: Japan's Multinational Trading Companies*. Boulder, Colo.: Westview Press, 1979.

    Describes the general trading companies and their development, activities, and roles in the Japanese and international economies.

c. Industrial Groups

589. Dodwell Marketing Consultants. *Industrial Groupings in Japan*. Rev. ed. Tokyo, 1975.

   A survey of the major industrial groups, affiliation analysis, industry strength, the general trading houses (sogo shoshas) and affiliated companies. Includes more information and covers more companies than the 1973 edition.

590. Goto, Akira. "Business Groups in a Market Economy." *European Economic Review* 19 (1982):53-70.

   Goto examines the nature and significance of the business groups in the context of a market economy. He discusses the characteristics of the two kinds of Japanese business groups: Type A, the "zaibatsu" (financial combines) successors and non-"zaibatsu" principal bank groups, and Type B, groups that center around large firms and their subsidiaries.

591. Okumura, Hiroshi. "Interfirm Relations in an Enterprise Group: The Case of Mitsubishi." *Japanese Economic Studies* 10 (1982):53-82.

   Japanese corporate capitalism is explained through an analysis of two types of inter-enterprise relationships and combinations: "Keiretsu," or vertical affiliates, and "Kigyoshudan," or horizontal enterprise groups.

592. Ozawa, Terutomo. "Japan's Industrial Groups." *MSU Business Topics* 28 (1980):33-41.

   Reviews the origins of the "Zaibatsu" (financial groups) and looks at how they were transformed into "Keiretsu" (linked groups) after World War II.

593. Roberts, John G. *Mitsui: Three Centuries of Japanese Business*. New York: Weatherhill, 1973.

   A comprehensive history of the world's oldest large-scale business enterprise, which symbolizes continuity and change and represents the economic growth and development of Japan during the past three hundred years. In addition, Mitsui is the prototype of the powerful combines, or "Zaibatsu," which emerged in the late nineteenth century and served as instruments of national policy in the building of a modern, industrial Japan. Roberts attributes Mitsui's success not only to its policy of recruiting talent, but also to its ability to maintain close ties with the government.

594. "Sumitomo: How the 'Keiretsu' Pulls Together to Keep Japan Strong." *Business Week* No. 2374 (March 31, 1975):43-48.

    Sumitomo is Japan's third largest business group (or "Keiretsu"), and the six big "Keiretsu" dominate the nation's commerce the way the "Zaibatsu" did before the war (they were outlawed after World War II). It is necessary for Japanese companies to maintain a solid relationship with the "Keiretsu" in order to survive. This article discusses the activities of Sumitomo and other "Keiretsu" within the context of the economy.

d. International Business Enterprises

595. Franko, Lawrence G. *The Threat of Japanese Multinationals: How the West Can Respond.* New York: J. Wiley, 1983.

    Examines the successes and failures of Japanese multinational companies in the context of international business competition. Also offers some advice on how Western multinational companies can be effective competitors against Japanese firms.

596. Ozawa, Terutomo. "The Emergence of Japan's Multinationalism: Patterns and Competitiveness." *Asian Survey* 15 (1975):1036-1053.

    Assesses the rapid growth of direct overseas operations of Japanese industry, with emphasis on the following questions: (1) what factors have motivated Japan's government and industry to suddenly switch from a traditional policy of building industries at home to a more international orientation of economic growth, and (2) how have Japanese firms attained the necessary advantages to manufacture directly in foreign markets.

597. —————. *Multinationalism, Japanese Style: The Political Economy of Outward Dependency.* Princeton, N.J.: Princeton University Press, 1979.

    Japan's multinationalism is discussed in light of its overseas investments. Examines the role of government and market forces (including resource dependency, and the influence of new competition from less-developed countries in Japan's traditional export markets) in shaping decisions to invest abroad. Also looks at how heavily the attitudes of host countries are affected by political, cultural, and other national attributes of multinational businesses. In addition, the role of the Japanese trading companies in fostering and financing foreign investment is assessed.

598. Sato, Sadayuki. "Japanese Multinational Enterprises: Potential and Limits." *Japanese Economic Studies* 9 (1980):68-85.

    Evaluates the possibilities and limitations of the multinationalization of Japanese enterprises. Also discusses whether emerging Japanese multinationals will become "Japanese-type" or "Japanese-style" multinationals.

599. Tsurumi, Yoshihiro. *The Japanese Are Coming: A Multinational Interaction of Firms and Politics.* Cambridge, Mass.: Ballinger, 1976.

    Studies the development of Japanese multinational firms within the context of Japan's postwar economic progress, and evaluates possible conflicts of interest between Japan and other countries.

600. Tung, Rosalie L. *Key to Japan's Economic Strength: Human Power.* Lexington, Mass.: Lexington Books, 1984.

    Tung compares and contrasts the selection and training procedures for foreign assignments among a sample of American and Japanese multinational companies. She analyzes the reasons for the success of the Japanese multinationals, and presents procedures that American multinationals can learn from their Japanese counterparts. Included are chapters on the following topics: characteristics of Japanese personnel management, training institutes for international management, Japanese trading companies, Japanese financial institutions, Japanese manufacturers of electrical machinery (SONY and Canon), and Japanese heavy industrial sector (Nissan Motor Co., Nippon Steel Corp.).

601. Yoshino, M.Y. *Japan's Multinational Enterprises.* Cambridge, Mass.: Harvard University Press, 1976.

    A study of the development and structural characteristics of Japanese multinational enterprises from 1868 to 1970, with comparisons of those of the United states and other countries. Most of the data were obtained from executives of Japanese enterprises. Includes discussions of the beginnings of multinationals, ventures in raw materials, the spread of manufacturing, the trading company, and the manufacturing firm.

e. Small Business

602. Hollerman, Leon. "Changes in Japanese Small Business." *Japan Quarterly* 19 (1972):211-217.

    Delineates changes in Japanese small business in the 1970s that were caused by a structural transition in the economy. Includes discussion of the historical aspects of the origin, role, and persistance of small business in the prewar era.

603. Japan. Ministry of International Trade and Industry. *Venture Businesses in Japan and VB Promotion Policies.* Tokyo, 1975.

    Examines the present situation and problems of venture businesses, which have become very common in Japan since the late 1960s. Also explains government policies that are being planned to encourage venture businesses.

5. MARKETING

604. Czinkota, Michael R. "Distribution in Japan: Problems and Changes." *Columbia Journal of World Business* 20 (1985):65-71.

    Reviews the major features of the Japanese distribution system, highlights the changes taking place, and analyzes their effects on imports. Also makes suggestions on how importers can take advantage of these changes in order to successfully penetrate the Japanese market. The information is based on a series of in-depth interviews carried out in Japan and the United States with individuals from public and private sector institutions.

605. ―――. *Japan's Market: The Distribution System.* New York: Praeger, 1986.

    Discusses the intricacies of the Japanese distribution system. Czinkota contends that the United States negotiations with Japan on problems of market access have only met with limited success when measured on a standard of increased sales because of the restrictiveness of the Japanese distribution system. This restrictiveness is the result of its complex nature and the close relationship among Japanese business groups who tend not to purchase from outside suppliers. Also explores the various groupings and special relationships that tie distributors to manufacturers and bind manufacturers among themselves, as well as the structures and operations of the wholesale and retail sectors. Includes information on how foreign companies can function within the system and where the best opportunities lie.

606. Dentsu Incorporated. *Marketing Opportunities in Japan*. New York: McGraw-Hill, 1978.

    Describes the requirements for entering the Japanese market for foreign companies as well as for effective marketing, and discusses Japanese marketing and management practices.

607. Haley, John Owen. "Marketing and Antitrust in Japan." *Hastings International and Comparative Law Review* 2 (1979):51-72.

    Because of the inefficiencies of the present distribution structure in Japan and consequent cost to consumers, a trend has developed in which there is greater manufacturer control in channelling distribution of their products. However, this has not met with the approval of the Japanese Fair Trade Commission (FTC). In a recent series of cases, the FTC has adopted a strict illegality approach and held one of the more typical manufacturer-imposed market channelling arrangements to constitute an unfair business practice in violation of Article 19 of the Japanese Antimonopoly and Fair Trade Law. Haley discusses these cases and their implications in the context of Japanese antitrust regulation of marketing.

608. Ishida, Hideto. "Anticompetitive Practices in the Distribution of Goods and Services in Japan: The Problem of Distribution 'Keiretsu.'" *Journal of Japanese Studies* 9 (1983):319-334.

    Ishida, who is on the staff of the Japan Fair Trade Commission, expresses the Japanese concern with exclusionary marketing practices by Japanese producers in order to assure control over the distribution of their goods and services. He also discusses the need for an efficient and competitive marketing system.

609. *Keys to Success in Japan's Industrial Goods Market: As Told by Foreign & Japanese Executives.* Tokyo: JETRO, 1981.

   A concise presentation of the opinions and advice of foreign and Japanese representatives of fourteen firms, all of whom have gone through the process of setting up a business in industrial goods in Japan. Special attention is given to those areas where the industrial goods market differs from the consumer goods market.

610. Kotler, Philip and Liam Fahey. "The World's Champion Marketers: The Japanese." *Journal of Business Strategy* 3 (1982):3-13.

   Japan's marketing skill is considered here to be a critical factor among several contributing to its commercial success. The Japanese carefully determine which industries to enter, which market segments to serve, and the appropriate approaches to penetrate these markets. The authors discuss some of the misconceptions regarding Japanese marketing as well as Japanese marketing strategies.

611. ———— and Somkid Jatusripitak. *The New Competition.* Englewood Cliffs, N.J.: Prentice-Hall, 1985.

   Analyzes the "new competition" from Japan that American and European firms have been faced with. Factors responsible for Japan's economic success, especially its marketing strategy, are discussed. Recommendations are offered on how Western-based companies can meet the marketing challenge of the "new competition."

612. Narayana, Chem L. "Aggregate Images of American and Japanese Products: Implications on International Marketing." *Columbia Journal of World Business* 16 (1981):31-35.

   Narayana reports and analyzes the results of research comparing United States and Japanese consumers' perceptions of the "Made in USA" and "Made in Japan" images. The images are derived and discussed in the context of international and domestic marketing strategies.

613. Rabino, Samuel and Elva Ellen Hubbard. "The Race of American and Japanese Personal Computer Manufacturers for Dominance of the US Market." *Columbia Journal of World Business* 19 (1984):18-31.

   Describes the key features of the marketing strategies

of leading American and Japanese manufacturers of personal computers. Comparisons between the strategies draw on the product life cycle model of firm behavior. Also compares some aspects of the Japanese strategy to past strategies in other industries.

614. Shimaguchi, Mitsuaki. *Marketing Channels in Japan.* N.P.: UMI Research Press, 1978.

    The unique structural and behavioral characteristics of Japan's marketing channels are discussed, as well as the cultural determinants of the manufacturers' administrative behavior toward wholesale channel members in the pharmaceutical, soap and detergent, and dentifrice and toiletry industries.

615. ———— and Larry J. Rosenberg. "Demystifying Japanese Distribution." *Columbia Journal of World Business* 14 (1979):32-41.

    Interprets Japan's distribution system for Western marketing practitioners. Explains the unique features of the system, trade customs, and cultural forces. The authors recommend six methods that will allow Western marketing practitioners to develop and plan an effective distribution strategy.

616. Wheatley, John J. and Sadaomi Oshikawa. "Marketing in Japan: Problems and Possibilities for American Business." *Journal of Contemporary Business* 8 (1979):63-79.

    Discusses marketing opportunities for American firms in Japan. The authors contend that these opportunities should improve somewhat because of changes in the business environment. However, they maintain that Japan is likely to continue to import an increasingly larger volume of goods from countries other than the United States and that in order to change this situation, the American government would have to behave more like the Japanese government with respect to international business activity. This would mean, for example, encouragement of cooperation among American businesses in exporting to Japan or the launching of joint ventures there.

617. Yoshino, M.Y. *The Japanese Marketing System: Adaptations and Innovations.* Cambridge, Mass.: MIT Press, 1971.

    An in-depth examination of significant trends and developments in Japan's marketing system, with emphasis on the field of consumer marketing.

618. ———. *Marketing in Japan: A Management Guide.* New York: Praeger, 1975.

 An analysis of the special features of Japan's marketing and distribution system, intended primarily for business people interested in entering the Japanese market.

6. TRANSFER PRICING AND VENTURE CAPITAL

619. Clark, Rodney. *Venture Capital in Britain, America and Japan.* New York: St. Martin's, 1987.

 Describes venture capital, which is an American institution, and explains how it has been adopted in Japan and Britain. Reviews the development and current state of venture capital activity in the three nations. While the British and American economic systems are similar, the Japanese system is very different and therefore provides an interesting contrast.

620. Tang, Roger Y.W. *Transfer Pricing Practices in the United States and Japan.* New York: Praeger, 1979.

 An explanation of the similarities and differences in transfer pricing practices of large companies in the United States and Japan. Deals with both domestic and international aspects.

7. FOREIGN ECONOMIC RELATIONS

621. Ballon, Robert J. and Eugene H. Lee, eds. *Foreign Investment and Japan.* Tokyo: Sophia University, in cooperation with Kodansha International, 1972.

 Chapters initially written as working papers for the International Management Development Seminars, sponsored by the Sophia University Socio-Economic Institute. Includes discussions of Japanese legal controls, management of foreign operations, and Japanese foreign ventures.

622. Bryant, William E. *Japanese Private Economic Diplomacy: An Analysis of Business-Government Linkages.* New York: Praeger, 1975.

 A study of the government-business relationship in the context of private economic diplomacy. Analyzes the major participants involved in private economic diplomacy, which include government ministries, business associations, companies, and business leaders.

623. Dahlby, Tracy. "Come Along, It's Time to Join the Human Race." *Far Eastern Economic Review* 100 (1978):65-71.

    Discusses attempts by the Japanese at image-making in order to counterbalance the often distorted foreign images it is subject to. This sense of being misunderstood by the outside world dominates Japan's new awareness of economic interdependency, and has become important primarily because it has become dangerous to Japan's interests.

624. Hollerman, Leon. "Disintegrative versus Integrative Aspects of Interdependence: The Japanese Case." *Asian Survey* 20 (1980):324-331.

    Concerned primarily with the economic and political aspects of Japan's interdependence on the multilateral free market system in the world economy.

625. Woronoff, Jon. *Japan's Commercial Empire*. Armonk, N.Y.: M.E. Sharpe, 1984.

    Woronoff attempts to present a more balanced, objective account of the success of Japan's foreign investments. He contends that other accounts have been exaggerated, one-sided, and more emotional than factual.

626. ─────. *World Trade War*. New York: Praeger, 1984.

    The author presents the view that other countries are as much to blame as Japan, which has been criticized the most, for causing trade conflicts. He presents information on Japan's foreign economic relations and international economic relations that can be used in resolving these conflicts.

a. Import Quotas and Joint Ventures

627. Ozaki, Robert S. *The Control of Imports and Foreign Capital in Japan*. New York: Praeger, 1972.

    A survey of the legal and administrative controls over imports and foreign investments in postwar Japan, together with discussions of related problems. These control measures constitute a feature of foreign economic policy and are components of the overall growth strategy in postwar Japan. Part One of the book discusses trade and exchange controls; Part Two deals with the control of foreign capital; and Part Three includes source materials, which consist of a collection of documents concerning the control of imports and foreign capital in postwar Japan.

628. Vaughan, Francis T. "Introduction to Joint Venturing in Japan." *Case Western Reserve Journal of International Law* 6 (1974):178-198.

    Discusses the procedures involved in establishing operations in Japan by a foreign company. Vaughan advises that things will move much more smoothly if the foreign investor engages in a joint venture with a Japanese partner.

629. Wright, Richard W. "Joint Venture Problems in Japan." *Columbia Journal of World Business* 14 (1979):25-31.

    Wright examines the results of in-depth interviews he conducted with executives of foreign investor companies, the Japanese partners, and the local subsidiary managers of twenty-five American and Canadian joint ventures in Japan from 1976 to 1977. He also looks at the cultural barriers to effective joint venturing in Japan, and makes several suggestions as to how problems may be avoided.

b. Negotiation

630. Guittard, Stephen W. "Negotiating and Administering an International Sales Contract with the Japanese." *International Lawyer* 8 (1974):822-831.

    Guittard's premise is that conduct of the parties prior and subsequent to the signing of an agreement depends more upon conformity with prevailing commercial custom than on adherence to established legal standards, especially when the agreements involve a Japanese party. He is concerned with attitudes and behavioral characteristics the parties consider to be appropriate conduct rather than with provisions of written law.

631. Hahn, Elliott J. "Negotiating Contracts with the Japanese." *Case Western Reserve Journal of International Law* 14 (1982):377-385.

    Written to acquaint Westerners with the unique features of Japan's negotiation process. Among the features discussed are the following: the relationship is expected to be longterm and based on friendship and trust; proper introductions are critical; negotiations take longer than Western ones do and include socializing; and lawyers are distrusted, as their presence may prevent the establishment of a harmonious relationship.

632. Rowland, Diana. *Japanese Business Etiquette: A Practical Guide to Success with the Japanese*. New York: Warner Books, 1985.

    A handbook of Japanese business customs and etiquette that is intended to promote understanding so that Western business people and professionals may have a means of interpreting the behavior they observe, and have a better idea of what is expected of them in return. Includes chapters on preliminaries of form and etiquette, negotiating, communications, social side of business, Japanese corporate culture, after business hours, and general information about Japan.

633. Van Zandt, Howard F. "How to Negotiate in Japan." *Harvard Business Review* 48 (1970):45-56.

    Describes important Japanese behavioral characteristics, advises Americans on how to conduct themselves in Japan, and explains how to negotiate more successfully with executives there.

634. Zimmerman, Mark. *How to Do Business with the Japanese*. New York: Random House, 1985.

    The author, a Western businessman who was closely involved in doing business with the Japanese, presents information and advice on conducting business with the Japanese. Includes social and cultural aspects of Japan, as well as information on negotiating, competing, and working with the Japanese. Has also been published by George Allen & Unwin in 1985 under the title: *Dealing with the Japanese*.

B. INDUSTRY

1. INDUSTRIES

635. Baranson, Jack. *The Japanese Challenge to U.S. Industry*. Lexington, Mass.: Lexington Books, 1981.

    Examines Japan's success in international competition to see what can be learned by United States policy and business practice, with emphasis on the consumer electronics industry. American and Japanese corporate practices are contrasted as well.

636. Boyer, Edward. "How Japan Manages Declining Industries." *Fortune* (Jan. 10, 1983):58-63.

   Japan's methods of managing declining industries are unique because of its Depressed Industries Law (1978). Discussed here are actual cases, problems encountered, and solutions.

637. Dore, Ronald P. *Structural Adjustment in Japan, 1970-82*. Geneva: International Labour Office, 1986.

   Explains the mechanisms by which the Japanese economy adjusted to the changes and challenges of the 1970s, such as the new concern with the environment, the oil price rise, the world recession, the strong protectionist reaction against rising Japanese exports, the acceleration of technological change, and the increasing competitive pressure from the newly industrializing countries of Asia, especially in labor-intensive branches of production. Discusses the following major agents of adjustment: the enterprise, the labor market, government and the business enterprise, textiles, and consumer electronics.

638. Ehrlich, Eva. *Japan: A Case of Catching Up*. Budapest: Academia Kiado, 1984.

   A quantitatively oriented study of Japan's economic growth and development from the nineteenth through the twentieth centuries, and of its success in catching up with the more economically advanced countries.

639. Guillain, Robert. *The Japanese Challenge*. Philadelphia: J.B. Lippincott, 1970.

   Guillain's intention is to show that Japan is primarily modern and that it is one of the most outstanding successes of our age. He sees the strength of its industries as being a major contributor to its success, and he analyzes and discusses this factor.

640. *Japan Company Handbook* (1974)-   . Tokyo: The Oriental Economist.

   An annual directory of Japanese corporations listed on the First Sections of the Tokyo, Osaka, and Nagoya Stock Exchanges. Issued in two parts: the 1st half contains listings as of January 3, and the 2nd half contains listings as of July 31.

641. *Market Share in Japan* (1978)- . Tokyo: Yano Economic Research Institute.

An annual summary of market share business categories and products, based on the *Industrial Statistics Survey*, prepared by the Ministry of International Trade and Industry (MITI).

642. Murata, Kiyoji, ed. *An Industrial Geography of Japan.* New York: St. Martin's, 1980.

Intended mainly for geographers and economists interested in Japanese industries, but for whom material in English is not available. Focuses on organization and location of industries, and is divided into six major sections. Parts One, Two, and Three examine the formation and the current state of the industrial areas. Parts Four and Five examine the major industries, and Part Six examines the role and contribution of the government in industrial development and support.

643. Mutoh, Hiromichi. *Development in Japan's Industrial Structure since the Oil Crisis.* Tokyo: Japan Economic Research Center, 1980.

Discusses the development of industry from 1960 to 1977, with emphasis on the way various industries coped with the situation in the post-oil crisis from 1973 to 1977. Compares the performances of industries in the indicators of various industrial sectors, such as value-added, employment, labor productivity, prices, plant and equipment investment and capital stock, exports and imports, and the consumption structure of households.

644. Patrick, Hugh, ed. *Japanese Industrialization and Its Social Consequences.* Berkeley: University of California Press, 1976.

A collection of papers originally presented at a conference in 1973 by Japanese and American economists, sociologists, and anthropologists, which explore the social consequences of Japan's industrialization. The papers are divided into three parts: those dealing with evolving sociological and economic aspects of the industrial workforce, those treating specific industries and the issues and problems associated with various features of industrial firms by size, and those examining certain important social consequences of industrialization.

645. Sato, Kazuo, ed. *Industry and Business in Japan*. White Plains, N.Y.: M.E. Sharpe, 1980.

Essays by Japanese experts on industrial organization that are intended to be a sampling of what goes on in Japanese economic studies in Japan. The essays are grouped into five major sections, as follows: (1) Japan's industrial organization and historical perspectives, (2) industry studies, (3) big business and business groups, (4) industrial policy, and (5) bibliographic studies.

646. Takezawa, Shin-ichi. *Improvements in the Quality of Working Life in Three Japanese Industries*. Geneva: International Labour Office, 1982.

Gives an account of a study on the changing patterns of the quality of working life in three major industries in Japan, which are shipbuilding, electrical machinery, and automobile manufacturing. It covers the period from the late 1960s to the latter half of the 1970s, a period when changes occurred most actively in relevant union, management and government programs.

647. Washington Researchers, Ltd. *How to Find Information about Japanese Companies and Industries*. Washington, D.C., 1984.

Intended to provide business researchers with sources of information about the commercial, economic, and political situation in Japan. The book is divided into five parts: (1) researching Japanese markets, (2) sources of information in the U.S., (3) sources of information in Japan, (4) worldwide organizations, and (5) sources of published information.

a. Automobile Industry

648. Chang, C.S. *The Japanese Auto Industry and the U.S. Market*. New York: Praeger, 1981.

An analysis of the growth of the Japanese automobile industry, with emphasis on management, and its impact on the United States market.

649. Cole, Robert E., ed. *The American Automobile Industry: Rebirth or Requiem?* Ann Arbor: Center for Japanese Studies, University of Michigan, 1984.

Proceedings of the fourth U.S.-Japan Automotive Industry Conference held at the University of Michigan in 1984. Among the topics discussed are industrial policy, the development and future problems of the Japanese auto industry, quality strategy at Ford Motor Company, and U.S.-Japanese tax structures.

650. ―――――, ed. *The Japanese Automotive Industry: Model and Challenge for the Future?* Ann Arbor: Center for Japanese Studies, University of Michigan, 1981.

Proceedings of the 1981 automobile conference held at Ann Arbor. Addresses the strengths and competitive aspects of the Japanese automotive industry in relation to the United States automotive industry, and U.S.-Japan trade relations.

651. Cusumano, Michael A. *The Japanese Automobile Industry: Technology and Management at Nissan and Toyota.* Cambridge, Mass.: Council on East Asian Studies, Harvard University, 1985.

A study of the development of the Japanese automobile industry from the 1930s through the early 1980s, with emphasis on the 1950s and 1960s. Focuses on the rivalry between Nissan and Toyota and the differences in their technology and management practices.

652. Sakiya, Tetsuo. *Honda Motor: The Men, the Management, the Machines.* New York: Kodansha International, 1982.

Examines the Honda Company's unique management system and strategies within the framework of Japanese politics, economics, culture, and psychology. Also traces Honda's history and development.

b. Beef Industry

653. Longworth, John W. *Beef in Japan: Politics, Production, Marketing & Trade.* St. Lucia, Queensland, Australia: University of Queensland Press, 1983.

A detailed account of the evolution of the postwar beef industry in Japan in the context of social and cultural changes. Examines the important role the Japanese government has played, and continues to play, in the development of the industry and in international trade

Commerce, Business, and Industry 173

in beef, and analyzes the nature of government-business relations in modern Japan, as well as trade issues between Japan and other countries.

c. Computer Industry

654. Feigenbaum, Edward A. and Pamela McCorduck. *The Fifth Generation: Artificial Intelligence and Japan's Computer Challenge to the World.* Rev. and updated. New York: New American Library, 1984.

Discusses Japan's Ministry of International Trade and Industry's national plan, Fifth Generation Computer Systems, which documents a ten-year research and development program on Knowledge Information Processing Systems, which is the next stage of computer technology. Implementation began in 1982 with the formation of the Institute for New Generation Computer Technology (ICOT) and with the coordination of laboratories of the major Japanese firms in the computer industry. Emphasis is on the nature of the Fifth Generation, how it will work, why the Japanese are so committed to it, how they will carry it out, and its impact on the United States.

655. Kawatani, Yukimaro. "Japan in the Computer Age." *Industrial Management & Data Systems* (Jan./Feb. 1982):24-28.

Assesses the present state of the Japanese computer industry. Emphasis is on the following topics: growth of the industry, telecommunications, computer-aided design and manufacturing, computer applications in the steel industry, and myths about Japan's role in the world of computers.

656. United States International Trade Commission. *64K Dynamic Random Access Memory Components from Japan: Determination of the Commission.* Washington, D.C., 1986.

Discusses an investigation conducted by the United States International Trade Commission concerning the effects of imports by Japan of 64K dynamic random access memory components of the N-channel metal oxide semiconductor type (64K DRAM'S) on American companies that manufacture 64K DRAM'S.

657. Yasaki, Edward Y. and Angeline Pantages. "Japan's Computer Industry." *Datamation* 22 (1976):91-102.

A commentary on the progress to date (1976) of various companies in the computer industry. With the assistance of the government, internal combines, and external joint ventures or licenses, Japan is engaged in catching up to the United States.

d. Electronics Industry

658. Gould, Rowland. *The Matsushita Phenomenon*. Tokyo: Diamond Sha, 1970.

   Traces the history and development of the Matsushita Electric Company from its beginnings in 1918. Describes the unique management philosophy developed by its founder, Konosuke Matsushita. This philosophy includes development of individual potential and the contribution of the company to society as the basic motivation for business.

659. Gregory, Gene. *The Japanese Electronics Industry*. Tokyo: Sophia University, 1981.

   Consists of articles originally published in the *Far Eastern Economic Review* and *Scientific American* between 1979 and 1981. They reflect the general hypothesis that Japan's emergence as a world industrial leader, which has coincided with the electronic technology revolution, is functionally related to the institutions and systems that Japanese industry has developed since the early years of its modern era for managing rapid technological change, for efficiently allocating scarce resources, and for the timely substitution of new competitive products before old ones have reached the point of diminishing returns on investment. Presents a unified and gradual pattern of industrial structural change, brought on by innovation and anticipatory industrial policies.

660. ―――. "Mega-Research Investment for Japanese Microelectronics." *Research Management* 26 (1983):14-19.

   Discusses the increased research and development programs of major Japanese manufacturers of electronic devices and equipment that will enable them to achieve even higher stages of technology development. These R&D programs include higher expenditures, reorganization, and the appointment of technical experts to top management posts.

661. *Japan Electronics Almanac*. New York: Dempa Publications.

   An annual directory of Japan's electronics industry and leading firms. The electronics industry section contains progress and trends of various types of industry, such as semiconductors, microprocessors, electronic parts and components, and factory automation, as well as a list of Japan's top 100 companies and electronics related organizations. Part Two contains information on Japan's leading electronics companies.

662. Lyons, Nick. *The SONY Vision.* New York: Crown Publishers, 1976.

    A nontechnical history of SONY from 1945 to 1975, which stresses the company's ideals of innovation, quality, and performance.

663. Morita, Akio. *Made in Japan: Akio Morita and SONY.* New York: E.P. Dutton, 1986.

    An autobiographical account of the history of the relationship between SONY and Akio Morita, one of its founders and present chairman. Morita discusses his views on management, the differences between Japanese and American management practices, U.S.-Japan trade relations, and the role of technology in preserving the future of mankind.

e. Manufacturing Industry

664. Fatemi, Ali M., Hossein Safizadeh and Marna Jo Young. "A Financial Comparison of Japanese and U.S. Manufacturers." *Asia Pacific Journal of Management* 2 (1984): 40-53.

    A study that compares and contrasts the financial policies of Japanese and comparable American manufacturing firms on the basis of fifteen financial ratios. In addition to human resource management, efficient management of financial resources is a vital component of a concern's management system, but according to the authors, there has not been much literature written about possible financial policy differences between Japan and the United States.

665. Ikeda, Katsuhiko and Noriyuki Doi. "Mergers and Economic Concentration in Japanese Manufacturing Industry." *Industrial Organization Review* 8 (1980):1-26.

    Analyzes the effects of mergers on overall concentration and individual industrial concentration since 1962. Also compares these effects with those of the United States and the United Kingdom.

666. ——————. "The Performances of Merging Firms in Japanese Manufacturing Industry: 1964-75. *Journal of Industrial Economics* 31 (1983):257-265.

A quantitative study of the microeconomic effects of mergers that focuses on the financial performances of merging firms. Tests the following indicators of performance: profitability, efficiency, firm growth, and research and development.

f. Steel Industry

667. Gold, Bela. "Factors Stimulating Technological Progress in Japanese Industries: The Case of Computerization in Steel." *Quarterly Review of Economics & Business* 18 (1978):7-21.

Examines the past roles of the following factors in stimulating technological progress in Japanese industries: management, government, organizational relationships within the firm, and market pressures. Emphasis is on the computerization of the steel industry. Attention is also given to the likelihood that such factors will help to continue Japanese leadership in the steel industry and related sectors of industrial operations as well. Gold bases his judgments on extensive field research on steel operations in the United States, Western Europe, and Japan.

668. Kawahito, Kiyoshi. *The Japanese Steel Industry: With an Analysis of the U.S. Steel Import Problem.* New York: Praeger, 1972.

A quantitative assessment of the postwar history to 1960 and economics of the Japanese steel industry. Discusses the reconstruction and development of the industry from 1945 to 1960 as well as its contemporary situation. Among the topics examined are production and markets; raw materials; distribution system; pricing method and price levels; finance, labor costs, and labor productivity. Also includes an analysis of United States steel imports from Japan.

669. ——————. "Relative Profitability of the US and Japanese Steel Industries." *Columbia Journal of World Business* 19 (1984):13-17.

Compares the relative profitability of United States and Japanese steel industries in the framework of an empirical expose of the irrelevancy of some profit indices when the capital structure of two firms is radically different. Presents alternative data and analyses of profitability that demonstrate that the American steel industry has been less viable than its Japanese counterpart. Also discusses several issues related to steel industry profitability.

2. TECHNOLOGICAL INNOVATION

670. Eto, Hajime and Konomu Matsui, eds. *R&D Management Systems in Japanese Industry*. New York: North-Holland, 1984.

    Reports of actual research and development (R&D) systems in Japanese industry. The following subjects are discussed: R&D for fifth generation computer systems, a policy guidance system for complex innovation, public investment and R&D investment as reflationary policy, Japanese creativity, information technology-based innovation, R&D and patents, behavior of Japanese R&D organizations, and soft science in Japan.

671. Lynn, Leonard H. *How Japan Innovates: A Comparison with the U.S. in the Case of Oxygen Steelmaking*. Boulder, Colo.: Westview Press, 1982.

    Lynn examines a prime example of Japan's industrial success, the introduction of steelmaking technology, which originated in Europe and which was adopted and improved by the Japanese. He utilizes this industrial technology in order to articulate clearly the conclusion made by economists that much of Japan's economic success is the result of its unique social capacity to adopt and improve foreign technology. A comparison is made of how Japan and the United States adopted a major new industrial technology, the basic oxygen furnace (BOF), which is now the world's most widely used steelmaking process. Japan's rapid introduction of the BOF was a major factor in the dramatic increase of international competitiveness of its steel industry in the 1960s.

672. Ozawa, Terutomo. *Japan's Technological Challenge to the West, 1950-1974: Motivation and Accomplishment*. Cambridge, Mass.: MIT Press, 1974.

    Describes Japan's postwar experience in both adapting Western technology and developing technological innovations within the industrial sector, which was a major force behind its high rates of economic growth.

a. Industrial Robots

673. Baranson, Jack. *Robots in Manufacturing: Key to International Competiveness*. Mt. Airy, Md.: Lomond Publications, 1983.

   Compares the implementation of AMES (Automated Manufacturing Equipment and Systems) between industrial sectors of the United States, Japan, and Western Europe. Explains the importance of automated manufacturing in today's emerging international economy, and the underlying reasons that have caused the United States to fall behind Japan and other countries in the adoption of AMES. In addition, a detailed analysis of factors that determine the rate of adoption of AMES in each of the country areas is presented. Also contains profiles of thirty-three AMES producers in Japan, Western Europe, and the United States.

674. Chacko, George K. *Robotics/Artificial Intelligence/Productivity: U.S.-Japan Concomitant Coalitions*. Princeton, N.J.: Petrocelli Books, 1986.

   Examines the productivity potential of the various technologies under robotics and artificial intelligence on the one hand, and the competitive cooperation between the United States and Japan to secure and share the advances and applications in these fields, on the other. The book is divided into two parts. Part One concentrates on productivity promises of robotics and artificial intelligence. Part Two deals with concomitant coalitions in cars and computers, with focus on trade and technology in Japan and the United States.

675. Hartley, John. *Flexible Automation in Japan*. New York: Springer-Verlag, 1984.

   A collection of articles on Japan's activities in advanced automated manufacturing technology, including industrial robots. Well illustrated with photographs and diagrams. Includes a compilation of specifications of Japanese robots currently being manufactured.

676. JMA Research Institute. *Robotization: Its Implications for Management*. Tokyo: Fuji Corp., 1983.

   Presents a basic understanding of present trends and innovations in the Japanese manufacturing industry, especially as they relate to industrial robots. Based on the investigation of actual cases of industrial robot utilization. Also examines how Japanese management is dealing with robot utilization. The following topics are discussed: trends in the development and utilization of industrial robots, roles and effects of industrial robots, management aspects, case histories of industrial robot utilization, and future outlook for industrial robots.

677. Sadamoto, Kuni, ed. *Robots in the Japanese Economy: Facts about Robots and Their Significance.* Tokyo: Survey Japan, 1981.

    An overall view of industrial robots in Japan, with emphasis on their development and economic significance.

IX
INDUSTRIAL MANAGEMENT, ORGANIZATION, AND PRODUCTIVITY

A. INDUSTRIAL MANAGEMENT

678. Abegglen, James C. and William V. Rapp. "Japanese Managerial Behavior and 'Excessive Competition.'" *Developing Economies* 8 (1970):427-444.

    The authors argue that many aspects of Japanese corporate behavior make the maintenance and expansion of market share an important objective of Japanese management. This concern results in "excessive competition," which is the degree of preemptive capital investment and pricing. Since Japanese firms rely heavily on price as a competitive weapon, this is a realistic consequence. The authors also explain the suitability of the Japanese business system for this type of pricing policy and the cost-effectiveness of high growth.

679. ────── and George Stalk, Jr. *Kaisha, the Japanese Corporation*. New York: Basic Books, 1985.

    Describes and explains the competitive behavior of Japan's companies ("Kaisha") to those Western business persons whose own competitive decisions and actions require a more complete understanding of the "Kaisha." Among the competitive fundamentals chosen by the successful "Kaisha" are a growth bias, a preoccupation with actions of competitors, the creation and ruthless exploitation of competitive advantage, and the choice of corporate financial and personnel policies that are economically consistent with all of the preceding. Covers the following topics: the dynamic economy, manufacturing competition, technological leadership, working with banks and shareholders, the foreign company in Japan, the multinational "Kaisha," and the future of the "Kaisha."

680. Alston, Jon P. *The American Samurai: Blending American and Japanese Managerial Practices.* New York: W. de Gruyter, 1986.

Focuses on Japanese consensus management and its development in Japanese history and culture. Also presents Japanese administrative practices, which according to Alston, because of their universal rather than exclusively Japanese values, American management can combine with American practices to create a successful synthesis that will enable them to increase productivity and meet the Japanese competition.

681. Aonuma, Yoshimatsu. "A Japanese Explains Japan's Business Style." *Across the Board* 18 (1981):41-50.

Discusses Japanese management characteristics, many of which, the author contends, are contradictory in nature and are difficult for the Japanese to understand. Among the characteristics examined are the sacrificing of personal interest for the nation and the company, the concept of the company as a family, and the emphasis that is placed on small groups.

682. Arai, Shunzo. *An Intersection of East and West: Japanese Business Management.* Tokyo: Rikugei Publishing House, 1971.

Arai presents his views on Japanese business management, which he contends should be practical, personalized, and humanistic. He discusses the lifetime employment and security system, collective decision-making, recruiting and training methods, and affiliated company systems, and points out their advantages and disadvantages. He also maintains that justice should be the foundation of business management, and because justice as expressed in the West coincides with the way of the Orient, managers should act as the intermediary between East and West to promote a deeper mutual understanding among nations.

683. Boisot, Max. *Intangible Factors in Japanese Corporate Strategy.* Paris: Atlantic Institute for International Affairs, 1983.

Dr. Boisot presents the hypothesis that cultural factors are an important and often neglected element of the differences between corporate strategies in Japan and the other industrial democracies. He contends that an in-depth analysis of such factors will contribute substantially to increased understanding of performance differentials in the industrial structures of the Western democracies. Dr. Boisot also examines the notion of convergence as it applies to the large Japanese firm. This notion intimates that countries, as they industrialize under different circumstances, become more similar in their attitudes, beliefs, values, and behavior.

684. Campbell, Donald J. "The Meaning of Work: American and Japanese Paradigms." *Asian Journal of Management* 3 (1985):1-9.

In an attempt to close the "productivity gap" between American and Japanese workers, many American firms have begun to adopt or experiment with various forms of Japanese management practices. However, Campbell notes that this interest shown by American firms has not been accompanied by a corresponding interest in the Japanese philosophy of work, and that this is necessary if they want to transfer successfully Japanese practices to the United States. He examines some fundamental differences in the way the meaning of work is conceptualized in each of the two cultures, which should provide additional insight into the transferability of Japanese management methods to American organizations.

685. Chao, Ke-lu and William I. Gorden. "Culture and Communication in the Modern Japanese Corporate Organization." *International and Intercultural Communication Annual* 5 (1979):23-36.

Describes the major characteristics of Japanese corporate organizations and their management style. The characteristics discussed here are lifetime employment, the seniority system, fringe benefits, and company based unions. In addition, important aspects of communication and decision-making are identified, among which are the norms of harmony and group cooperation.

686. Clark, Rodney. *The Japanese Company*. New Haven, Conn.: Yale University Press, 1979.

Considers the organization and management of the Japanese company. Discusses lifetime employment, the nature of authority, company influence on the labor market, aging, employee attitudes, and the influence of the company on society as well as the factors contributing both to company stability and change.

687. Cole, Robert E. "Learning from the Japanese: Prospects and Pitfalls." *Management Review* 69 (1980):22-28, 38-42.

    The prospects of Americans learning from the Japanese in the area of worker-management relations are discussed through two approaches: (1) the experience with the Japanese in borrowing from the Americans in this area, and (2) the concrete example of Japanese quality control circles (QC circles). Also looks at the introduction of QC circles in the United States and the problems encountered with them.

688. Cooper, C.L. and N. Kuniya. "Participative Management Practice and Work Humanisation in Japan." *Personnel Review* 7 (1978):25-30.

    Gives examples of work humanization projects in Japan, which are centered mainly on autonomous work groups. Presents an account of the social and historical background of participative management in Japan and the role of the Japanese labor unions concerning participative management.

689. De Mente, Boye. *The Japanese Way of Doing Business*. Englewood Cliffs, N.J.: Prentice-Hall, 1981.

    A revised edition of the author's *Japanese Manners & Ethics in Business* (1961). A practical approach that includes Japanese social life and customs as well as business practices. Discusses the Japanese company and management, the concept of "amae" in Japanese manners and ethics, working and living in a vertical society, and the spirit of Japan.

690. Dickerman, Allen. *Training Japanese Managers*. New York: Praeger, 1974.

    Traces the development of Japanese management from the late nineteenth century to the present. Emphasis is on such management practices as the decision-making process and employee relations. Also includes information about the structure of Japanese business education and management training programs, as well as American business activity in Japan.

691. Diebold, John. "Management Can Learn from Japan." *Business Week* (Sept. 29, 1973):14-19.

    Diebold discusses his ideas on the two most distinctive Japanese management practices, lifetime employment, and payment by age and length of service, which he contends can be adopted by American business. He also suggests that other successful features of the Japanese business system could be emulated as well, such as the generally supportive relations between the Japanese bureaucracy and business, the emphasis Japanese trading houses put on understanding the distribution systems employed abroad, and the capability for constant retraining that comes from the lifetime employment system.

692. Dillon, Linda S. "Adopting Japanese Management: Some Cultural Stumbling Blocks." *Personnel* 60 (1983):73-78.

Dillon suggests that cultural factors may inhibit the easy transferability of some Japanese management practices to the West. The only elements, she argues, that the West may borrow are perhaps those that Japan borrowed from the West in the process of industrialization.

693. Doktor, R. "Culture and the Management of Time: A Comparison of Japanese and American Top Management Practice." *Asia Pacific Journal of Management* 1 (1983):65-71.

Compares the amount of time chief executive officers (CEO's) and upper-level managers in Japan and the United States spend working alone and with others and on each activity in order to ascertain patterns of time utilization as functions of culture.

694. Dreyfack, Raymond. *Making It in Management--The Japanese Way*. Rockville Centre, N.Y.: Farnsworth, 1982.

Advice for American industrial management on how to practice more effective management techniques in order to increase productivity and product quality. Dreyfack stresses the successful philosophy and management style of Konosuke Matsushita, founder and chief executive of Matsushita Electric Industrial Co.

695. Drucker, Peter F. "What We Can Learn from Japanese Management." *Harvard Business Review* 49 (1971):110-122.

Drucker discusses those features of Japanese management that are major contributing factors to Japan's economic achievement and that the United States should emulate (not imitate) in order to solve some of its problems. Among the features discussed here are decision by consensus, lifetime employment, continuous training, and the godfather system.

696. Dunphy, Dexter C. and Bruce W. Stening. *Japanese Organization Behaviour and Management: An Annotated Bibliography*. Hong Kong: Asian Research Service, 1984.

   Provides a listing of materials published in English that discuss Japanese management and organization behavior as related to the Japanese enterprise. Includes both monographs and journals, and coverage is from 1970 to October 1983. Among the topics covered here are employment practices, decision-making, use of groups, work attitudes, management style and organizational structure, corporate strategies, overseas operations, the importability of non-Japanese management practices, and the exportability of Japanese management practices.

697. Endo, Calvin M. "Formal Management Relations Practices in Japanese Business and Industrial Organizations." *International Journal of Contemporary Society* 11 (1974):23-33.

   Describes the practices of lifetime employment, the recruitment system, and the wage and promotion system in contemporary Japanese firms.

698. England, George W. and Ryohji Koike. "Personal Value Systems of Japanese Managers." *Journal of Cross-Cultural Psychology* 1 (1970):21-40.

   Analyzes the personal value systems of Japanese managers and their impact on organizational behavior.

699. Ford, Bill, Millicent Easther and Ann Brewer. *Japanese Employment and Employee Relations: An Annotated Bibliography*. Canberra: Australian Government Publishing Service, 1984.

   Consists of 536 annotated citations of monographs and periodicals in English, on the subject of Japanese employment and employee relations, especially in relation to such key issues as skills formation, technological change, quality of working life, and employee participation. Much of the material has been based on the experiences of large Japanese organizations, since there is little research and few publications on employment in small and medium-sized enterprises in Japan that are available in English. Most of the material selected for inclusion was published between 1970 and 1981.

700. Fox, William M. "Japanese Management: Tradition under Strain." *Business Horizons* 20 (1977):76-85.

   Compares Japanese and American management practices, analyzes the factors responsible for the success of Japanese management, and looks at the potential problems traditional Japanese management practices may be faced with. Fox contends that these practices are being challenged by young people who are not as accepting of traditional values and by changing circumstances both at home and abroad.

701. Fruin, W. Mark. "The Japanese Company Controversy." *Journal of Japanese Studies* 4 (1978):267-300.

   Analyzes the practices of lifetime employment and seniority-based compensation of a major Japanese foods industry during the period from 1918 to 1976. The results present new data on the controversy over Japanese personnel policies and company practices.

702. Furstenberg, Friedrich. *Why the Japanese Have Been So Successful in Business*. London: Leviathan House, 1974.

   Discusses the successful management systems and practices of large Japanese companies. The following topics are included here: organizational structure, information and decision-making, planning and research, personnel policy and practice, wage system, managerial and worker training, and methods of promotion and worker participation. Also presents the findings of the author's survey of management practices of eight large Japanese companies.

703. Garvin, David A. "Japanese Quality Management." *Columbia Journal of World Business* 19 (1984):3-12.

   A comparison of the quality management practices of United States and Japanese manufacturers of room air conditioners in order to explain the Japanese success with product quality. Specific practices are identified, among which are process control, quality systems and staffing, management attitudes, and government policies.

704. Gibney, Frank. *Miracle by Design: The Real Reasons behind Japan's Economic Success*. New York: Times Books, 1982.

   Describes the successful Japanese methods of doing business as well as their applicability in the United States. Gibney lived and worked in Japan from 1966 to

1976 and came to admire much in Japanese business and society, and found many things that the United States could adopt. He discusses the Japanese work ethic, management, company integrity, successful company unions, how to deal with legal issues without lawyers, and doing business in Japan.

705. Hamada, Tomoko. "Winds of Change: Economic Realism and Japanese Labor Management." *Asian Survey* 20 (1980): 397-406.

Hamada analyzes the socioeconomic and cultural factors that may possibly have led to the emergence of the Japanese employment system. He also examines recent managerial actions in large companies in order to ascertain the degree of traditionalism and rigidity in the employment system and to predict how the system will change. Emphasis is on seniority rule and the life-long employment system.

706. Harbron, John D. "How Japanese Executives Manage the New Zaibatsu." *Business Quarterly* 45 (1980):15-18.

The vertically integrated nature of Japan's "zaibatsu" (historical industrial combines) enhances the Japanese style of management in which group action and consensus are the main features. Harbron looks at the management practices of Japanese executives within "zaibatsu" companies. He contends that they attach great importance to consensus and are very close to their managers and workers, and their workers respond with loyalty and hard work. The presidents of "zaibatsu" companies practice "inter-group teaming" and others help formulate overall economic policy through their roles in Keidanren (the Federation of Economic Organizations). Senior Japanese executives do not issue unilateral company directives, but work with others.

707. Hatakeyama, Yoshio. *Manager Revolution! A Guide to Survival in Today's Changing Workplace*. Stamford, Conn.: Productivity Press, 1985.

Translation of a work originally written for Japanese managers, but has applications for Western managers as well. Outlines the fundamentals of being a manager, and discusses various work and personal problems. Hatakeyama, who is president of the Japan Management Association, has written this book as a suggestion that managers need to change themselves in order to deal with the social responsibilities of their jobs.

708. Hattori, Ichiro. "A Proposition on Efficient Decision-Making in the Japanese Corporation." *Columbia Journal of World Business* 13 (1978):7-15.

    Analyzes the decision-making process, with emphasis on the role of top management in creating the optimal conditions and rules for an efficient process.

709. Hatvany, Nina and Vladimir Pucik. "An Integrated Management System: Lessons from the Japanese Experience." *Academy of Management Review* 6 (1981):469-480.

    Japanese management in large companies is viewed as being characterized by its focus on human resources, and this has resulted in high productivity, low turnover and absenteeism.

710. ──────. "Japanese Management Practices and Productivity." *Organizational Dynamics* 9 (1981):5-21.

    Focuses on successful management practices, which are influenced by a concern for human resources, and which have contributed to high industrial productivity.

711. Hayes, Robert H. "Why Japanese Factories Work." *Harvard Business Review* 59 (1981):56-66.

    Hayes attributes the success of Japanese factories to their managerial emphasis on the equal importance of every stage of the manufacturing process and on their goals of perfect products and error-free operations.

712. Hazama, Hiroshi. "Formation of the Management System in Meiji Japan; Personnel Management in Large Corporations." *Developing Economies* 15 (1977):402-419.

    The author describes the industrialization process in Japan, factory conditions, and the problems that led to changes in personnel management in the Meiji period. He uses Kanebo (Kanegafuchi Spinning Company) to illustrate these changes. According to Hazama, Japanese private enterprises at that time copied the personnel welfare policies of Western nations, and the characteristics of the contemporary Japanese management system have their forerunners in private enterprises such as Kanebo.

713. *How Japan Works*. Boston: Harvard Business Review, 1982.

    A collection of articles reprinted from the *Harvard Business Review*, 1961 to 1981. They are arranged according to three topics: (1) lessons from Japanese management, (2) Japan's competitive threat, and (3) succeeding in the Japanese market.

714. Howard, N. and Y. Teramoto. "The Really Important Difference between Japanese and Western Management." *International Management* 21 (1981/3):19-30.

The authors discuss their thesis that the difference between Japanese and Western management lies in the ability to understand the functions of social practices. The Japanese, through their culture, understand how decisions are made, while Westerners do not. The Japanese regard decision-making as a matter of cybernetic games, which requires the management of vast amounts of variety and the reaching of understanding between different parties with different preferences. This thesis is tested against a list of observable differences between Japanese and Western management practices.

715. Iwata, Ryushi. *Japanese-Style Management: Its Foundations and Prospects*. Tokyo: Asian Productivity Organization, 1982.

Originally written for Japanese businessmen. Describes the structure, mechanism, and foundations of Japanese management practices, fluctuations in environmental conditions and their responses to such changes, and the future of Japanese management. Emphasis is on the social and cultural uniqueness of Japanese society, due to the author's major concern with the compatibility between Japanese management and the social and cultural factors in Japanese society.

716. Juran, J.M. "Japanese and Western Quality: A Contrast in Methods and Results." *Management Review* 67 (1978): 27-45.

Using the color TV set as a case example, the quality of Japanese and Western products is compared. In addition, some of the differences and reasons concerning quality are evaluated, and implications for the future are suggested.

717. Karatsu, Hajime. "What Makes Japanese Products Better?" *Advanced Management Journal* 47 (1982):4-7.

The author, managing director of Matsushita Communications Industrial Company, Ltd., discusses his view that good management is more responsible for Japan's economic success than cultural factors. According to Karatsu,

Japan's cultural advantage would count for nothing if it were not for good leadership, as is demonstrated by Japan's problem-riddled companies such as Japan National Railways. He also discusses quality control circles (QC) and total quality control (TQC), management techniques he considers to be prime reasons for Japan's success.

718. Kaufmann, Felix. "Decision Making--Eastern and Western Style." *Business Horizons* 13 (1970):81-86.

    Kaufmann suggests a way to synthesize the best elements of the Japanese and Western systems into a decision-making process suitable for the West. He contends that this will require the development and utilization of professional strategic analysts.

719. Kawase, Takeshi and Tadaaki Nemoto. "An Empirical Study on Ideal Personal Characteristics of Japanese OR/MS Leaders." *Interfaces* 9 (1979):56-62.

    Analyzes the results of an empirical study of the personal characteristics of Japanese OR/MS (Operations Research/Management Science) leaders that are regarded as important factors affecting the successful survival and promotion of OR/MS activities in the organization at three phases of organization evolution. Emphasis is on those factors peculiar to the OR/MS group leaders and dependent upon phases of the growth of the OR/MS group.

720. Kobayashi, Maurie K. and W. Warner Burke. "Organization Development in Japan." *Columbia Journal of World Business* 11 (1976):113-123.

    Discusses some of the differences in organization development between the United States and Japan, as well as the distinctive characteristics of the Japanese form.

721. Kono, Toyohiro. "Japanese Management Philosophy: Can It Be Exported?" *Long Range Planning* 15 (1982):90-102.

    Analyzes the major characteristics of Japanese management, with emphasis on style. The author maintains that certain of these practices can be transferred to other countries.

722. ———. *Strategy and Structure of Japanese Enterprises*. Armonk, N.Y.: M.E. Sharpe, 1984.

    Examines the product-market strategy, the organizational structure, and strategic decisions of relatively large and successful Japanese corporations, focusing especially on the strategic aspects of Japanese management. Covers the following topics: top management, organizational goals, product and diversification, vertical integration, multinational management, competition strategy, new-product development, long-range planning, organizational structure and resource structure, and personnel management.

723. Krauss, W. Paul. "Will Success Spoil Japanese Management?" *Columbia Journal of World Business* 8 (1973):26-30.

   The strengths and weaknesses of the Japanese system are analyzed with respect to operating and controlling foreign companies. Also discusses procedures to perform this successfully.

724. Lee, Sang M. and Gary Schwendiman, eds. *Japanese Management: Cultural and Environmental Considerations.* New York: Praeger, 1982.

   Contains selected empirical and conceptual studies written by well-known Japanese and American scholars that were presented at the Japan-United States Business Conference, Lincoln, Nebraska, 1981. The studies analyze Japanese management systems and the possibilities of transferring them to American companies. Addresses the following topics: learning from the Japanese, Japanese culture and management, and the Japanese management environment.

725. ——————, eds. *Management by Japanese Systems.* New York: Praeger, 1982.

   Based on papers presented at a conference on Japan-United States Business, Lincoln, Nebraska, 1981, by leading Japanese and American management scholars and business executives and administrators, as well as those specially written for this volume. Emphasis is on the following key issues of Japanese management systems: overall Japanese management style, various aspects of quality circles, Japanese operations management systems and marketing systems, comparative analysis of Japanese and American management, and the transferability of Japanese management systems to the United States.

726. Long, William A. and K.K. Seo. *Management in Japan and India, with Reference to the United States.* New York: Praeger, 1977.

   The authors present the thesis that management practices in any country are deeply rooted in the historical and religious origins of the country's culture, customs, and traditional social values, as well as in its economic and social systems, and that successful management practices must be tailored to the customs and culture of the country. Japan was chosen for inclusion because it has achieved economic success with management practices that are quite opposite to those of the United States. India, on the other hand, offers an opportunity to study a developing nation that has chosen democratic socialism rather than capitalism or communism. The United States is used here as a basis for comparison, and is not meant by the authors to be used as a standard to be emulated by other countries. Most of the discussions are limited to management practices in the larger business enterprises of each country. Among the topics covered are cultural attributes, management structures and ideology, selection and training of managers, employment policies and industrial relations, and relationships between government and business.

727. Marengo, Franco. "Learning from the Japanese: What or How?" *Management International Review* 19 (1979):39-46.

   Examines current Western interpretations of Japanese organizational and managerial behavior, concentrating on "groupism," consensual decision-making, and reliance on growth rather than profit, and demonstrates that these interpretations are generally biased by Western perspectives.

728. Marsh, Robert M. and Hiroshi Mannari. *Modernization and the Japanese Factory.* Princeton, N.J.: Princeton University Press, 1976.

   Relates three sets of variables: technological modernization, the modernization of social organization, and organizational performance or effectiveness, to the Japanese industrial manufacturing firm. The main theoretical problem is the validity of the paternalism-lifetime commitment model of the Japanese factory and the convergence theory of modernization, which holds that as societies become more highly modernized they tend to become more alike in their social and cultural structure. The authors contend that the paternalism model exaggerates the uniformity, traditionalism, and uniqueness of Japanese factories, and that the most successful firms have moved in the direction of a more modern organizational structure.

729. Marshall, Byron K. "Japanese Business Ideology and Labor Policy." *Columbia Journal of World Business* 12 (1977):22-29.

Discusses the development of Japan's contemporary system of management and paternalistic labor policies.

730. Maruta, Yoshio. "The Management of Innovation in Japan: The Tetsuri Way." *Research Management* 23 (1980):39-41.

The author, who is the president of Kao Soap Company, Ltd., Tokyo, discusses the origin of the concept of "Tetsuri" (refers to the absolute truth that governs the universe as well as the world of theoretical physics and molecular biology) in Japan, and how it provides guidelines for the everyday management and R&D of the Kao Soap Company.

731. McMillan, Charles J. "Is Japanese Management Really So Different?" *Business Quarterly* 45 (1980):26-31.

McMillan develops the view that the Japanese system of management is neither unique nor novel. What is different, he maintains, is that the Japanese are applying textbook management principles, and these principles are economically sound, managerially rational, and equally applicable to any industrial society.

732. ─────. *The Japanese Industrial System.* 2d rev. ed. New York: W. de Gruyter, 1985.

A study of the Japanese industrial system and the evolving management strategies of the 1980s. Examines the Japanese model at three fundamental levels: (1) government (national industrial policy), (2) microeconomic sector analysis, and (3) the corporation.

733. Misumi, Juji. *The Behavioral Science of Leadership: An Interdisciplinary Japanese Research Program.* Ann Arbor: University of Michigan Press, 1985.

Based on leadership and management studies sponsored by the Chair of Group Dynamics at the Faculty of Education, Kyushu University, and by the Institute for Group Dynamics, Fukuoka City. Develops a Performance-Maintenance (PM) theory of leadership, which describes and explains leadership behavior according to two basic group functions: leadership that promotes goal achievement (P) and leadership that maintains social stability (M). Both P and M functions are present in leadership behavior at the same time. The research consists of field surveys and laboratory studies.

734. Monden, Yasuhiro. *Innovations in Management: The Japanese Corporation.* Norcross, Ga.: Industrial Engineering and Management Press, 1985.

    Explores the total hierarchical system inherent in Japanese management. Covers the philosophical, strategic, managerial, and operational levels of modern Japanese management as well as in-depth investigations of operational management in fields such as human-resource management, production management, finance, and marketing. Includes examples of various empirical numerical data.

735. Moran, Robert T. "Japanese Participative Management—Or How 'Ringi Seido' Can Work for You." *Advanced Management Journal* 44 (1979):14-22.

    Observes some basic differences in management and business practices between Japan and the United States, and discusses some Japanese management practices that can or cannot be transferred to the United States.

736. Musahi, Miyamoto. *A Book of Five Rings.* New York: Overlook Press, 1982.

    The author, who completed this book in 1645, is considered to be the greatest samurai in Japanese history. The work is regarded as a classic guide to strategy by business persons. It draws heavily from Confucianism, Shintoism, and Zen, and its conceptual basis and structure are provided by the Five Greats, or the elements of the universe, of Buddhism. Japanese businessmen, who are especially appreciative of tradition, apply this philosophy to any business situation where plans and tactics can be used, especially in the implementation of strategy, and it perpetuates the foundations for the work ethic of contemporary Japanese businessmen.

737. Oh, Tai K. "Japanese Management—A Critical Review." *Academy of Management Review* 1 (1976):14-25.

    Oh explores Japan's permanent employment system ("Nenko") in the context of an interdependent part of the socioeconomic structure of Japanese industry and contends that it has created a highly efficient dual wage and labor market system. Oh also examines some of its social and economic costs, among which is the exclusion of two-thirds of the Japanese labor force from its benefits. He also posits the question of compatibility of the system with American behavior patterns and value orientations, and concludes that Japanese managerial effectiveness cannot be understood and probably cannot be duplicated outside the context of the Japanese industrial relations system.

738. Okamoto, Yasuo. "The Grand Strategy of Japanese Business." *Japanese Economic Studies* 10 (1982):3-52.

Focuses on the development and characteristics of those product-market managerial strategies that have significantly changed the characteristics of the firms in this study, and that have had a long-term impact on other firms. The study is limited to large manufacturing firms.

739. Ouchi, William G. *Theory Z: How American Business Can Meet the Japanese Challenge.* Reading, Mass.: Addison-Wesley, 1981.

Ouchi contrasts the characteristics of Japanese and American companies, and suggests that American companies should incorporate the best of Japanese techniques and values by applying the "Theory Z" approach to management. This theory maintains that involved workers are the key to increased productivity, and Ouchi contends that those American companies that have applied "Theory Z" to their management practices (Hewlett-Packard, IBM, Eli Lilly, and Proctor & Gamble, to name a few) are more productive than the "Type A" or typical American organizations.

740. ─────. "Organizational Paradigms: A Commentary on Japanese Management and Theory Z Organizations." *Organizational Dynamics* 9 (1981):36-43.

The author offers his comments and reflections on the article "Japanese Management Practices and Productivity" (Hatvany and Pucik, *Organizational Dynamics* 9 (1981):4-21), and on the interview with Richard D. Wood, chief executive officer of Eli Lilly Company, a "Theory Z" organization (*Organizational Dynamics* 9 (1981):22-35). Ouchi recommends that typical American firms should adopt a management philosophy based on that which underlies Japanese and "Theory Z" organizations.

741. Pascale, Richard Tanner. "Communication and Decision Making across Cultures: Japanese and American Comparisons." *Administrative Science Quarterly* 23 (1978):91-110.

   Presents research results of a study in which the communications and decision-making practices of Japanese firms operating in Japan and the United States were compared with American firms operating in the United States.

742. ―――――. "Zen and the Art of Management." *Harvard Business Review* 56 (1978):153-162.

   Analyzes the results of a 1974 study of Japanese-managed companies in the United States and Japan in order to ascertain what elements of the communications and decision-making processes contributed to the reported high performance of Japanese companies. The results indicate that the Zen-like quality of ambiguity that Japanese managers use in interpersonal communication appears to account for more effective organizational functioning.

743. ―――――― and Anthony G. Athos. *The Art of Japanese Management: Applications for American Executives*. New York: Simon and Schuster, 1981.

   The authors contend that American firms cannot imitate the Japanese, but rather should use the best of Eastern traditions to strengthen their own areas of weakness. They examine Matsushita Electric Co., ITT, United Airlines, and IBM. Stresses the subtleties of Japanese management, such as the use of ambiguity and implicit communication instead of forced directness, and the emphasis on cooperation instead of competitive individualism. The success of many Japanese companies is attributed to a "7-S" management model in which the Japanese pay meticulous attention to staff skills, style, and superordinate goals. In contrast, Western companies have tended to stress strategy, structure, and style.

744. Pegels, C. Carl. *Japan vs. the West: Implications for Management*. Boston: Kluwer-Nijhoff, 1984.

   Provides a thorough background on the practice of Japanese management. Also presents suggestions and directions for Western management on how to adopt or adapt to Japanese management practices and operations. Pegels contends that all Japanese management practices are transferable to the West. The book consists of four parts. Part One provides an overview of Japanese industry versus Western industry. Part Two discusses Japanese management as practiced by the Japanese. Part Three explores the effects of the Japanese influence on Western management practices. And Part Four looks at industrial world competition in the future.

745. Prochaska, Robert J. "The Management of Innovation in Japan: Why It Is So Successful." *Research Management* 23 (1980):35-38.

    The author, a vice president of a company in Osaka, Japan, presents his observations on the innovation process and compares it with that of the United States. He attributes Japan's success in innovation management to the following factors: it is a remote island community, and as a result has a homogenous society; emphasis is on high product quality, good customer service, and the ability to satisfy a specific customer need; customer-orientation; the elevation of the needs of the company above personal needs of the employee; bottom-up organization of the Japanese company and the consensus decision-making process; and long-term job experience of the Japanese worker within each job assignment.

746. Pucik, Vladimir. "White Collar Human Resource Management: A Comparison of the US and Japanese Automobile Industries." *Columbia Journal of World Business* 19 (1984):87-94.

    A comparative review of contemporary conditions of white collar employment in American and Japanese automobile industries. Emphasis is on corporate Human Resource Management (HRM) policies. Analyzes white collar labor force composition and demographic profiles. Also discusses the role of the personnel function and specific HRM functions targeted at white collar employees. In addition, current trends and their implications for future HRM policies are summarized.

747. Rehder, Robert R. "Japanese Management: An American Challenge." *Human Resource Management* 18 (1979):21-27.

    Analyzes the Japanese management and organization system and the reasons for its success in Japan. Also addressed the issue of whether the system is exportable to the United States and other advanced nations.

748. ──────. "What American and Japanese Managers Are Learning from Each Other." *Business Horizons* 24 (1981):63-70.

Focus is on newly emerging nontraditional American and Japanese management and organization systems, and the identification of those management innovations from both countries that may hold promise as creative solutions to common problems in the competitive race for world industrial supremacy.

749. Santora, Joseph C. *Japanese Management, 1970-1981: A Selected Guide to Periodical Literature*. Monticello, Ill.: Vance Bibliographies, 1982.

Contains approximately 120 citations to periodical articles on Japanese management published during 1970 to 1981. Not annotated.

750. Sasaki, Naoto. *Management and Industrial Structure in Japan*. New York: Pergamon Press, 1981.

A discussion of the cultural and economic aspects, as well as the decision-making process, of Japanese management and industry. Among the topics covered are the cultural and economic backgrounds, the management of human resources, decision-making, decision-making and policy coordination among industries and government, the changing international environment and its impact on Japanese management, and present changes.

751. Sato, Kazuo and Yasuo Hoshino, eds. *The Anatomy of Japanese Business*. Armonk, N.Y.: M.E. Sharpe, 1984.

Essays on various aspects of Japanese business management written by Japanese experts. A sequel to *Industry and Business in Japan*, K. Sato, ed. (1980), which concentrates on Japanese industrial and business organization. The book consists of four parts. Part One discusses management, Part Two deals with business groups, Part Three presents case studies of production systems and quality control in Japanese corporations, and Part Four is concerned with business strategy.

752. Schonberger, Richard J. *Japanese Manufacturing Techniques: Nine Hidden Lessons in Simplicity*. New York: Free Press, 1982.

Schonberger's thesis is that in order for the United States to catch up with Japan, it is more important to change industrial management policies than to change tax, trade, regulatory, and labor laws and policies, since it is Japan's industrial management that has given it a decisive edge. He explains Japanese just-in-time manufacturing control (JIT) and total quality control (TQC), and discusses a few early, successful attempts at implementing JIT/TQC in American plants.

753. Sekiguchi, Shiro. "How Japanese Business Treats Its Older Workers." *Management Review* 69 (1980):15-18.

   Summarizes how various Japanese companies and industries are responding to the social and economic problems that are being created by a growing group of aging workers.

754. Sethi, Narendra K. "The Japanese Managerial Scene: An Introductory View." *Marquette Business Review* 17 (1973):201-206.

   A brief introduction to Japanese management practices written primarily for the potential Western investor or exporter.

755. Sethi, S. Prakash. "Japanese Management Practices." Part 1. *Columbia Journal of World Business* 9 (1974): 94-104.

   Examines those aspects of management decision-making and personnel policies that are regarded as being characteristic of Japanese management. These aspects are decision-making by consensus, lifetime employment, and seniority-based wage system.

756. ─────, Nobuaki Namiki and Carl L. Swanson. *The False Promise of the Japanese Miracle: Illusions and Realities of the Japanese Management System*. Boston: Pitman, 1984.

   Analyzes the Japanese management system in terms of the values and norms of Japanese society, and attributes its success to political and governmental support. The limitations and drawbacks of the system are pointed out, and the authors recommend that American business can improve its productivity and efficiency, not by imitating the Japanese system, but by developing indigenous procedures. Includes an extensive bibliography.

757. Shimabukuro, Yoshiaki. *Consensus Management in Japanese Industry*. Tokyo: I.S.S. Inc., 1982.

   Concentrates primarily on the activities of quality circles (QC) in industry. The author attributes the increase of productivity in Japanese industry to these small groups of employees and their participation in management.

758. Sullivan, Jeremiah J. "A Critique of Theory Z." *Academy of Management Review* 8 (1983):132-142.

   Addresses the following questions: What is Theory Z? On what theoretical and empirical foundations is it based? How are employees motivated to increase their industrial productivity? Does empirical support for the theory exist? What contradictions does the theory contain? And what further research needs to be done?

759. Takagi, Haruo. *The Flaw in Japanese Management*. Ann Arbor, Mich.: UMI Research Press, 1985.

   A revision of the author's doctoral thesis, Harvard University, 1984, in which a study was made of a number of engineers employed by a large manufacturing company in 1982 in order to better understand the process of career development and integration within the organization under the conditions of the lifetime employment system. The results, the author finds, partially contradict Ouchi's Theory Z.

760. Thurow, Lester C., ed. *The Management Challenge: Japanese Views*. Cambridge, Mass.: MIT Press, 1985.

   Insights into Japanese management practices by Japanese economists and business leaders. At the end of each chapter, the editor provides a short essay that analyzes some of the implications for improving American economic practices and institutions. Among the topics covered are motivation and productivity, impact of Japanese culture on management, Japanese industrial relations, the firm and the market in Japan, Japanese financial system, product diversification, Japan's industrial policy, strategy for overseas markets, and economic planning in Japan.

761. Tsurumi, Yoshihiro. *Japanese Business: A Research Guide with Annotated Bibliography*. New York: Praeger, 1978.

   Covers such topics as the development of Japan's industries, the industrial relations system, and Japanese management in America. Each chapter is followed by an appendix of issues for further study. The annotated bibliography is comprehensive.

762. Tung, Rosalie L., ed. *Strategic Management in the United States and Japan: A Comparative Analysis*. Cambridge, Mass.: Ballinger, 1986.

Based on papers given at a conference held at the Wharton School, University of Pennsylvania, 1984, by Japanese and American scholars and practitioners. Topics include strategic issues in the management of government-business relationships and of general trading companies, and strategic management in the manufacturing and financial sectors.

763. Ueda, Yoshio and George P. Craighead. "Patience in Human Relations: Key to Doing Business in Japan." *Management Review* 67 (1978):57-59.

A discussion of the six most common mistakes made by American companies in Japan in management staffing and human relations because of ignoring the unique character of Japan's business environment. These mistakes are (1) unqualified executives, (2) too rapid rotation of the expatriate manager, (3) too many Americans, (4) not enough authority, (5) advancement closed to Japanese executives, and (6) poor communications.

764. Vandenbrink, John, ed. *Corporate Strategy & Structure: Japan and the USA*. Chicago: Chicago Council on Foreign Relations, 1983.

Several of the papers included here were initially prepared for a conference on Corporate Strategy and Structure: Japan and the USA, held in 1982 in Wisconsin. One of the chief tasks of the conference was to assess the nature and magnitude of the Japanese competitive challenge. The papers address a variety of topics, among which are the nature of Japan's challenge, the decline in America's rate of productivity growth, U.S. and Japanese industrial policy, and the steel and pharmaceutical industries.

765. Wakabayashi, Mitsuru. *Management Career Progress in a Japanese Organization*. N.p.: UMI Research Press, 1980.

A longitudinal study of achievement levels reached by new managerial employees of a large industrial organization in Japan. Discusses those factors that determine the level of progress during the early periods of organizational career development.

766. Wallace, William McDonald. "The Secret Weapon of Japanese Business." *Columbia Journal of World Business* 7 (1972):43-52.

    The success of Japan's business enterprises is attributed to the "esprit de corps," or team spirit and fraternalism, which underlies the structure of their personnel policies.

767. Wheelwright, Steven C. "Japan--Where Operations Really Are Strategic." *Harvard Business Review* 59 (1981):67-74.

    Wheelwright contends that the involvement of Japanese manufacturing managers in the strategic operations policy of their companies has contributed to Japan's industrial success.

768. Woronoff, Jon. *Japan's Wasted Workers*. Tokyo: Lotus Press, 1981.

    Originally written for the Japanese public, this work examines some of the weaknesses of the average to mediocre Japanese companies. Emphasis is on white collar workers who continue to work, using traditional methods that have become inefficient, and on a number of sectors that have become a drain on the economy. Also brings out dissatisfaction with the management system and the possibility of implementing reforms.

769. Yang, Charles Y. "Management Styles: American Vis-a-Vis Japanese." *Columbia Journal of World Business* 12 (1977):23-31.

    Compares the management styles of Japan ("organic type") and the United States ("system type"), with emphasis on their strengths and weaknesses. Yang also suggests modifications of both styles that are needed to cope with the new situation of low-growth economy, external pressures, and technological leadership that both countries share.

1. EMPLOYEES

770. Atsumi, Reiko. "'Tsukiai'--Obligatory Personal Relationships of Japanese White-Collar Company Employees." *Human Organization* 38 (1979):63-70.

    A study of the extent to which personal relationships among Japanese white-collar employees are "tsukiai," or based on social necessity or feelings of obligation.

771. Cole, Robert E. *Work, Mobility, and Participation: A Comparative Study of American and Japanese Industry.* Berkeley: University of California Press, 1979.

    A comparative study of the male labor force in Detroit and Yokohama, which focuses on interfirm and intrafirm mobility. Practices of work design at the Toyota Auto Body factory are examined, with special attention given to quality control circles. Also observes Japanese and American work ethics.

772. Helvoort, Ernest van. *The Japanese Working Man: What Choice? What Reward?* Vancouver: University of British Columbia Press, 1979.

    Looks into the way personnel management is being conducted in Japan, and discusses the following issues: how people are motivated to work, the basic principles of reward and promotion, training and education in relation to the industrial scene, the unique features of decision-making, participation and communication, quality control and safety features, and unions. Throughout the work is the underlying question of how the Japanese workers feel about the way they are being dealt with.

773. Inoue, Ken. *The Education and Training of Industrial Manpower in Japan.* Washington, D.C.: World Bank, 1985.

    Traces the development of industrial manpower education and training in Japan from 1868 to the present. Also discusses the role of companies and government in the upgrading of and utilization of manpower.

774. Kamata, Satoshi. *Japan in the Passing Lane.* London: Allen and Unwin, 1983.

    Originally published in Japan in 1973, this work is the diary of a Japanese freelance journalist who worked as a temporary worker in the Toyota Motor Company in Japan for just over six months. Kamata indicts the company for its inhumane treatment of temporary workers on the assembly line, and he makes use of his own reactions as well as the reactions and conversations of his fellow workers in order to convey the details of the situation. He also shows the unquestioning adherence to the system.

775. Levine, Solomon B. and Hisashi Kawada. *Human Resources in Japanese Industrial Development*. Princeton, N.J.: Princeton University Press, 1980.

   Discusses the process through which Japan has generated human skills and talents required by modern economic activities since the beginning of Japanese industrialization more than one hundred years ago. Focus is on institutions established or utilized in major large-scale modern industries, and these institutions are examined against the background of Japan's overall economic and educational development. Among the industries included here are steel and shipbuilding; railways and telecommunications; banking; textiles; mining; and heavy machinery, electrical equipment and chemicals.

776. Plath, David W., ed. *Work and Lifecourse in Japan*. Albany: State University of New York Press, 1983.

   Consists of case studies of the dimensions of development in various occupational careers. Presents three modes of investigation: an examination of adult career development ("lifecourse"), an examination of the social organization of industrial work, and the consideration of culture and behavior in modern Japan. Includes overview chapters on employment trends in the Japanese economy.

777. Suzuki, Norihiko. "Spin-Out Employees in Japanese Business Society: Their Problems and Prospects." *Columbia Journal of World Business* 16 (1981):23-30.

   "Spun-out" managers are those managers who have been dismissed, transferred and/or demoted because of an excess of managers in Japanese companies. This employment policy is more modern than the policy of lifetime employment, and it creates financial, promotional, and psychological problems for the "spun-out" managers. Suzuki examines these problems and the evaluation of the Japanese lifetime employment system by these managers.

778. Rohlen, Thomas P. "'Spiritual Education' in a Japanese Bank." *American Anthropologist* 75 (1973):1542-1562.

   Rohlen describes a bank company spiritual training

program for new employees in which he was a participant in 1969. This philosophy of spiritualism is based on a set of ideas about human psychology and character development, and it can be traced to the traditional Zen, Confucian, and samurai traditions. It emphasizes social cooperation and responsibility, an acceptance of reality, and perseverance.

779. Sengoku, Tamotsu. *Willing Workers: The Work Ethics in Japan, England, and the United States.* Westport, Conn.: Quorum Books, 1985.

Based on the results of comparative surveys of willingness to work attitudes conducted in factories in Japan, the United States and Great Britain in 1979. The central theme is why is a Japanese worker willing to work just because the job is there? This concept is totally different from the American or British motivation to work. The book is divided into three sections. Part One deals with the sociological aspects of the employment structure and willingness to work from the comparative perspective. Part Two focuses on the psychological mechanism of willingness to work. And Part Three discusses willingness to work on the part of youth.

780. Tanaka, Hiroshi. "The Japanese Method of Preparing Today's Graduate to Become Tomorrow's Manager." *Personnel Journal* 59 (1980):109-112.

Describes the educational process of new employees by major companies. Two dimensions of this process are emphasized here: preemployment education, or the training given before the entrance ceremony, and initial managerial education, which begins immediately after the ceremony. The data on which this study is based is derived from interviews with fifty of Japan's major corporations conducted during the spring of 1978. Concerned with the training given to male university graduates, who are the future management candidates.

781. ―――. "New Employee Education in Japan." *Personnel Journal* 60 (1981):51-53.

Examines the systematic educational procedure for training new employees by Japanese companies. The dominant trend in new employee education is learning through experience, which includes practical work experience, teamwork exercises, and self-discipline skills. It is intended to help prepare employees mentally, physically, and emotionally for the increasingly complex and rapidly changing challenges of corporate life.

2. EMPLOYMENT SYSTEM

782. Abegglen, James C. *Management and Worker: The Japanese Solution.* Tokyo: Sophia University Press, 1973.

    A study of the Japanese employment system during 1956, 1966, and 1972, periods of tremendous economic growth. Includes an update and partial reprinting of the author's earlier book: *The Japanese Factory: Aspects of Its Social Organization*, which is a report on studies carried out in 1955 and 1956 of the organization and personnel practices of Japanese companies. This work briefly describes and analyzes in some detail the nature, consequences, and prospects of Japan's employment system as viewed in the 1970s. It also presents a report of a study conducted in 1966 comparing that time with 1956.

783. Alston, Jon P. "Awarding Bonuses the Japanese Way." *Business Horizons* 25 (1982):46-50.

    Contrasts Japanese and American employment philosophies regarding workers. The Japanese emphasize the familial model, in which rewards are given as equally as possible to the work group rather than to the individual, and group awards are given to the work group, which helps to promote group harmony and cooperation. The American philosophy, on the other hand, emphasizes the individual, and bonuses are awarded on an individual basis, which Alston contends creates jealousy and rivalry.

784. Cole, Robert E. "Functional Alternatives and Economic Development: An Empirical Example of Permanent Employment in Japan." *American Sociological Review* 38 (1973):424-438.

    Cole argues for the superiority of the functional alternative approach over other approaches, such as convergence and historicism, for conceptualizing the structural changes associated with modern economic development. He compares selected employment characteristics of Japan and the United States, and concludes that there is evidence for partial convergence as well as the functional alternative approach, which allow both societies to motivate individuals so that their advanced technologies are maintained.

785. ─────. "The Late-Developer Hypothesis: An Evaluation of Its Relevance for Japanese Employment Practices." *Journal of Japanese Studies* 4 (1978):247-265.

Presents a critique of R. Dore's thesis that Japan's late-developer status, which argues that later industrializing countries advanced by borrowing from already industrialized nations, was responsible for the development of its employment system. Cole contends that the late-developer hypothesis does not adequately explain Japan's development process.

786. ─────. "Permanent Employment in Japan: Facts and Fantasies." *Industrial and Labor Relations Review* 26 (1972):615-630.

A quantitative comparison of differences between Japanese permanent employment practices and those of the United States. Cole maintains that his data provide strong evidence for an explanation of the differences on the basis of "functional alternatives."

787. ─────. "The Theory of Institutionalization: Permanent Employment and Tradition in Japan." *Economic Development and Cultural Change* 20 (1971):47-70.

Cole attempts to reconcile the sociological and economic explanations of permanent employment within the framework of the institutionalization process. He also examines the potential for the permanent employment system to change as well as the changes that are already occurring.

788. Crawcour, S. "The Japanese Employment System." *Journal of Japanese Studies* 4 (1978):225-245.

Discusses the development of the employment system, which Crawcour contends is a reaction to the shortage of skilled labor and is of relatively recent origin. He describes the characteristics of the system, which are lifetime employment and seniority, and the concept of the firm as a community. He also discusses the ways in which the system could be affected by the economic developments of the 1970s.

789. Dore, Ronald P. "More about Late Development." *Journal of Japanese Studies* 5 (1979):137-151.

In this response to Cole's article, "The Late Developer Hypothesis," Dore argues that the later development occurs, the more likely the country will have an employment system based on paternalism, employee loyalty, and permanent commitment of employer and employee.

790. Haitani, Kanji. "Changing Characteristics of the Japanese Employment System." *Asian Survey* 18 (1978):1029-1045.

The author examines the influence of change upon the employment system that occurred in the 1970s. These changes, which include decreased economic growth, increasing age levels of the workforce, and the increasing proportion of tertiary management, have created two major problems, according to Haitani: increasing workforce costs, and inflation of the managerial sector.

791. Hanami, Tadashi A. "The Lifetime Employment System in Japan: Its Reality and Future." *Atlanta Economic Review* 26 (1976):35-39.

Describes various aspects of the Japanese employer-employee relationship, including recruitment of regular employees, the role of temporary employees, and the seniority wage system. The author also discusses the lifetime employment system in the context of changes in the labor market and in the era of multinationals.

792. Harari, Ehud. "Unemployment in Japan: Policy and Politics." *Asian Survey* 18 (1978):1013-1028.

Although Japan has had low unemployment rates and an affirmative unemployment policy, the question of how to cope with unemployment is a frequent and sometimes major issue in Japanese politics. Harari analyzes those factors that have contributed to the controversiality of the issue and the various patterns of conflicts that have arisen over it. Among those factors analyzed are economic, technological, and demographic factors affecting the definition of unemployment policy; characteristics of the populations directly affected by unemployment policy; and characteristics of party and bureaucratic politics.

793. Hashimoto, Masanori. "Bonus Payments, On-the-Job Training, and Lifetime Employment in Japan." *Journal of Political Economy* 87 (1979):1086-1104.

A model of on-the-job training is developed in order to analyze the determination of the amounts and the sharing of investment in specific human capital. Evidence indicates that education and firm size, which are often said to be positively associated with the profitability of on-the-job training in Japan, together with years of experience in the current firm, are positively correlated with the bonus-earnings ratio.

794. Japan. Social Insurance Agency. *Outline of Social Insurance in Japan.* Tokyo, 1983.

Published irregularly. There is a 1985 edition that was not available for examination. Presents an outline of social security in Japan, and describes the various categories of social insurance and their provisions and benefits. Included are administrative organization of social insurance; international cooperation; health, day-laborer's health, and national health insurance; health and medical services for the aged; seamen's, employees' pension, national pension, and farmers' pension; mutual aid associations; children's allowance; workmen's accident compensation and employment insurance; and management of social insurance systems. The appendix includes charts of social insurance schemes, organization of the Ministry of Health and Welfare, administrative organs for the operation of social insurance schemes, and a chronological table of main social insurance schemes in Japan.

795. Marsh, Robert M. and Hiroshi Mannari. "Lifetime Commitment in Japan: Roles, Norms, and Values." *American Journal of Sociology* 76 (1971):795-812.

An examination of the extent to which the lifetime commitment system disconfirms theories of economic development and of social and political modernization that assert that there is an increase in differentiation of the identity of the employee from that of his firm, which accompanies greater industrialization.

796. ―――. "A New Look at 'Lifetime Commitment' in Japanese Industry." *Economic Development and Cultural Change* 20 (1972):611-630.

Approaches the problem of lifetime commitment in terms of factors that maintain or strengthen it and factors that weaken it. Examples of the former are the seniority system, characteristics of the job itself, and social relationships on the job. Examples of the latter are the labor shortage, school recruits and employees recruited with previous experience, job advertisements in newspapers, size of firm, and the shift from seniority to job classification.

797. Organisation for Economic Co-operation and Development. *Manpower Policy in Japan.* Paris, 1973.

A final report by the OECD that is based on the findings of a team of examiners that visited Japan in 1970 in order to investigate its manpower policies. Includes a report by a Japanese team of authorities that explains and describes the policies.

798. Ozawa, Terutomo. "Japanese World of Work: An Interpretive Survey." *MSU Business Topics* 28 (1980):45-55.

Delineates the key features and characteristics of Japanese business organization. Among the features discussed are paternalism, labor mobility and training, participatory management, and education. The mode of organization is based on the familial, in which workers are treated like family members. As a consequence of this, Japanese employees are very proud of the success of their company, and they identify with the company, which engenders a sense of competition both externally with other companies, and internally in loyalty to their own company.

799. Reischauer, Edwin O. "The Japanese Way." *Across the Board* 14 (1977):34-42.

Observes some of the distinctive features of Japanese business and industry that have contributed to Japan's economic success. Among the features discussed are lifetime employment patterns, wages determined by seniority, personal loyalty between bosses and workers, and close cooperation between government and business.

800. Yashiro, Naohiro. "Male Female Wage Differentials in Japan: A Rational Explanation." *Japanese Economic Studies* 9 (1980-81):28-61.

A statistical look at the present state of male-female wage differentials. Gives a brief account of recent developments in the economics of wage discrimination and draws comparisons with Japan's labor market. Yashiro proposes a hypothesis of "technical discrimination" (viz., wage differentials are determined by the rational behavior of firms in the competitive market rather than by irrational factors like prejudice), and attempts to test it empirically.

B. INDUSTRIAL ORGANIZATION

801. Aoki, Masahiko, ed. *The Economic Analysis of the Japanese Firm.* New York: North-Holland, 1984.

    An explanation of certain features of the Japanese firm by means of an econometric rationale that goes beyond the neoclassical economic view of the firm. Covers the following topics: labor, corporate finance, external relationships with business partners and the government, and managerial efficiency and the motivation system.

802. Ballon, Robert J. "Non-Western Work Organizations." *Asia Pacific Journal of Management* 1 (1983):1-14.

    Examines the Japanese work organization. Describes Japanese industrial society and employment, as well as the relationship between worker and machine, the production system, quality control circles, personnel relationships, unionism, and decision-making.

803. Caves, Richard E. and Masu Uekusa. *Industrial Organization in Japan.* Washington, D.C.: Brookings Institution, 1976.

    Presents a quantitative economic analysis of Japanese industry and industrial policy that focuses on the following areas: industrial organization, the structure of industry, patterns of competition, the role of intermarket groups, allocative and technical efficiency, imported technology and industrial progress, and government policy toward industry. Makes extensive comparisons between the Japanese and American industrial systems.

804. Marsh, Robert M. and Hiroshi Mannari. "Technology and Size as Determinants of the Organizational Structure of Japanese Factories." *Administrative Science Quarterly* 26 (1981):33-57.

    Discusses the results of a study done to ascertain the effects of technology and size (i.e., number of personnel) on organizational structure in Japanese factories.

805. Ouchi, William G. and Alfred M. Jaeger. "Type Z Organization: Stability in the Midst of Mobility." *Academy of Management Review* 3 (1978):305-314.

    A comparison of the "ideal types" of Japanese and American forms of corporate organization. Relates them to their respective socio-cultural backgrounds, and presents a hybrid organizational "ideal type," "Type Z."

806. Ozaki, Robert S. "Japanese Views on Industrial Organization." *Asian Survey* 10 (1970):872-889.

Surveys recent views of Japanese economic policy makers in the government, representatives of big business, and modern economists on industrial organization in the modern sector of the economy. Two issues are addressed specifically: the business-government coalition, and the Yawata-Fuji steel merger of 1968.

807. Rohlen, Thomas P. *For Harmony and Strength: Japanese White-Collar Organization in Anthropological Perspective.* Berkeley: University of California Press, 1979.

A study of a large, modern Japanese bank that the author, a cultural anthropologist, undertook in 1968-69, using the participant observer approach. "Harmony and strength" is the official motto of the bank. Rohlen's intention here is primarily to demonstrate the general applicability of the anthropological perspective to the study of modern organizations. Among the topics discussed are song, ceremonies, and the bank's ideology; entrance, departure, and lifelong commitment; the office group; the union; dormitories and company apartments; and marriage and the family.

808. Rotwein, Eugene. "Economic Concentration and Monopoly in Japan--A Second View. *Journal of Asian Studies* 36 (1976):55-77.

This study is a supplement to an earlier study by the author, "Economic Concentration and Monopoly in Japan," *Journal of Political Economy* 72 (1964), which deals with the patterns of Japanese industrial organization prevailing during the 1950s. This article covers a substantially longer time span, and introduces new material in considering three questions discussed in the earlier study: (1) the extent of economic concentration in Japan as indicated by broad market measures, (2) the importance of business groups ("Keiretsu") in the Japanese economy, and (3) the domestic impact of cartels that have been legalized. Also presents a general appraisal of the contemporary scene and detects trends that may have a significant influence in the future.

809. Tracy, Phelps and Koya Azumi. "Determinants of Administrative Control: A Test of a Theory with Japanese Factories." *American Sociological Review* 41 (1976):80-94.

   Attempts to test the adequacy of Western concepts of organizational structure, which rest largely upon the notions of rationality and economic efficiency, in Japanese manufacturing plants. It combines theoretical insights from both Weberian and decision-making traditions within a single model (which also includes the factors of size, uncertainty, and technology), which is then tested with data from forty-four Japanese manufacturing plants. The basic issue here is one of determining structural regularities among organizations in different cultural settings.

810. Vogel, Ezra F., ed. *Modern Japanese Organization and Decision-Making.* Berkeley: University of California Press, 1975.

   A collection of papers that were presented at the Conference on Japanese Organization and Decision-Making, Hawaii, 1973, which include analyses of Japanese political, cultural, and educational organizations. In these papers a number of concepts that currently dominate Western work on Japanese organization have been criticized and modified, while others have been reinforced, extended, or applied to additional phenomena. Among those concepts that have been criticized are Japan, Inc.; "Ringi Sei," which is a decision-making process; seniority and permanent employment systems; growth without profit; and school cliques. Among those concepts that have been reinforced and extended are groupism; long-range goal orientation; "Nemawashi," which is the practice of broad consultation before taking action; fair share; bureaucratic elitism; and business leadership.

C. INDUSTRIAL PRODUCTIVITY

811. Burnham, John M. *Japanese Productivity: A Study Mission Report.* N.p.: American Production and Inventory Society, 1983.

   A summary of the results of the International Study Mission on Japanese Productivity, Production, and Inventory Techniques on Japanese industrial plants in 1982.

812. Christainsen, Gregory B. and Jan S. Hogendorn. "Japanese Productivity: Adapting to Changing Comparative Advantage in the Face of Lifetime Employment Commitments." *Quarterly Review of Economics and Business* 23 (1983):23-39.

   The authors examine the co-existence of Japan's productivity growth with the practice of lifetime employment. Productivity growth has been encouraged by the government policy of transferring resources (including labor) out of declining industries and into expanding ones, and lifetime employment is a constraint that many companies face. They also discuss how declining industries adapt their labor-management practices to government policy within the restriction of lifetime employment.

813. Clutterbuck, David. "What Makes Japanese Car Manufacturers So Productive?" *International Management* 33 (1978):17-20.

   Describes the reasons for the high productivity levels of Mitsubishi Motors Corp. and Toyota Motor Co., which include strategic use of automation, the general approach to assembly methods, and total involvement of the workers in cost reductions and efficiency improvements.

814. Davidson, William H. "Small Group Activity at Musahi Semi-Conductor Works." *Sloan Management Review* 23 (1982):3-14.

   Analyzes the small group activity (SGA) at Hitachi's Musahi Semiconductor Works. SGA is a system for promoting employee motivation and productivity by generating self-selected proposals from worker groups, or by managerial direction of group effort toward particular projects, and it is used extensively throughout Japanese industry. It includes production workers as well as clerical, support, and certain managerial personnel.

815. Gerstenfeld, Arthur and Keyi Sumiyoshi. "The Management of Innovation in Japan: Seven Forces That Make the Difference." *Research Management* 23 (1980):30-34.

   The success of Japanese innovation is attributed to the following factors: high propensity for risk taking, employee reward structure, marketing-R&D interface, cooperation by unions, consensus decision-making, government/industry cooperation, and the collectiveness orientation of the Japanese culture.

816. Grossman, Elliot S. *Comparative Productivity Dynamics: Japan and the United States.* Houston, Tex.: American Productivity Center, 1982.

A study that is the result of collaborative efforts of the American Productivity Center and the Japan Productivity Center. It provides labor productivity data for the domestic economy, for the major sectors, and for the manufacturing industries. It also includes "total factor" and capital productivity growth rates, and trends in the capital/labor ratio.

817. Hirono, Ryokichi. *Factors Which Hinder or Help Productivity Improvement in the Asian Region: National Report--Japan.* Tokyo: Asian Productivity Organization, 1980.

Reviews the process of the overall economic growth in postwar Japan under which structural changes took place, re-examines the productivity performance in selected industries, and analyzes the major factors affecting the productivity performance at the national and the industrial/firm levels, in order to examine the prospect of productivity improvement in Japanese industry and economy during the 1980s. Looks at long-term trends during the last two decades in various economic, technological, and social factors affecting productivity performance in the selected industries. Included in the selected industries are the following: iron and steel, chemical; textile; food processing; and electrical machinery.

818. Keegan, Warren J. "Productivity: Lessons from Japan." *Long Range Planning* 8 (1975):61-71.

Compares Japanese productivity on an industry basis with the United States and European companies, and then examines the factors and methods that are responsible for Japan's success, in order to determine what, if any, lessons Western companies can learn from the Japanese approach. Among the key factors Keegan considers to have contributed to Japanese productivity are commitment to economic growth and the objective of world economic leadership, high savings and investment, national strategy, government/business cooperation, strategic business analysis, employment and job security, team spirit, and decision-making by consensus.

819. Ozawa, Terutomo. *People and Productivity in Japan.* New York: Pergamon, 1982.

A brief review of recent publications in English that address the issue of Japan's success in industrial expansion and productivity. Includes such topics as unparalleled productivity growth, industrial policy and expansion of aggregate demand, technological borrowing, dual industrial structure, labor-management relations, participatory management, and on-the-job training.

820. U.S. Congress. Joint Economic Committee. Subcommittee on International Trade, Finance, and Security Economics. *Japanese Productivity: Lessons for America: Hearing.* 97th Cong., 1st sess., 1981. Washington, D.C.: GPO, 1982.

Hearings held on the subjects of how Japan has achieved its high productivity growth and on those contributing factors that can be applied to the American economy.

1. QUALITY CIRCLES

821. Alexander, C. Philip. "Learning from the Japanese." *Personnel Journal* 60 (1981):616-619.

Discusses the management perspectives that are indispensable for quality circles to have the same kind of continuing success as in Japan. Among these are trust, commitment to quality, open communication, supportive management, and training and development.

822. Bocker, H.J. and H.O. Overgaard. "Japanese Quality Circles: A Managerial Response to the Productivity Problem." *Management International Review* 22 (1982):13-19.

Focuses on the functions and interactions of QC (quality circle) activities and operations. Also explains how to set up a QC program, and points out areas of concern, obstacles, and potential problems.

823. Konz, Stephan. "Quality Circles: Japanese Success Story." *Industrial Engineering* 11 (1979):24-27.

A brief observation of the operation of quality circles at Matsushita Electric and illustrates how defects can be minimized when workers discover and deal with the problems. Also presents a summary of the results of eighty-seven quality circles at Sumitomo Electric.

824. Nemoto, Masao. *Total Quality Control for Management: Strategies and Techniques from Toyota and Toyota Gosei*. Englewood Cliffs, N.J.: Prentice-Hall, 1987.

Nemoto, who is president of Toyota Gosei, a company that has made major parts for Toyota, since 1982, and a former managing director of Toyota Motors, where he was instrumental in the promotion of total quality control (TQC), presents to American managers his advice for utilizing human resources efficiently in a technological environment. Consists of two parts. Part One contains the author's previous book, which was published in Japanese in 1983, and which deals with his own experiences in strengthening corporate attributes and motivating employees. Part Two is the sequel, which was published in 1986, and it relates events leading to the awarding to Toyota Gosei the Deming application prize in 1985 for strengthening its special corporate attributes through the practice of TQC, and also discusses the concept of groupwide TQC and offers suggestions for diversifying QC circle activities.

825. *Quality Control Circles at Work: Cases from Japan's Manufacturing and Service Sectors*. Tokyo: Asian Productivity Organization, 1984.

A collection of sixteen case studies published in the Japanese magazine *Quality Control for the Foreman*, from 1976 to 1980, which discuss the contribution of QC circles to various industrial fields in the manufacturing and service sectors. Each study provides explanations in detail on how the QC circle defined the problem, how it discussed possible solutions, how it implemented solutions, what results were obtained, and how the results were consolidated so that the problem did not recur. Emphasis is on the importance of maintaining good personal relations at the workshop.

826. Ross, Joel E. and William C. Ross. *Japanese Quality Circles and Productivity*. Reston Va.: Reston Pub. Co., 1982.

A practical guide for those considering implementing quality circles.

827. Sasaki, Naoto and David Hutchins, eds. *The Japanese Approach to Product Quality: Its Applicability to the West*. New York: Pergamon, 1984.

Collected papers presented to the past four conferences

of QC Circle, held in London since 1979, on the quality control (QC) circle method of industrial quality and productivity control. The QC circle is a small-group activity in which workers apply basic tools of statistical quality control to their own work on the shop floor. Among the topics discussed are quality control groups in particular companies, the historical development of quality control in the West, and establishing a quality control circle program.

2. QUALITY CONTROL

828. Ishikawa, Kaoru. *Guide to Quality Control*. 2d rev. ed. Tokyo: Asian Productivity Organization, 1982.

   A complete guide to quality control techniques for department and section managers that may be used either as a textbook or for self study. It does not deal with the concept of QC or the reasons behind it. Includes instructions for the making and reading of graphs, Pareto diagrams, histograms, scatter diagrams, etc., as well as for the use of binomial probability paper, and practice problems.

829. ———. *What Is Total Quality Control? The Japanese Way*. Englewood Cliffs, N.J.: Prentice-Hall, 1985.

   A practical approach to starting and operating a sound total quality control program, written by Japan's foremost authority in the field.

830. Japan External Trade Organization. *Productivity and Quality Control: The Japanese Experience*. Tokyo, 1981.

   Presents the findings of in-depth interviews with seven Japanese companies concerning the nature and contribution of QC circles. The following companies are included here: Minolta Camera Co., Nippon Steel Corp., Nisshin Steel Co., Wacoal Corp., Kayaba Industry Co., and TDK Electronics Co.

3. RESEARCH AND DEVELOPMENT

831. Glicksman, Maurice. "R&D in Japan: A Future That Will Challenge the U.S." *Research Management* 14 (1971):28-37.

   An analysis of the Japanese commitment to increasing

scientific and technological research in the coming decades. In order to understand and assess research in Japan, the following five factors are discussed: state of the economy and the motivation for devotion of resources to research, the planning and financial commitments to research and development, the organization of research and development, including the roles played by industry and government, the areas of research emphasized, and the capabilities of the scientific and technical personnel and establishments. Glicksman predicts that by the end of the 1970s Japan's growth of industrial research and its application to saleable products and processes should approach comparable strength with the United States.

832. Johnson, Steven B. "Comparing R&D Strategies of Japanese and U.S. Firms." *Sloan Management Review* 25 (1984):25-34.

Compares the R&D (research & development) investments of Japanese and American firms during the period from 1965 to 1981 in terms of strategic approach and level of return earned. Explores how the R&D investment strategies of Japanese and United States firms have differed over the past twenty years, how differences in the governmental/institutional environment of both countries may have contributed to this disparity, and why the basic R&D investment strategies of many Japanese firms during the period from 1965 to 1981 outperformed those of their American counterparts. Also looks at the strategic and policy-making implications of the findings.

X
INDUSTRIAL RELATIONS

833. Allinson, Gary D. "Public Servants and Public Interests in Contemporary Japan." *Asian Survey* 20 (1980):1048-1068.

    Discusses problems that concern organized workers in Japan's municipal governments. Most of the workers belong to "Jichiro," (All-Japan Prefectural and Municipal Workers' Union), which had become Japan's largest labor union by the 1970s. Analyzes a case study of a prolonged conflict between a Jichiro union in a Tokyo suburb and local authorities. In addition, there is a brief interpretation of past and present relations among local authorities, public unions, and the Japanese citizenry.

834. Cole, Robert E. *Japanese Blue Collar: The Changing Tradition*. Berkeley: University of California Press, 1971.

    An empirical study of the everyday activities and thoughts of Japanese blue collar workers at two different companies, where Cole held blue collar positions in order to get material for his research. Among the topics covered are the wage system; the promotion system; permanent employment; worker unity; and the relationship between the workers, the company, and the union.

835. Connaghan, Charles J. *The Japanese Way: Contemporary Industrial Relations*. Ottawa, Ontario: Labour Canada, 1982.

    A brief outline of the Japanese industrial relations system, based largely on interviews with leading Japanese industrial relations practitioners in trade unions, management, and government. Includes extracts from individual labor laws.

836. *The Development of Industrial Relations Systems: Some Implications of Japanese Experience: Report Prepared after a Multi-National Study Group Visit, 20th September-4th October, 1975*. Paris: Organisation for Economic Co-operation and Development, 1977.

Discusses the key features of the Japanese industrial relations system, which include lifetime employment, seniority wages, and enterprise unionism. Reviews the main institutions and procedures involved in industrial relations, such as trade unions and employer's associations, collective bargaining and joint consultation, labor disputes, and the role of government and law. Emphasizes the importance of the decision-making process in the Japanese enterprise as well as the attitudes that workers and managers bring to the enterprise. Concludes with a discussion of possible trends in Japan in relation to what is happening in other countries, as well as the implications of such trends for industrial relations systems.

837. Hanami, Tadashi A. *Labor Relations in Japan Today*. Tokyo: Kodansha International, 1979.

Studies the unique character of conflict in Japanese industrial relations and of dispute settlement.

838. Harari, Ehud. *The Politics of Labor Legislation in Japan: National-International Interaction*. Berkeley: University of California Press, 1973.

A revised and updated version of the author's doctoral dissertation, University of California, Berkeley, 1968. It examines the interrelationship of politics at the local-provincial, national, and international levels, and focuses on Japan's ratification of International Labor Organization Convention 87 (Freedom of Association and Protection of the Right to Organize) and related domestic legislation. Includes a glossary of Japanese individuals, organizations, and laws associated with the labor movement.

839. Japan Productivity Center. *In Search of a New Industrial Relations Model: Summary of 1984 White Paper on Labor Management Relations*. Tokyo: Asian Productivity Organization, 1985.

Analyzes the structural changes that are occurring in Japan's industrial society and their effects on labor-management relations. Much attention is given to the problem of the aging workforce.

840. Odaka, Kunio. *Toward Industrial Democracy: Management and Workers in Modern Japan.* Cambridge, Mass.: Harvard University Press, 1975.

The author discusses changes in managerial ideologies and practices, as well as the reactions of workers to technological advances, their thoughts on their companies and labor unions, their motivations for work, and the meaning of their leisure time.

841. Okochi, Kazuo, Bernard Karsh and Solomon B. Levine, eds. *Workers and Employers in Japan: The Japanese Employment Relations System.* Princeton, N.J.: Princeton University Press, 1974.

A study of the characteristics of the industrial relations system on the national level, as it has developed since the end of World War II. Emphasis is on change in political configurations and in ideological and value systems, which is brought about by industrialization. Covers such topics as the labor market, management, workers and organizations, collective bargaining, labor disputes, wages and benefits, and social security.

842. Pascale, Richard Tanner and Mary Ann Maguire. "Comparison of Selected Work Factors in Japan and the United States." *Human Relations* 33 (1980):433-455.

Compares industrial relations practices in Japanese companies in Japan and the United States with those of American companies. Two theoretical models underlie these comparisons: cultural diversity, which emphasizes cultural variables as crucial in explaining employee attitudes and behavior, and sociology of organizations, which emphasizes organizational variables. These models are compared in terms of their ability to explain the differences in work climates, styles of supervision, and the behavior and attitudes of non-managerial employees in Japanese and American-owned companies. Analyzes survey and organizational data from thirty-seven companies in ten industries.

843. Shirai, Taishiro, ed. *Contemporary Industrial Relations in Japan.* Madison: University of Wisconsin Press, 1983.

Essays by Japanese industrial relations experts on

industrial relations in Japan as they compare to other advanced industrial societies. Among the topics covered are the Japanese appraisal of Western literature on industrial relations; labor relations in the small and medium-sized firm sector, in government enterprises, and in the civil service; internal processes of enterprise unions; current Marxist interpretation of industrial relations in Japan; the function of law in the labor relations field; the structure and strategy of collective bargaining; and the labor movement in politics.

844. Taira, Koji. *Economic Development & the Labor Market in Japan.* New York: Columbia University Press, 1970.

A review of the workings of the labor market and its interactions and institutional factors in the course of Japan's economic development in the last one hundred years. The work is divided into two parts: Part One is concerned with relative wages in the equilibrating process, and Part Two deals with institutions in the labor market process.

845. Versagi, Frank J. "What American Labor/Management Can Learn from Japanese Unions." *Management Review* 71 (1982):24-28.

Versagi maintains that in order to avert a crisis in an already lagging American economy, management, labor, and government must abandon their antiquated adversarial positions. He discusses the Japanese labor unions, which have learned to achieve "conflict in harmony" with labor and management, and argues that there is much that American managers can learn from Japanese labor-management relations.

846. Whitehill, Arthur M. and Shin-ichi Takezawa. "Workplace Harmony: Another Japanese 'Miracle'?" *Columbia Journal of World Business* 13 (1978):25-39.

An analysis of the results of a cross-national survey of Japanese and American production workers in order to ascertain industrial relations trends in both countries and to assess the extent to which the experiences of each provides lessons for the other.

XI
UNITED STATES-JAPAN RELATIONS (GENERAL)

847. Barnds, William J., ed. *Japan and the United States: Challenges and Opportunities.* New York: New York University Press, 1979.

    Essays by specialists on Japanese affairs, United States-Japan relations, and key issues in political, security, and economic relations between the two countries.

848. Bereday, George Z.F. and Shigeo Masui. *American Education through Japanese Eyes.* Honolulu: University Press of Hawaii, 1973.

    Between 1964 and 1968, selected Japanese teachers came to the United States to study American classrooms and American people. They were part of the Japanese-American Teacher Program, whose aim was to exchange teachers between the two countries. This work renders an account of the experiences and observations of the Japanese teachers. Among the areas under examination are school administrations, theory and practice in the classroom, the teaching of subject matter, special issues in the curriculum, and the status and duties of teachers.

849. Clapp, Priscilla and Morton H. Halperin, eds. *United States-Japanese Relations: The 1970's.* Cambridge, Mass.: Harvard University Press, 1974.

    A collection of revised papers from a 1973 conference by American and Japanese scholars on the political and economic aspects of American and Japanese relations. Covers the following topics: U.S. domestic politics and relations with Japan, future U.S.-Japanese economic relations, Asian economic growth, the influence of the United States on Japan, summit talks, Japan and China, Japan's security, and U.S.-Japanese security relations.

850. Clemens, Walter C., Jr. "SALT, the NPT, and U.S.-Japanese Security Relations." *Asian Survey* 10 (1970):1037-1045.

   Clemens speculates on the significance that the SALT (Strategic Arms Limitations Talks) negotiations between United States and Soviet representatives in Vienna may have for the future of Japanese-United States defense relations, which are presently characterized by a lightly armed Japan linked to the United States through a bilateral security pact. He also considers the impact of SALT on the effectiveness and scope of the Nuclear Nonproliferation Treaty (NPT).

851. Curtis, Gerald L., ed. *Japanese-American Relations in the 1970s*. Washington, D.C.: Columbia Books, 1970.

   Writings by Japanese and American scholars on the outlook for the bi-national relationship in the 1970s in view of the political, economic, and social conditions of each country as well as in other countries of Asia. The papers collected here were originally presented at the second Japanese-American Assembly, which met in Shimoda, Japan, in 1969.

852. Denoon, David B.H. "Japan and the U.S.--The Security Agenda." *Current History* 82 (1983):353-394.

   A discussion of the contemporary United States-Japan security relationship as well as previous ones. According to Denoon, this relationship has changed within the last five years for basically two reasons: the election of President Reagan, who is committed to a rapid modernization and expansion of United States military strength; and recognition by the Japanese Liberal Democratic Party leadership that the Soviet military threat is tangible and that Japan would have to take on an expanded military role to maintain at least the semblance of adequate defense sharing with the United States.

853. Ebinger, Charles K. and Ronald A. Morse, eds. *U.S.-Japanese Energy Relations: Cooperation and Competition*. Boulder, Colo.: Westview Press, 1984.

   As energy relations between the United States and Japan have become a barometer of the diplomatic relationship between the two countries, this work focuses on the major problems and challenges in the United States-Japan energy relationship. Among the topics discussed are energy security differences and uncertain oil markets; U.S.

crude oil exports to Japan; and nuclear, coal, and solar cooperation.

854. Iriye, Akira, ed. *Mutual Images: Essays in American-Japanese Relations*. Cambridge, Mass.: Harvard University Press, 1975.

Consists of papers presented at a binational conference held on Kauai, Hawaii, in 1972, which represent studies by Japanese and American scholars of mutual perceptions held by diverse groups of Japanese and Americans. The essays are concerned with the issue of how we can come to a better understanding of Japanese history, American history, and Japanese-American relations by tracing the interaction between Japanese and American mutual and self images.

855. *Japan-America Dialogue: A Survey of Organizational Activities*. New York: United States-Japan Foundation, 1981.

A listing and description of private organizations in Japan and the United States that function to foster relations between the two countries in the areas of commerce, education, policy studies, the media, the arts, and science, as well as in other areas.

856. Jauregui, Jacqueline. "Index of Selected Bilateral Treaties: United States and Japan." *Hastings International and Comparative Law Review* 2 (1979):105-127.

Has two purposes. The first one is to provide the student or practitioner with an overview of treaty relations between the United States and Japan. The second purpose is to aid researchers dealing with questions touching on United States-Japan relations to determine whether any applicable treaty in force exists. The treaties are grouped into four categories. The first category consists of those treaties entered into in the aftermath of the second World War. The second group is composed primarily of specific projects, often defense-related, that were undertaken jointly. In the third category are environmental protection treaties. The final category consists of miscellaneous treaties that seem basically to perform a housekeeping function for both nations and private citizens.

857. Johnson, Sheila K. *American Attitudes toward Japan, 1941-1975*. Washington, D.C.: American Enterprise Institute for Public Policy Research, 1975.

   The author is an anthropologist who has lived in Japan. Factors that influenced American attitudes towards postwar Japan are gleaned from the examination of books and popular magazine articles about Japan, as well as from movies, business relations and exports, art exhibits, and tourism.

858. Kamiya, Fuji. "Japanese-U.S. Relations and the Security Treaty: A Japanese Perspective." *Asian Survey* 12 (1972):717-725.

   Kamiya discusses his view that the 1951 San Francisco Peace Treaty should continue to be in effect, even though it no longer serves the purposes for which it was originally created. He contends that the Treaty has taken on new importance as a symbol of the political relationship between the United States and Japan, especially in light of a new system of political relations developing in East Asia.

859. Kaplan, Morton A. and Kinhide Mushakoji, eds. *Japan, America, and the Future World Order*. New York: Free Press, 1976.

   A symposium volume jointly planned and financed by scholarly groups in both Japan and the United States. It is concerned with United States-Japan relations that will play a major role in the development of the international system, and the problems and prospects that face both nations and the world. The chapters fall into the following categories: external policy issues, internal processes and images, economic issues, and technological and environmental issues.

860. Kitamura, Hiroshi. *Psychological Dimensions of U.S.-Japanese Relations*. Cambridge, Mass.: Center for International Affairs, Harvard University, 1971.

   A brief essay on the sources of psychological problems that exist in Japanese-American relations.

861. Kodama, Sanehide. *American Poetry and Japanese Culture*. Hamden, Conn.: Archon Books, 1984.

   Traces historically how American poets have encountered Japan and how they have been inspired by Japanese subjects, forms, attitudes, and values since the time of

Whitman and Longfellow through that of Kenneth Rexroth and Gary Snyder. The author makes the point that although recent Japanese economic and technological development has attracted the attention of critics throughout the world, and economists and engineers are now looking for models in Japan, the American poets have been absorbing Japanese values for a long time.

862. Lester, Richard K. "U.S.-Japanese Nuclear Relations: Structural Change and Political Strain." *Asian Survey* 22 (1982):417-433.

Discusses United States-Japanese nuclear relations in which civil nuclear policy has been one of the most serious points of contention in recent years. Also examines the problems of the nuclear industries of each country.

863. Michael, Franz and Gaston J. Sigur. *The Asian Alliance: Japan and United States Policy.* N.p.: National Strategy Information Center, 1972.

A study of Japanese political affairs since the end of World War II, with emphasis on the contemporary political scene, the economy, armed forces, relations with the United States, and its foreign policy. Among the topics covered are Japan's governing structure; political opposition; the news media and intellectuals; postwar economic growth; foreign trade, aid, and investment; postwar military structure; Peking's policy and the United States-Japanese reaction; and the future of the alliance.

864. Morse, Ronald A. and Shigenobu Yoshida, eds. *Blind Partners: American and Japanese Responses to an Unknown Future.* Lanham, Md.: University Press of America, 1985.

Papers that were presented at a 1984 conference by American and Japanese scholars in which the cultures of both countries are compared and contrasted, with emphasis on how they have prepared the two countries to respond to the challenges of the future.

865. ───── and Edward A. Olsen. "Japan's Bureaucratic Edge." *Foreign Policy* 52 (1983):167-180.

The authors contend that one important reason for American economic and political failures in the relationship with Japan is the lack of qualified personnel and organization on the part of the United States foreign policy bureaucracy, which prevents it from dealing effectively with Japan. In contrast, Japan has a very proficient bureaucracy for dealing with America, which has given Japan a great bureaucratic edge over the United States. They discuss various problems with the American foreign policy bureaucracy, and also present some possible solutions.

866. Ogata, Sadako. "Some Japanese Views on United States-Japan Relations in the 1980s." *Asian Survey* 20 (1980):694-706.

Examines the relationship between the United States and Japan in light of its problems and prospects. Various sources of economic and political friction are discussed. Ogata contends that in order to confront the issues of the 1980s, especially those having to do with access to energy and other raw materials, development of science and technology, defense sharing, trade balance, and assistance to developing countries, it is essential that each country reevaluate the relationship, paying particular attention to the needs, plans, and responsibilities of the other in the global context.

867. Olsen, Edward A. *U.S.-Japan Strategic Reciprocity: A Neo-Internationalist View*. Stanford, Calif.: Hoover Institution Press, 1985.

An evaluation of the past, present, and future course of United States-Japan military and security relations. Olsen contends that the purpose of this book is to improve clarity of mutual perceptions so that each nation will know, understand, and appreciate the interests and attitudes of the other. He presents some factual background information on how United States-Japan security relations have reached their present status. In addition, the present relationship is assessed from the standpoint of both countries, and the range of possible options open to each is analyzed. Finally, Olsen concludes with a set of policy recommendations for the United States and he estimates their impact on Japan and other interested countries.

868. Pillsbury, Michael. "A Japanese Card?" *Foreign Policy* 33 (1978-79):3-33.

An examination of the changes in Japan's attitudes towards national defense policy and their consequences for American defense policy in Asia. Today the postwar generation of Japanese favors the U.S.-Japan Mutual Security Treaty (1952) and the Japanese Self-Defense Forces (created in 1954), which reflects a significant shift in views that has helped to lay the foundation for new defense plans in Japan.

869. Rosovsky, Henry, ed. *Discord in the Pacific: Challenges to the Japanese-American Alliance.* Washington, D.C.: Columbia Books, 1972.

    Background papers for the third Japanese-American Assembly, which met in Shimoda, Japan, in 1972. They discuss a wide range of social, political, and economic issues of concern to both countries. Emphasis is on narrowing the communications gap, and the recommendations, for the most part, have to do with the media and with education and exchange programs, both official and unofficial.

870. Sato, Hideo. "United States-Japanese Relations: A Japanese View." *Current History* 68 (1975):154-182.

    Addresses the issue of the continued viability of United States-Japanese relations following President Ford's 1974 visit to Japan, despite changing domestic and international conditions.

871. Shapiro, Isaac. "The Risen Sun: Japanese Gaullism?" *Foreign Policy* 41 (1980-81):62-81.

    Shapiro discusses Japan's desire for a gradual movement away from the West, toward greater self-reliance, and the importance for United States policy makers to understand this situation and to make the necessary adjustments, rather than allowing misunderstanding, conflict, and antagonism to occur. Shapiro maintains that the thirty-five year old United States-Japan alliance, which United States policy makers have assumed is based on shared values, economic interdependence, and security considerations, will be affected, and that both Japan and the United States need to begin efforts now to adjust to a new relationship.

872. Shiels, Frederick L. *Tokyo and Washington: Dilemmas of a Mature Alliance.* Lexington, Mass.: Lexington Books, 1980.

    A consideration of the alliance, from World War II to the 1980s, in terms of foreign policy making and political science.

873. Tsurutani, Taketsugu. *Japanese Policy and East Asian Security*. New York: Praeger, 1981.

   The issues of Japan's own defense and its role in East Asian regional security in the 1980s are discussed from the perspective of Japan-United States bilateral security.

874. U.S. Congress. House. Committee on Foreign Affairs. Subcommittee on Asian and Pacific Affairs. *United States-Japan Relations: Hearings*. 98th Cong., 2d sess., 1984. Washington: GPO, 1984.

   Presents an overview of United States-Japan relations, with particular emphasis on whether developments in the past two years represent a coming to terms with the changes that must gradually occur if the relationship is to meet the new challenges facing both countries, or merely a temporary solution to the underlying tensions. Also addresses the issues of United States-Japan security relations, economic relations, and United States administration policies toward Japan.

875. *U.S.-Japanese Relations: What Should the Future Hold?* Washington, D.C.: American Enterprise Institute for Public Policy Research, 1981.

   Contains edited transcripts of an interview in Tokyo with former Japanese Prime Minister Zenko Suzuki and an American Enterprise Institute Public Policy Forum held in Washington, D.C. in 1981. Among the topics included are U.S.-Japan cooperation to alleviate the energy shortage, Japan's international economic and defense responsibilities, and protectionism and United States free trade.

XII
UNITED STATES-JAPAN ECONOMIC RELATIONS

876. Abegglen, James C. *The Strategy of Japanese Business*. Cambridge, Mass.: Ballinger, 1984.

    A collection of articles previously prepared, which cover United States-Japan trade issues, Japanese management, foreign investment in Japan, and research and development in Japan.

877. ────── and Thomas M. Hout. "Facing Up to the Trade Gap with Japan." *Foreign Affairs* 57 (1978):146-168.

    An analysis of the realities of United States competitive performance in Japan and the trade imbalance. Emphasis is on the American international economic competitive position, which the authors contend is in urgent need of review.

878. Alexander, Arthur J. and Hong W. Tan. *Case Studies of U.S. Service Trade in Japan*. Santa Monica, Calif.: Rand, 1984.

    Compilation of case studies on United States service industries in Japan, with an examination of Japanese trade barriers to American trade in these industries. A companion volume to a Rand report entitled: *Barriers to U.S. Service Trade in Japan* (A. Alexander, H.W. Tan, 1984).

879. Amano, Matt M. "New Thinking in Japanese-American Trade." *Journal of Contemporary Business* 8 (1979):7-15.

    Amano takes issue with many of the reasons Americans claim are responsible for the American deficit against Japan (i.e., the exchange rate advantage of the yen over the dollar, the Japanese government's protectionist policies, mystical Japanese trading customs, and cheap labor), and presents a new viewpoint on the trade problem. He also examines the situations the Japanese and American people experienced after World War II, and he discusses contemporary changes as an important influence on American trade with Japan.

880. Bergsten, C. Fred and William R. Cline. *The United States-Japan Economic Problem*. Washington, D.C.: Institute for International Economics, 1985.

A discussion of the key analytical issues underlying the current economic imbalance between the United States and Japan, which includes recommendations for a series of policy actions for both countries. Examines macroeconomic factors such as the overvalued dollar; rapid U.S. recovery; imbalance in both countries between saving and resource use for investment and fiscal deficits; and protection, which includes tariffs, tangible non-tariff barriers, intangible protection, such as government procurement, regulation, oligopoly behavior, and industrial targeting.

881. Blaker, Michael K., ed. *The Politics of Trade: US and Japanese Policymaking for the GATT Negotiations*. New York: East Asian Institute, Columbia University, 1978.

Concerned with the structure and processes of domestic decision-making of Japan and the United States that are relevant to formulating policies for the Tokyo Round of multilateral trade negotiations. Focus is on the trade policies of the two countries and the GATT (General Agreement on Tariffs and Trade).

882. Borden, William S. *The Pacific Alliance: United States Foreign Economic Policy and Japanese Trade Recovery, 1947-1955*. Madison: University of Wisconsin Press, 1984.

Borden's goal here is to provide an overall understanding of the environment within which American foreign policy toward Japan developed in the postwar period. He demonstrates that Japan was the key to all Asian policy and that intervention in Southeast Asia was central to the success of policy concerning Japan. Borden also explains why the United States nurtured Japan's recovery after World War II and how American officials coped with the economic challenges and the task of cementing the Pacific Alliance. He explores and analyzes the dual American response to the dilemma of achieving multilateral goals in a badly unbalanced world economy, with emphasis on the threat of economic deterioration and its impact.

883. Borrus, Michael, James Millstein and John Zysman. *Responses to the Japanese Challenge in High Technology: Innovation, Maturity, and U.S.-Japanese Competition in Microelectronics.* Berkeley: Berkeley Roundtable on the International Economy, University of California, 1983.

A sequel to *U.S.-Japanese Competition in the Semiconductor Industry* (M. Borrus, J. Millstein, J. Zysman, 1982). The authors argue that the United States can meet the Japanese challenge in high technology and in microelectronics in particular, and that American firms can retain international leadership. It is divided into three sections. The first part examines the evolution of the United States semiconductor industry. The second section describes the competitive strength and the strategy of the Japanese semiconductor producers; it examines the impact of the Japanese government's policies on the international competitive position of Japanese firms; and it evaluates the state of current United States-Japanese competition. The third section looks at the general trade predicament confronting United States policymakers, and it proposes a policy response to the dilemma of United States-Japanese semiconductor competition.

884. ———. *U.S.-Japanese Competition in the Semiconductor Industry: A Study in International Trade and Technological Development.* Berkeley: Institute of International Studies, University of California, 1982.

Originally prepared as a study for the Joint Economic Committee, U.S. Congress. It details the evolution, operation, and distinctive features of the United States and Japanese semiconductor industries. It also describes how the Japanese utilized a controlled domestic market and financial leverage to enter the United States market in the late 1970s. Finally, it considers how United States policy might reconcile United States interests in maintaining leadership in this industry with those of Japan and Europe.

885. Bronfenbrenner, Martin. "A Japanese-American Economic War?" *Quarterly Journal of Economics and Business* 11 (1971):7-16.

Written before the Nixon economic policies of August 15, 1971 were promulgated, the author discusses five factors that have contributed to economic conflict between the United States and Japan. These factors are export and import quotas set up by the United States, Japanese tariff and nontariff restrictions on imports, alleged Japanese "dumping" in U.S. markets, restrictions by Japan on United States firms in its domestic market, and American pressure for revaluation of the yen.

886. Brzezinski, Zbigniew. "Japan's Global Engagement." *Foreign Affairs* 50 (1972):270-282.

   Discusses the problems that exist in United States-Japan relations, such as economics and security, and the necessity and importance of resolving them.

887. Castle, Emery N. and Kenzo Hemmi, eds. *U.S.-Japanese Agricultural Trade Relations*. Washington, D.C.: Resources for the Future, Inc., 1982.

   Papers by United States and Japanese scholars intended for use by policymakers in Japan and the United States. They present a thorough analysis of the subject, as well as of the agricultural economies of each country and of their internal problems.

888. Cohen, Jerome B., ed. *Pacific Partnership: United States-Japan Trade; Prospects and Recommendations for the Seventies*. Lexington, Mass.: Lexington Books, 1972.

   Explores United States-Japanese economic relations and presents policy recommendations formulated by the Businessman's Advisory Committee of the Japan Society and the Committee on Economic Policy Studies of the Japan Society. Examines the following aspects of United States-Japanese economic relations: the competitive impact of Japanese growth, Japan's balance of payments and its changing role in the world economy, Japan's foreign trade, Japan-United States trade, evolution of foreign direct investment, the U.S. and Japan, the textile confrontation, Japanese steel and automobile industries, and policy recommendations.

889. Cohen, Stephen D. *Uneasy Partnership: Competition and Conflict in U.s.-Japanese Trade Relations*. Cambridge, Mass.: Ballinger, 1985.

   A synthesis of the different perceptions of bilateral trade problems by the United States and Japan, and an analysis of the trade relationship as seen from the perspectives of the role of government, management, corporate structure, and culture.

890. Committee for Economic Development. *Toward a New International Economic System: A Joint Japanese-American View*. New York, 1974.

A statement by the Research and Policy Committee of the Committee for Economic Development, and Keizai Doyukai, the Japan Committee for Economic Development. Defines the common ground between Japan, the United States and the European Community that can be used in creating a new international economic system that will accommodate the rapidly changing economic relationships among countries

891. Curtis, Gerald L. "The Textile Negotiations: A Failure to Communicate." *Columbia Journal of World Business* 6 (1971):72, 75.

Curtis analyzes both the Japanese and American attitudes toward the textile negotiations, and he sees a serious breakdown in communications at all levels. He discusses the various dimensions of the communications problem between Japan and the United States.

892. Destler, I.M., Haruhiro Fukui and Hideo Sato. *The Textile Wrangle: Conflict in Japanese-American Relations, 1969-1971*. Ithaca, N.Y.: Cornell University Press, 1979.

Explains and analyzes the textile dispute that arose in 1969 between the United States and Japan, when the Nixon administration demanded that Japan enforce comprehensive controls on sales of man-made fiber and wool textile products to the American market and the Japanese government declined to do so. Negotiations to resolve the dispute dominated the economic relations of the two governments during the period from 1969 to 1971. The authors treat the dispute as a political crisis rather than an economic one, and they look at the reasons why this trade dispute generated a broader political crisis. They also look inside each country and government for reasons why particular policy steps were taken.

893. ———— and Hideo Sato, eds. *Coping with U.S.-Japanese Economic Conflicts*. Lexington, Mass.: Lexington Books, 1982.

Case studies of five sources of trade conflicts between

the United States and Japan during the period from 1977 to 1981 are presented, as well as their development and resolution. The sources discussed are steel trade, automobiles, agricultural products, telecommunications equipment, and macroeconomic policy coordination.

894. Deutsch, Mitchell F. *Doing Business with the Japanese.* New York: New American Library, 1984.

    A practical approach based largely on the advice of experienced American and Japanese business people who work in the United States and in Japan. Covers such topics as the problem of doing business with the Japanese, the Japanese company, a guide to correct behavior, bargaining and negotiation, working for a Japanese company, and doing business in Japan. Includes a compendium of key concepts and ideas for doing business in Japan.

895. Dickey, William L. "Aspects of the Legal, Political and Policy Issues That Will Confront the U.S.-Japan Trading Community During the Remainder of the 1980's." *Case Western Reserve Journal of International Law* 15 (1983):445-468.

    Explores aspects of the legal, political, and policy issues that will confront United States-Japan trade relations during the remainder of the 1980s, with emphasis on some considerations faced by United States policy makers. Among the issues discussed are competition in high technology areas, overvaluation of the dollar, and high United States interest rates.

896. Duncan, William Chandler. *U.S.-Japan Automobile Diplomacy: A Study in Economic Confrontation.* Cambridge, Mass.: Ballinger, 1973.

    Concentrates on the attempt of the American automobile industry to acquire a share of the Japanese market during the period from 1967 to 1971. This was a time of frustrating negotiations that contributed significantly to increasing strains in Japanese-American relations. Part One deals with the automobile negotiations, and Part Two with the development and growth of the Japanese automobile industry that was necessary so that liberalization could take place.

897. Frankel, Jeffrey A. *The Yen/Dollar Agreement: Liberalizing Japanese Capital Markets.* Washington, D.C.: Institute for International Economics, 1984.

    A study of the 1983-84 negotiations between the United

States and Japan over liberalization of the Japanese capital markets. Addresses the question of whether the Yen/Dollar Agreement achieved the basic purpose set out by the American and Japanese government leaders, which was to reduce, even eliminate, the serious misalignment in the exchange rate relationship between the dollar and the yen, which had been a prime contributor to international imbalances in 1984.

898. Fried, Edward R., Philip H. Trezise and Shigenobu Yoshida, eds. *The Future Course of U.S.-Japan Economic Relations.* Washington, D.C.: Brookings Institution, 1983.

　　Papers presented at a conference at the Brookings Institution in 1983 on trade and financial issues in United States-Japan relations.

899. Fugate, Wilbur L. "Antitrust Aspects of U.S.-Japanese Trade." *Case Western Reserve Journal of International Law* 15 (1983):505-525.

　　Illustrates the effect of United States and Japanese antitrust laws and related import trade laws on bilateral trade. Emphasis is on measures taken and under consideration by the United States in response to the perceived threat of unfair competition by major Japanese industries and the Japanese government. Also examines the nature and extent of the "unfairness" that exists in United States-Japanese trade relations.

900. Googins, Brian A. and James A. Greene. "The Industrial Targeting Practices of Japan and the Domestic Machine Tool Industry." *Case Western Reserve Journal of International Law* 15 (1983):469-487.

　　The authors examine the current state of United States-Japanese trade relations as it relates to the attempts by the domestic machine industry to compete with increased Japanese imports.

901. Graham, John L. "A Hidden Cause of America's Trade Deficit with Japan." *Columbia Journal of World Business* 16 (1981):5-15.

　　Graham compares the negotiating techniques of American and Japanese businessmen. He argues that because Americans do not understand the Japanese art of negotiation, much business is unnecessarily lost.

902. ——— and Yoshihiro Sano. *Smart Bargaining: Doing Business with the Japanese.* Cambridge, Mass.: Ballinger, 1984.

Advice for American business people on how to achieve successful business negotiations with the Japanese. Focus is on commercial and technical issues. The following topics are discussed: American and Japanese negotiating styles, negotiator selection and team assignment, negotiation preliminaries, at the negotiating table, after negotiations, culture and personality issues, and experiences of four American companies.

903. Gresser, Julian. *High Technology and Japanese Industrial Policy: A Strategy for U.S. Policymakers.* Washington, D.C.: GPO, 1980.

A study commissioned by the United States State Department to examine the issues and problems of United States-Japan trade in the high technology industries. Part One discusses Japan's industrial policy and the development of its semiconductor, computer and telecommunications industries. In Part Two Gresser argues that the United States approach to foreign competition in high technology will not meet the challenge, and that current trends in trade and investment need to be watched. In addition, Gresser contends that a new perspective is required. Part Three discusses a new industrial policy for the United States for high technology industries.

904. ———. *Partners in Prosperity: Strategic Industries for the United States and Japan.* New York: McGraw-Hill, 1984.

The author considers the deterioration of the United States-Japan relationship as being wasteful and unnecessary, and he presents three proposals to reverse the present situation. The first proposal provides psychological insight into the cultural perspectives that divide Japanese and Americans. The second proposal advances the conception of joint economic growth that would require close collaboration between the two countries, as if their respective strategic industries were actually those of one country. Finally, the third proposal involves showing how a new negotiation process with Japan can begin, and how joint economic growth can be achieved.

905. Haynes, Stephen E., Michael M. Hutchison and Raymond F. Mikesell. *Japanese Financial Policies and the U.S. Trade Deficit.* Princeton, N.J.: International Finance Section, Dept. of Economics, Princeton University, 1986.

   A short essay that examines the validity of the allegation that much of the increase in United States trade deficits from 1980 through 1984 was caused by the undervalued yen and on Japan's trade and financial policies. It also looks at the changes in the United States and Japanese trade balances and exchange rates between 1980 and 1984.

906. ————. "U.S. Japanese Bilateral Trade and the Yen-Dollar Exchange Rate: An Empirical Analysis." *Southern Economic Journal* 52 (1986):923-932.

   An empirical exploration of the response of the United States-Japanese trade balance in manufacturing to movements in the yen-dollar rate. It provides a test of the conventional view that the weak yen has been a major factor in explaining the Japanese penetration of the United States manufacturing sector, while Japanese protectionism has effectively insulated Japan's markets from United States competition.

907. Hodgson, James D. *James D. Hodgson, U.S. Ambassador to Japan, 1974-1977, Speaks on the U.S. Trade Deficit with Japan.* Stanford, Calif.: Hoover Institution, Stanford University, 1979.

   A brief overview of the trade deficit issue that discusses the following topics: how the issue appears to both Japan and the United States, its importance to the relationship between the two countries, and a suggestion for its solution. This was a speech delivered by Hodgson at the Symposium on the Changing U.S.-Japanese Economic Partnership "Outlook for the 80s," held in San Francisco in 1979.

908. ————. *The United States and Japan: An Economic, Cultural, and Political Thicket.* Stanford, Calif.: Hoover Institution, Stanford University, 1980.

   Based on a speech by the former U.S. Ambassador to Japan, delivered at the Hoover Institution in 1980. It offers insight into the Japanese dedication to economic matters, and into Japan's unique and integrated culture, which influences almost every aspect of national behavior. Hodgson contends that these two aspects are very influential in Japan's relations with the United States.

909. Hollerman, Leon, ed. *Japan and the United States: Economic and Political Adversaries.* Boulder, Colo.: Westview Press, 1980.

Essays by Japanese and American government officials, business leaders and academics on issues central to the United States-Japan controversy. Among the issues covered are interventionism and foreign trade statistics in occupied Japan; Japan's postwar technological superiority; Japan-U.S. relations in science and technology; U.S. trade problems, particularly with Japan; Japan's foreign trade policy; the evolution and future of U.S.-Japan relations; and U.S. protectionism.

910. ―――. "The Politics of Economic Relations between the United States and Japan." *Journal of Contemporary Business* 8 (1979):87-97.

Hollerman discusses his view that political manipulation has progressively displaced the role of economic rationality in United States-Japan relations in recent years. Politicization may take the form not only of barriers to imports but also of pressure applied by one country against another for economic advantage. Hollerman contends that a basic cause of this situation is the misperception or misrepresentation of the relation between economic cause and effect.

911. ―――. "United States Protectionism in Economic Relations with Japan." *Asian Survey* 17 (1977):491-496.

The author maintains that the overriding issue in United States and Japanese economic relations at present concerns American protectionism, and he suggests ten reasons why the United States may be increasingly protectionist in its future relations with Japan.

912. Japan Economic Research Center. *A Long-Term Outlook of Japanese and U.S. Economies, 1980.* Abridged translation. Tokyo, 1973.

Consists of projections of the course of economic relations between Japan and the United States for the period from 1970 to 1980. Among the topics included are the Japanese and U.S. economies, Japan's trade, Japan-U.S. trade, U.S. trade, direct investments, balance of international payments, and the international environment.

913. Japan-United States Economic Relations Group. *Appendix to the Report of the Japan-United States Economic Relations Group.* Washington, D.C., 1981.

 Contains the background studies that the Japan-United States Economic Relations Group referred to in reaching its conclusions and recommendations on Japan-United States economic relations.

914. ————. *Report of the Japan-United States Economic Relations Group.* Washington, D.C., 1981.

 Contains recommendations by the Group concerning United States-Japan economic relations that stress that a number of problems need to be addressed in order to improve the bilateral relationship. These problems include inadequate consultative mechanisms between the two governments, mistaken or outdated perceptions of each country by the other country, inadequate American economic performance, lagging liberalization of market access in Japan, and often, a failure by the governments and private sectors of both countries to face up to difficult problems.

915. ————. *Supplemental Report of the Japan-United States Economic Relations Group.* Springfield, Va.: National Technical Information Service, 1981.

 The final official activity of the Group. Discusses the comments of the American and Japanese governments and private sectors on its Report. Also reviews some important issues in the economic relationship of the two countries, as well as the need for international economic leadership, United States and Japanese trade policies, potential bilateral economic issues, energy issues, and a possible comprehensive partnership. Includes further recommendations.

916. *The Japan-U.S. Assembly: Proceedings of a Conference on Japan-U.S. Economic Policy.* Washington, D.C.: American Enterprise Institute for Public Policy Research, 1975.

 Consists of the proceedings of a 1974 conference on Japan-U.S. economic relations, sponsored by the Conference Board on U.S.-Japan Economic Policy, in which the Japanese and American participants reviewed the history of Japan-U.S. economic relations and explored the possibilities of the two countries achieving a better understanding and cooperation in the formulation of economic policy. The book is divided into five sections. Part One discusses energy problems and the international economy. Part Two is concerned with the current situation of and prospect for the United States and Japanese economies. Part Three deals with inflation. Part Four looks at United States-Japan economic problems. And finally, Part Five consists of discussion on cooperation in Japanese and American economic policy.

917. *The Japanese Challenge and the American Response: A Symposium.* Berkeley: Institute of East Asian Studies, University of California, 1982.

    Papers and discussions from a conference held at Berkeley in 1981 that analyze the uneven United States-Japan economic relationship.

918. Kaji, Motoo. "Japan-U.S. Economic Relations." *Japan Quarterly* 20 (1973):268-274.

    An observation of the Japanese-United States economic relationship as seen in the context of changes in the international economy.

919. Kawahito, Kiyoshi. "The Steel Dumping Issue in Recent U.S.-Japanese Relations." *Asian Survey* 20 (1980):1038-1047.

    Between 1969 and 1974, which was a period of voluntary restraint agreements, the protectionist movement in the United States against steel imports was fairly subdued. However, it began to intensify in 1975, when free trade was resumed, and in 1977 Japanese producers were charged with having engaged in massive steel dumps in the United States market, especially in 1976. Kawahito argues here that Japanese producers generally did not dump steel in the United States market. Rather, this dumping issue was brought about by American misjudgment, and he offers an explanation of the American causes of this misconception as well as the Japanese causes.

920. Krause, Walter and Wilbur F. Monroe. "Prospects for United States-Japan Trade Relations." *Columbia Journal of World Business* 16 (1981):18-22.

    The authors discuss the large trade imbalance between the United States and Japan. They compare the major differences in how the Reagan Administration proposes to deal with the methods that were used by the Carter Administration.

921. Langdon, Frank. "Japan-United States Trade Friction: The Reciprocity Issue." *Asian Survey* 23 (1983):653-666.

Langdon examines issues involved in the increasing Japan-United States trade friction. Focus is on reciprocity, which is the American demand that the Japanese market be as open to American exports as the American one is to Japanese exports, such as automobiles, television sets, video tape recorders, and integrated circuits.

922. Lyons, James M. "Japan's Quantitative Restrictions on the Importation of Agricultural Products." *Case Western Reserve Journal of International Law* 15 (1983):569-586.

Discusses the effects of Japan's restrictive agricultural trade on United States-Japanese economic relations. Japan's Liberal Democratic Party, dependent upon the farm vote, has been reluctant to make sacrifices that would seriously affect the Japanese agricultural community. Meanwhile, the United States is indignant over Japanese unwillingness to open its borders to American agricultural goods. Lyons contends that if this situation remains unchanged, a further deterioration in trade relations will result.

923. Matsushita, Mitsuo and Lawrence Repeta. "Restricting the Supply of Japanese Automobiles: Sovereign Compulsion or Sovereign Collusion?" *Case Western Reserve Journal of International Law* 14 (1982):47-81.

The authors discuss the events that led to the May 1, 1981 announcement by the Japanese government that it would adopt measures to restrict the export of Japanese automobiles to the United States over a three-year period. They also examine the question as to whether Japan's government was compelled or persuaded to do this by the United States government. This case is unique in that the Japanese government explained its actions in terms designed for analysis under American law, even before a dispute had arisen. This unusual step was taken to ensure that those Japanese automakers who would restrict sales in the United States market in response to measures taken by the Japanese government would not subsequently be exposed to liability for resulting violations of American antitrust law.

924. McCreary, Don R. *Japanese-U.S. Business Negotiations: A Cross-Cultural Study*. New York: Praeger, 1986.

   An analysis of Japanese and American communicative negotiation styles from a Soviet sociocultural psycholinguistic perspective. The author addresses the problems of lack of information and misperceptions about differences in values and negotiation styles that lessen the chances of reaching negotiation agreements.

925. Moran, Robert T. *Getting Your Yen'$ Worth: How to Negotiate with Japan, Inc*. Houston: Gulf Publishing, 1985.

   Offers practical information for American business people who plan to negotiate with the Japanese. Some historical and cultural background is presented, but primary focus is on the Japanese negotiating style and on presenting information that American negotiators can apply.

926. Nevin, John J. "Can U.S. Business Survive Our Japanese Trade Policy?" *Harvard Business Review* 56 (1978):165-177.

   Nevin, who is chairman of Zenith Radio Corporation's board, maintains that some American industries, such as television, are on the low end of the trade balance and are even having difficulty competing in their home markets because the Japanese government grants subsidies to exporters and places high import quotas that restrict the entry of foreign goods into Japan, and because some Japanese manufacturers are dumping their products on the U.S. market. Nevin further contends that American government diplomatic attitudes interfere with the Treasury and Justice departments in carrying out law enforcement duties against Japanese manufacturers and United States importers, and will cause even more economic damage in the future.

927. Okimoto, Daniel I., Takuo Sugano and Franklin B. Weinstein, eds. *Competitive Edge: The Semiconductor Industry in the U.S. and Japan*. Stanford, Calif.: Stanford University Press, 1984.

   An assessment of the technological, financial, and political factors affecting the competitive relationship between the United States and Japanese semiconductor industries.

928. Okita, Saburo. "Japan, China and the United States: Economic Relations and Prospects." *Foreign Affairs* 57 (1979):1090-1110.

   Analyzes conflicts over economic issues between the United States and Japan, as well as the role that each country should play in its relation with China.

929. ————. "The Textile Negotiations: Japan's Point of View." *Columbia Journal of World Business* 6 (1971):73-78.

   Okita discusses Japan-United States communications problems in the context of the textile negotiations, in which Japan was faced with a serious choice of either pushing forward the general policy of liberalization of both trade and investment, or moving a step backward and compromising with the request from the United States government. He looks at import pressure on Japan, trade and investment liberalization, lack of knowledge about Japan on the part of the United States, United States protectionism and isolationism, and lack of trust as being among those factors contributing to poor United States-Japan communications problems.

930. Ozaki, Robert S. "United States-Japanese Economic Relations." *Current History* 82 (1983):357-391.

   Points out various issues and problems behind the troubled United States-Japan economic relationship. According to Ozaki, the controversy centers on the United States fixation with Japan's trade surplus with the United States.

931. Ozawa, Terutomo. "Should the United States Restrict Technology Trade with Japan?" *MSU Business Topics* 20 (1972):35-44.

   Ozawa argues that technology trade should not be restricted since American technology has helped Japan attain its status as a highly industrialized country and it should therefore be considered as an investment. In addition, Ozawa contends that the United States should expand trade and direct investments and that it should also benefit from Japan's newly developed technology.

932. Petri, Peter A. *Modeling Japanese-American Trade: A Study of Asymmetric Interdependence.* Cambridge, Mass.: Harvard University Press, 1984.

A quantitative examination of the structure of interdependence in the Japanese-American economic relationship, or how events in one economy influence those of the other. Looks at the development of interdependence over time and traces the causes of the growing intensity of the bilateral relationship. Among the issues addressed here are the structural determinants of bilateral trade and the reasons for its prominence in policy debate.

933. Pugel, Thomas A., ed. *Fragile Interdependence: Economic Issues in U.S.-Japanese Trade and Investment.* Lexington, Mass.: Lexington Books, 1986.

Consists of revised papers that were presented at a conference hosted by the Center for Japan-U.S. Business and Economic Studies of the Graduate School of Business Administration, New York University, 1984. Concentrates on the economic issues that contribute to stress in United States-Japan trade and investment relations, and provides discussion of the issues of market access, international investment, and international technological competition by experts in these fields.

934. Rapp, William V. "What the United States Has to Do to Compete with Japan." *Journal of Contemporary Business* 8 (1979):17-26.

Rapp presents his views on the importance and necessity of the United States being able to compete with Japan. He maintains that in order to meet this challenge, a fundamental political economic reorientation is necessary, which should include a substantial resource allocation shift towards investment, trade and technology, and a change in regulatory policies and in the sharing of regulatory costs.

935. Richmond, Frederick W. *How to Beat the Japanese at Their Own Game.* Englewood Cliffs, N.J.: Prentice-Hall, 1983.

An analysis of those aspects of the Japanese economic system that the author considers to be the most pertinent for the United States in the continuing industrial struggle between the two countries. Richmond also proposes steps that can be taken to meet the Japanese competition. In addition, questions are raised concerning the political future of the Liberal Democratic Party with its shrinking minority of supporters. The source of the LDP's hold on the rural vote is due to the huge government subsidies to farmers, which are larger than most other items in Japan's domestic budget. This is also the reason for Japan's restrictive policies toward American imports, especially agricultural products. Richmond contends that should the LDP lose control of the government, United States-Japan friction will be alleviated.

936. Sanderson, Fred H. *Japan's Food Prospects and Policies.* Washington, D.C.: Brookings Institution, 1978.

Focuses on the future of United States-Japan agricultural relations and trade with regard to postwar food consumption trends in Japan, the costs and limits of expanding food production in Japan, and the capacity of the United States and other agricultural exporting countries to meet prospective Japanese and world import demands. Since the end of World War II, Japan's food system has undergone a radical transformation, in which a diet of rice and fish has shifted to a Western style diet, with a large component of meat products. Because it is lacking the resources needed to produce livestock feed, Japan now depends on imports for half of its total food requirements, and over half of these are supplied by the United States.

937. Sato, Hideo. "Japanese-American Economic Relations in Crisis." *Current History* 84 (1985):405-436.

As assessment of the current crisis in United States-Japan economic relations, which appears substantively different from earlier ones because it has been exacerbated by the Reagan Administration's lack of effective macroeconomic policy actions, according to Sato.

938. ―――. "Japanese-American Relations." *Current History* 75 (1978):145-181.

Addresses the issue of the strain economic factors have put on United States-Japan relations.

939. Saxonhouse, Gary R. "A Review of Recent U.S.-Japan Economic Relations." *Asian Survey* 12 (1972):726-752.

Discusses the tensions in United States-Japan economic relations, which in the author's view have occurred primarily because Japan has been increasingly seen as a threat to American jobs and markets. In addition, the evolution of the Japanese economy has been regarded as a menace to the postwar international economic system.

940. ———— and Kozo Yamamura, eds. *Law and Trade Issues of the Japanese Economy: American and Japanese Perspectives.* Seattle: University of Washington Press, 1986.

Essays that were originally presented at a 1983 workshop sponsored by the Committee on Japanese Economic Studies (U.S.) on legal institutions and U.S.-Japanese economic relations. They analyze the domestic legal frameworks of both Japan and the United States, which because of their institutional differences, are important in shaping the character of bilateral economic relations as well as the very nature of the relationship itself. The book is divided into three parts. Part One deals with the Japanese legal framework and domestic economy institutions. Part Two is concerned with Japan's legal framework and foreign access to its market. And Part Three addresses the American legal framework and bilateral issues.

941. Shimeall, Warren G. "Strategic Planning for the Protection of U.S. Technology and Intellectual Property in the Trade Relationship between the United States and Japan." *Case Western Reserve Journal of International Law* 15 (1983):611-622.

Discusses the intensity of the Japanese commitment to the development of science and technology, which has had a tremendous impact on United States-Japan trade relations. Shimeall contends that reevaluation of American policy should be done specifically with respect to Japan, focusing on long-range strategic and technological goals.

942. Siegel, Nancy L. and Noah Sherman. "The Chips Are Down: Legal Implications of Alleged Japanese Unfair Practices in the United States Semiconductor Industry." *Hastings International and Comparative Law Review* 2 (1979):129-180.

An examination of alleged Japanese trade secret violations in the United States semi-conductor industry, and various protective mechanisms available to United States industry on both domestic and international levels.

943. Sobel, Robert. *IBM vs. Japan: The Struggle for the Future.* New York: Stein and Day, 1986.

Explains those factors that have contributed to the

success of IBM and to its ability to withstand competition, so far, from Japanese information processing companies. Also discusses the strategies and experiences of Japanese computer companies in dealing with IBM.

944. Taira, Koji. "Power and Trade in U.S.-Japanese Relations." *Asian Survey* 12 (1972):980-998.

Explores the effects of the new economic policy of August 15, 1971, of the United States, on Japan, with emphasis on the following issues: why Japan was perceived as a primary target of the new policy, how the United States extracted concessions from Japan, and how Japan responded to United States pressure.

945. Tasca, Diane, ed. *U.S.-Japanese Economic Relations: Cooperation, Competition, and Confrontation.* New York: Pergamon, 1980.

Papers resulting from a series of monthly seminars, held at the Lehrman Institute from 1978 to 1979, by Japanese and American scholars, businessmen, bankers, and government officials, which analyzed the reasons for the problems in economic relations between the United States and Japan, and which also propose recommendations for their resolution.

946. Taylor, Allen, ed. *Perspectives on U.S.-Japan Economic Relations.* Cambridge, Mass.: Ballinger, 1973.

Papers presented at the U.S.-Trade Council Economic Conference, held in Washington, D.C. in 1973, that address, among others, the issues of the trade imbalance, the economic impact of Japanese imports, and U.S.-Japanese industrial structure and international competitiveness.

947. Tung, Rosalie L. *Business Negotiations with the Japanese.* Lexington, Mass.: Lexington Books, 1984.

Examines Japanese attitudes and values concerning business negotiations and the processes involved in United States-Japan business negotiations. Based on a survey of 114 American firms that have negotiated with Japanese firms.

948. U.S. Congress. House. Committee on Foreign Affairs. *United States-Japan Economic Relations: Hearings and Markup*. 96th Cong., 2d sess., 1980. Washington, D.C.: GPO, 1981.

Hearings held for the purpose of clarifying issues involved in United States-Japan economic relations and in industrial policy of both countries. Among the topics covered are restraint on the export of Japanese cars to the United States, market access, nontariff barriers, and investment opportunities.

949. ―――――. Subcommittee on Foreign Economic Policy. *United States Foreign Economic Policy toward Japan: Hearings*. 92d Cong., 1st. sess., 1971. Washington, D.C.: GPO, 1972.

Hearings held with the goal of improving United States-Japan economic and political relations, which had seriously deteriorated in the aftermath of the "Nixon Shocks" of 1971.

950. U.S. Congress. House. Committee on Science and Technology. Subcommittee on Science, Research and Technology. *The Role of Technical Information in U.S. Competiveness with Japan: Hearings*. 99th Cong., 1st. sess., 1985. Washington, D.C.: GPO, 1985.

An investigation of the availability of Japanese scientific information in the United States and of the comparative strength of the United States and Japan in selected high technology fields.

951. U.S. Congress. House. Committee on Ways and Means. Subcommittee on Trade. *Current Exchange Rate Relationship of the U.S. Dollar and the Japanese Yen: Hearing*. 97th Cong., 2d sess., 1982. Washington, D.C.: GPO, 1983.

A discussion of the causes and effects of the exchange rate relationship and its implications for United States trade policy.

952. ―――――. *Japanese Voluntary Restraints on Auto Exports to the United States: Hearings*. 99th Cong., 1st. sess., 1985. Washington, D.C.: GPO, 1985.

An examination of the issue of whether the voluntary restraints, which are due to expire on March 31, 1985, should be allowed to expire, or be extended, or modified.

953. ———. *Trade with Japan: Hearings.* 96th Cong., 2d sess., 1980. Washington, D.C.: GPO, 1980.

Discusses subjects germane to Japan-United States trade, including nontariff barriers and investment issues, negotiations relating to the MTN agreement on government procurement, recent trends in Japanese auto exports, and prospects for long-range improvement in trade relations.

954. ———. *United States-Japan Trade Relations: Hearings.* 98th Cong., 1st. sess., 1983. Washington, D.C.: GPO, 1983.

Hearings held in order to discuss various aspects of the United States-Japan bilateral trade situation, with emphasis on the degree of openness of the Japanese market for American markets. Among the topics covered are Japanese industrial policy, the exchange relationship of the yen and the dollar, and other tariff and nontariff barriers to specific United States exports. Held in preparation of a United States trade mission to Japan.

955. U.S. Congress. Joint Economic Committee. Subcommittee on Economic Goals and Intergovernmental Policy. *Japan's Economy and Trade with the United States: Selected Papers.* Washington, D.C.: GPO, 1985.

A collection of essays that examine the Japanese economy and its relationship with the United States from a diversity of viewpoints. While emphasis is on trade, also explored are Japanese domestic economic policies that affect the United States. Written by specialists on Japan for the purpose of providing information on the Japanese economy for United States legislators and policymakers.

956. U.S. Congress. Joint Economic Committee. Subcommittee on International Trade, Finance, and Security Economics. *U.S.-Japanese Economic Relations: Hearings.* 97th Cong., 1st. sess., 1981. Washington, D.C.: GPO, 1981.

Hearings held in order to explore ways in which the imbalance of United States-Japan trade relations can be corrected.

957. U.S. Congress. Senate. Committee on Banking, Housing, and Urban Affairs. Subcommittee on International Finance and Monetary Policy. *Semiconductor Trade and Japanese Targeting: Hearing.* 99th Cong., 1st. sess., 1985. Washington, D.C.: GPO, 1985.

   Looks at the problems of unfair trade practices and Japanese barriers to trade in the semiconductor industry.

958. U.S. General Accounting Office. *United States-Japan Trade: Issues and Problems.* Washington, D.C., 1979.

   An analysis of the economic factors underlying the United States-Japan trade imbalance and of the differences in trade policies between the two countries. Case studies of seven American industries that illustrate problems in the Japanese market are presented. These industries are computers, automobiles, telecommunications, color television, machine tools, logs and lumber, and soybeans.

959. U.S. Industry and Trade Administration. *U.S. Export Opportunities to Japan.* Washington, D.C., 1978.

   A survey of fourteen Japanese industrial market sectors and the possibilities for American export. Also presents information on marketing in Japan.

960. *U.S.-Japan Economic Relations: A Symposium on Critical Issues.* Berkeley: Institute of East Asian Studies, University of California, 1980.

   Papers delivered at a conference on Japanese-American economic relations at Berkeley in 1979 that address the following issues: U.S.-Japan trade competition in the 1980s, Japan-U.S. economic relations, U.S.-Japan trade relations, Japanese quality, economic rearmament for the United States and Japan, Japan's fiscal and monetary policy, and United States-Japan financial cooperation in the Pacific.

961. *U.S.-Japan Economic Relations Yearbook.* 1984-85- Washington, D.C.: Japan Economic Institute of America.

   Continues the *Yearbook of U.S.-Japan Economic Relations*, 1978-1983, published by the U.S.-Japan Trade Council. An annual review of the economic relationship between Japan and the United States. Also considers both the economic developments of the year and the policy discussions and decisions that shaped the nature of bilateral economic activity. Looks at political and security developments and the world economy as well. The appendices contain a chronology of events for the year and statistical tables.

962. Vernon, Raymond. *Two Hungry Giants: The United States and Japan in the Quest for Oil and Ores.* Cambridge, Mass.: Harvard University Press, 1983.

   Vernon sees the search response by the United States and Japan for raw energy materials as having been greatly influenced by their respective histories and cultures. He relates this to the broader issues of international relations and cultural differences.

963. Viksnins, George J. "U.S.-Japanese Trade: Perceptions and Reality." *Asian Survey* 19 (1979):205-229.

   Analyzes two major topics: first, recent trends in United States-Japanese economic relations, and second, American and Japanese interests in the Pacific Asian region.

964. Weil, Frank A. and Norman D. Glick. "Japan--Is the Market Open? A View of the Japanese Market Drawn from U.S. Corporate Experience." *Law and Policy in International Business* 11 (1979):845-902.

   Although Japan recently agreed to lower its formal import quotas, foreign business people, among them many from the United States, continue to encounter difficulties in establishing their goods in the Japanese market. To illustrate the nature of these problems, the authors analyze cases filed by American business people with the Joint United States-Japan Trade Facilitation Committee, which was set up to ease the entry into Japan of American goods.

965. Wilbur F. Monroe Associates, Inc. *Japanese Exports to the United States: Analysis of "Import-Pull" and "Export-Push" Factors.* Washington, D.C.: United States-Japan Trade Council, 1978.

   A study conducted on behalf of the U.S.-Japan Trade Council on the effects of both "import-pull" and "export-push" factors on six major American industries.

AUTHOR INDEX
The references below are to entry numbers.

A

Abegglen, James C. 365, 678, 679, 782, 876, 877
Adams, L. Jerold 349, 350
Adelman, Kenneth L. 351
Akao, Nobutoshi 552
Alexander, Arthur J. 878
Alexander, C. Philip 821
Algarin, Joanne P. 62
Allen, G.C. 366, 367, 468
Allinson, Gary D. 248, 833
Alston, Jon P. 680, 783
Amano, Ikuo 73, 92
Amano, Matt M. 879
Ames, Walter L. 68
Amnesty International 69
Anderson, Alun M. 182
Anderson, Ronald S. 72
Anderson, William S. 368
Anthony, D.F. 579
Aoki, Masahiko 801
Aoki, Michiko Y. 36
Aonuma, Yoshimatsu 681
Arai, Shunzo 682
Arthur Andersen & Co. 246
Aso, Makoto 73
Athos, Anthony G. 743
Atsumi, Reiko 770
Auerbach, Morton 267
Austin, Lewis 144, 249
Azuma, Hiroshi 106
Azumi, Koya 809

B

Baerwald, Hans H. 250, 251, 252, 299, 300, 301, 302, 303, 317, 329
Bailey, Jackson H. 37
Ballon, Robert J. 621, 802
Banoff, Barbara Ann 242
Baranson, Jack 635, 673
Barnds, William J. 847
Barnhart, Michael A. 369
Barnlund, Dean C. 117
Barrett, M. Edgar 567
Bartels, R. 565
Barthes, Roland 38
Beasley, W.G. 1, 2
Beauchamp, Edward R. 74
Beer, Lawrence Ward 108, 109, 196, 215, 229
Befu, Harumi 39, 127
Bellah, Robert N. 132
Benjamin, Roger W. 197, 253, 330
Bereday, George Z.F. 848
Bergsten, C. Fred 880
Bhuinya, Niranjan 254
Bieda, K. 370
Birmingham, Hobart McK. 469
Blaker, Michael K. 304, 881
Blumenthal, Tuvia 371, 526
Bocker, H.J. 822
Boisot, Max 683
Boltho, Andrea 372

Bolz, Herbert F. 232
Borden, William S. 882
Borrus, Michael 883, 884
Bowen, Roger Wilson 255
Bowes, John E. 145
Bowman, Mary Jean 75
Bownas, Geoffrey 559
Boyer, Edward 636
Brett, Cecil C. 318
Brewer, Ann 699
Brockman, Rosser H. 549
Bronfenbrenner, Martin 885
Bronte, Stephen 531, 532
Bryant, William E. 622
Brynildsen, Richard J. 305
Brzezinski, Zbigniew 256, 886
Buckley, Roger 3
Bunge, Frederica M. 21
Bunke, Harvey C. 373
Burke, W. Warner 720
Burks, Ardath W. 22
Burnham, John M. 811
Busch, Noel F. 4
Business Intercommunications, Inc. 374
Buzbee, B.L. 184

C
Caiger, J.G. 16
Campbell, Donald J. 684
Campbell, John Creighton 533
Castle, Emery N. 887
Caudill, William A. 40, 100
Caves, Richard E. 803
Chacko, George K. 674
Chang, C.S. 648
Chao, Ke-lu 685
Cheng, Peter P. 257
Choi, Sung-il 258, 306, 319
Christainsen, Gregory B. 812
Christopher, Robert C. 118
Clapp, Priscilla 849
Clark, Rodney 619, 686
Cleaver, Charles Grinnell 41
Clemens, Walter C., Jr. 850
Clifford, William 70
Cline, William R. 880

Clutterbuck, David 813
Codrea, John E. 470
Cohen, Jerome B. 888
Cohen, Stephen D. 889
Cole, Robert E. 649, 650, 687, 771, 784, 785, 786, 787, 834
Coleman, Samuel 101
Committee for Economic Development 890
Condon, John C. 119
Connaghan, Charles J. 835
Conroy, Hilary 20
Conroy, Mary 102
Cook, Alice H. 172
Cooper, C.L. 688
Copper, John F. 307
Courdy, Jean-Claude 120
Craig, Albert M. 19, 42
Craighead, George P. 763
Crawcour, S. 788
Cummings, William K. 76, 77, 78, 90, 91, 92
Curtis, Gerald L. 259, 308, 309, 357, 851, 891
Cusumano, Michael A. 651
Czinkota, Michael R. 604, 605

D
Dahlby, Tracy 260, 623
Dardess, Margaret B. 36
Davidson, William H. 814
Davies, Derek 261
Davis, Winston 133
De Mente, Boye 23, 689
Denoon, David B.H. 852
Dentsu Incorporated 606
Destler, I.M. 892, 893
Deutsch, Mitchell F. 894
De Vos, George A. 110, 111, 112, 121
Dickerman, Allen 690
Dickey, William L. 895
Diebold, John 691
Dillon, Linda S. 692
Dodwell Marketing Consultants 589

Author Index

Doi, Noriyuki 665, 666
Doi, Takeo 122, 123
Doi, Teruo 239
Doktor, R. 693
Donnelly, Michael W. 375
Dore, Ronald P. 455, 637, 789
Downs, Ray F. 5
Dreyfack, Raymond 694
Drucker, Peter F. 456, 457, 508, 695
Drummond, Richard Henry 134
Dubro, Alec 71
Duke, Benjamin C. 79, 98
Duncan, William Chandler 896
Dunphy, Dexter C. 696
Duus, Peter 6

E
Earhart, H. Byron 135, 136
Easther, Millicent 699
Ebinger, Charles K. 853
The Economist 377
Edelstein, Alex S. 145
Ehrlich, Eva 638
Elliott, James 262
Ellwood Robert S., Jr. 43
Emery, Robert F. 534
Emmerson, John K. 331, 344
Endicott, John E. 263, 358
Endo, Calvin M. 696
England, George W. 698
Entwistle, Basil 7
Eto, Hajime 670
Evans, Robert, Jr. 378
Ewald, R.H. 184

F
Fahey, Liam 610, 611
Fatemi, Ali M. 664
Feigenbaum, Edward A. 654
Fields, George 44
Financial Times 379
Flanagan, Scott C. 264, 287, 310
Fodella, Gianni 146
Ford, Bill 699

Foster, James J. 332
Foster, Mark Edward 217
Fox, William M. 700
Frank, Isaiah 381, 382
Frankel, Jeffrey A. 897
Franko, Lawrence G. 595
Fried, Edward R. 898
Fruin, W. Mark 568, 569, 701
Fugate, Wilbur L. 899
Fujikura, Koichiro 237
Fujita, Yasuhiro 198, 218
Fukai, Shigeko N. 333, 334
Fukui, Haruhiro 265, 335, 336, 509, 892
Fukutake, Tadashi 147, 148
Furstenberg, Friedrich 702
Furuhashi, Yusaku 472
Fuse, Toyomasa 149

G
Gale, Roger W. 352
Garvin, David A. 703
Gehrke, Judith Ann 567
Gerstenfeld, Arthur 815
Gibney, Frank 45, 704
Glick, Norman D. 964
Glicksman, Maurice 831
Gold, Bela 667
Goldsmith, Raymond W. 535
Goldsmith, Scott K. 219
Goldstein, Bernice Z. 64
Googins, Brian A. 900
Gorden, William I. 685
Goto, Akira 570, 590
Gotoda, Teruo 320
Gould, Rowland 658
Graham, John L. 901, 902
Greene, James A. 900
Gregory, Ann 383
Gregory, Gene 384, 659, 660
Gresser, Julian 237, 903, 904
Grootaert, Christiaan 385
Grossberg, Kenneth A. 46
Grossman, Elliot S. 816
Guillain, Robert 639
Guittard, Stephen W. 630

H

Hadley, Eleanor M.   205, 510
Hah, Chong-do   113
Hahn, Elliott J.   220, 631
Haitani, Kanji   386, 553, 790
Hakuta, Kenji   106
Haley, John Owen   199, 221, 607
Hall, John Whitney   8
Hall, Robert B.   387
Halliday, Jon   388
Halperin, Morton H.   849
Hamada, Tomoko   389, 705
Han, Sungjoo   359
Hanami, Tadashi A.   241, 791, 837
Hane, Mikiso   9, 150
Harari, Ehud   266, 792, 838
Harbron, John D.   706
Hardacre, Helen   137
Harsel, Sheldon M.   145
Hartley, John   675
Hartman, F.L.   222
Hashimoto, Akira   252
Hashimoto, Masanori   793
Hatakeyama, Yoshio   707
Hattori, Ichiro   708
Hattori, Takaaki   216
Hatvany, Nina   709, 710
Hayashi, Hiroko   172
Hayes, Robert H.   711
Haynes, Stephen E.   905, 906
Hazama, Hiroshi   712
Helou, Angelina   580
Helvoort, Ernest van   772
Hemmi, Kenzo   887
Henderson, Dan Fenno   216, 576
Hendry, Joy   103
Hibino, Kazuyuki   189
Hidaka, Rokuro   458
Higashi, Chikara   563
Higgins, Mary Faith   206
Higuchi, Yoshio   179
Hildebrand, James L.   207, 210, 223
Hirono, Ryokichi   382, 817

Hirschmeier, Johannes   279, 390, 554
Ho, Alfred K.   564
Hodgson, James D.   907, 908
Hogendorn, Jan S.   812
Holden, Constance   185
Hollerman, Leon   391, 555, 602, 624, 909, 910, 911
Hoover, Thomas   47
Horne, James   536
Horvath, Dezso   511
Hoshino, Yasuo   751
Hout, Thomas M.   482, 877
Howard, N.   714
Hrebenar, Ronald J.   311, 337
Hubbard, Elva Ellen   613
Huddle, Norie   190
Hulten, Charles R.   423
Hunsberger, Warren S.   393
Hunter, Janet   10
Hutchins, David   827
Hutchison, Michael M.   905, 906

I

Iga, Mamoru   151, 267
Ike, Brian   512
Ike, Nobutaka   268, 269, 394, 459
Ikeda, Hideo   75
Ikeda, Katsuhiko   665, 666
Imai, Masaaki   556
Inoguchi, Takashi   360
Inoue, Ken   773
Iriye, Akira   854
Isenberg, Irwin   11
Ishida, Eiichiro   48
Ishida, Hideto   608
Ishida, Takeshi   152, 153
Ishida, Tsuyoshi   467
Ishii, Ryosuke   270
Ishikawa, Kaoru   828, 829
Itoh, Hiroshi   229, 271
Iwao, Seiichi   12
Iwata, Ryushi   715
Iyori, Hiroshi   208

J

Jaeger, Alfred M. 805
Janow, Merit E. 430
Jansen, Marius B. 24
Japan. Agency for Cultural Affairs 138
Japan. Business History Institute 527
Japan Center for International Exchange 25
Japan. Central Council for Education 93
Japan. Economic Planning Agency 396, 473, 474, 475
Japan Economic Research Center 397, 912
Japan External Trade Organization 830
Japan. Ministry of Foreign Affairs 398
Japan. Ministry of International Trade and Industry 603
Japan Productivity Center 839
Japan. Social Insurance Agency 794
Japan. Supreme Court 233
Japan-United States Economic Relations Group 913, 914, 915
Japan-U.S. Study Group 477
Jauregui, Jacqueline 856
Jenney, B.W. 452
JMA Research Institute 676
Johnson, Chalmers 272, 478, 513, 514, 515
Johnson, Mark S. 224
Johnson, Sheila K. 857
Johnson, Steven B. 832
Jones, H.J. 173, 174, 175
Jorgenson, Dale W. 401
Juran, J.M. 716

K

Kahn, Herman 402, 403
Kaji, Motoo 918
Kamata, Satoshi 774
Kamiya, Fuji 858
Kan, Ori 330
Kanamori, Hisao 404
Kaneko, Yoshio 405
Kaplan, David E. 71
Kaplan, Eugene J. 516
Kaplan, Morton A. 859
Karatsu, Hajime 717
Karsh, Bernard 841
Kato, Hiroki 61
Kato, Shuichi 32
Kaufmann, Felix 718
Kawada, Hisashi 775
Kawaguchi, Hiroshi 528
Kawahito, Kiyoshi 668, 669, 919
Kawase, Takeshi 719
Kawatani, Yukimoro 655
Keegan, Warren J. 818
Keller, Sherry Yajima 176
Kelley, Allen C. 406
Kiefer, Christie W. 80
Kim, Chin 230
Kim, Chong Lim 273
Kim, Hong N. 338
King, Henry T., Jr. 225
Kinmonth, Earl H. 154
Kirby, Stuart 437
Kirkpatrick, Maurine A. 155
Kitamura, Hiroshi 478, 479, 860
Kitamura, Kazuyuki 92
Kitaoji, Hironobu 104
Kobayashi, Maurie K. 720
Kobayashi, Victor Nobuo 78, 81
Kodama, Sanehide 861
Koike, Ryohji 698
Kojima, Kazuto 49
Kojima, Kiyoshi 480, 582
Kono, Toyohiro 721, 722
Konz, Stephan 823
Kornhauser, David 407
Kosai, Yutaka 408, 409
Kosaka, Masataka 274
Koschmann, J. Victor 156
Koshi, George M. 235
Kotabe, Masaaki 481, 517

Kotler, Philip 610, 611
Koyano, Shogo 157
Kraar, Louis 577
Krause, Walter 920
Krauss, Ellis S. 158, 326
Krauss, W. Paul 723
Kumon, Shumpei 50, 275
Kuniya, N. 688
Kurihara, Kenneth K. 410
Kuroda, Yasumasa 327
Kuwabara, Takeo 51

L
Langdon, Frank 345, 921
Langer, Paul F. 339
Lapp, Christopher C. 113
Lebra, Joyce 177
Lebra, Takie Sugiyama 124, 125, 178
Lebra, William P. 125
Lee, Changsoo 114
Lee, Eugene H. 621
Lee, Jooinn 340
Lee, O-young 126
Lee, Sang M. 724, 725
Lee, Tosh 312
Lehmann, Jean Pierre 13
Lester, Richard K. 862
Levine, Solomon B. 460, 461, 775, 841
Lewis, Catherine C. 96
Lifson, Thomas B. 586
Lin, Ching-yuan 538
Livingston, Jon 14
Lobb, John C. 518
Long, William A. 726
Longworth, John W. 653
Lorenzo, Richard M. 234
Loss, Louis 242
Lu, David John 15
Lynn, Leonard H. 186, 187, 671
Lyons, James M. 922
Lyons, Nick 662

M
MacDougall, Terry Edward 341
Maeda, Daisaku 164

Magaziner, Ira C. 482
Maguire, Mary Ann 842
Mahajan, V.S. 411
Maki, John M. 231
Mannari, Hiroshi 127, 571, 728, 795, 796, 804
Marengo, Franco 727
Marsh, Robert M. 728, 795, 796, 804
Marshall, Byron K. 729
Maruta, Yoshio 730
Masatsugu, Mitsuyuki 159
Mason, R.H.P. 16
Massey, Joseph A. 276
Masui, Shigeo 848
Matsui, Konomu 670
Matsukawa, Michiya 557
Matsumoto, Keiji 227
Matsushita, Konosuke 483
Matsushita, Mitsuo 207, 209, 210, 923
McCorduck, Pamela 654
McCraw, Thomas K. 519
McCreary, Don R. 924
McKean, Margaret A. 342
McKinnon, Jill L. 228
McKinsey & Company, Inc. 578
McMillan, Charles J. 511, 731, 732
McNelly, Theodore 277
Mellon, Joan 33
Mendel, Douglas H., Jr. 353
Michael, Franz 863
Middleton, B. Jenkins 497
Mikesell, Raymond F. 905, 906
Miller, Roy Andrew 65, 66, 67
Millstein, James 883, 884
Minami, Hiroshi 128
Minami, Ryoshin 412, 413
Minor, Michael 346
Misumi, Juji 733
Mitchell, Douglas D. 278
Miyazaki, Isamu 484
Miyoshi, Shuichi 414
Mizoguchi, Toshiyuki 529
Mochizuki, Mike 347

Author Index

Monden, Yasuhiro 733
Monroe, Wilbur F. 414, 415, 919
Moore, Joe 14
Moran, Robert T. 735, 925
Morioka, Kiyomi 139
Morishima, Akio 237
Morishima, Michio 417
Morita, Akio 663
Moritani, Masanori 188
Morley, James William 160, 354
Morrison, Charles E. 294
Morsbach, Helmut 52
Morse, Ronald A. 485, 853, 864, 865
Morton, W. Scott 17, 82, 94
Munger, Frank 195
Murakami, Hyoe 53, 279
Murakami, Shigeyoshi 140
Murakami, Teruyasu 572
Murakami, Yasusuke 129, 280
Muramatsu, Michio 321
Murata, Kiyoji 642
Musahi, Miyamoto 736
Mushakoji, Kinhide 859
Mutoh, Hiromichi 643

N
Nagasu, Kazuji 418
Najita, Tetsuo 281
Nakamura, Takafusa 419, 420
Nakane, Chie 161
Nakayama, Shigeru 183
Namiki, Nobuaki 756
Namiki, Nobuyoshi 558
Nanto, Dick K. 421
Narayana, Chem L. 612
Nemoto, Masao 824
Nemoto, Tadaaki 719
Nevin, John J. 926
Nishibe, Susumu 54
Nishikawa, Shunsaku 179, 422
Nishimizu, Mieko 401, 423
Noda, Yosiyuki 201
Norbeck, Edward 462
Norbury, Paul 559

O
Odaka, Kunio 840
Ogata, Sadako 866
Ogino, Yoshitaro 409
Oh, Tai K. 737
Ohkawa, Kazushi 424, 425
Ohmae, Kenichi 426
Ohta, Thaddeus Y. 29
Okamoto, Yasuo 738
Okimoto, Daniel I. 361, 486, 927
Okita, Saburo 928, 929
Okochi, Kazuo 841
Okumura, Hiroshi 591
Oldfather, Felicia 14
Olsen, Edward A. 427, 865, 867
O'Neill, P.G. 30
Ono, Setsuko 55
Organisation for Economic Co-operation and Development 86, 162, 191, 428, 487, 540, 797
Organisation for Economic Co-operation and Development. Directorate for Scientific Affairs 87
Organisation for Economic Co-operation and Development. Group on Urban Affairs 192
Oshikawa, Sadaomi 616
Ouchi, William G. 739, 740, 805
Overgaard, H.O. 822
Ozaki, Robert S. 130, 627, 806, 930
Ozawa, Terutomo 429, 582, 592, 596, 597, 672, 798, 819, 931
Ozeki, Toshio 541

P
Palenberg, John 499
Palmore, Erdman B. 163, 164
Pantages, Angeline 657
Park, Yung Ho 88, 282, 322
Pascale, Richard Tanner 573, 741, 742, 743, 842

Passin, Herbert 313, 463
Patrick, Hugh 488, 644
Paulson, Joy 177
Pegels, C. Carl 744
Pempel, T.J. 89, 283, 355, 489, 490
Pepper, H.W.T. 550
Pepper, Thomas 403, 430
Petri, Peter A. 932
Pezeu-Massabuau, Jacques 431
Pharr, Susan J. 180
Picken, Stuart D.B. 141
Piggott, Juliet 63
Pillsbury, Michael 868
Plath, David W. 165, 776
Pollack, David 56
Powers, Elizabeth 177
Powles, Cyril 142
Prindl, Andreas R. 530
Prochaska, Robert J. 745
Pucik, Vladimir 583, 709, 710, 746
Pugel, Thomas A. 491, 933
Pyle, Kenneth B. 348

Q
Quester, George H. 362
Quirk, Peter J. 542

R
Rabino, Samuel 613
Ramseyer, J. Mark 211, 212
Rapp, William V. 492, 678, 934
Rebischung, James 432
Reed, Steven R. 284, 285
Rehder, Robert R. 434, 747, 748
Reich, Michael 190
Reischauer, Edwin O. 18, 19, 57, 799
Repeta, Lawrence 923
Richardson, Bradley M. 286, 287, 310, 328, 435
Richie, Donald 34
Richmond, Frederick W. 935
Rix, Alan G. 323
Roberts, John G. 593

Robins-Mowry, Dorothy 181
Rohlen, Thomas P. 97, 158, 343, 573, 778, 807
Rose, Sanford 560
Rosenberg, Larry J. 615
Rosovsky, Henry 424, 436, 488, 869
Ross, Joel E. 826
Ross, Steven 566
Ross, William C. 826
Rotwein, Eugene 808
Rowland, Diana 632
Ryang, Key Sun 288

S
Sadamoto, Kuni 677
Safizadeh, Hossein 664
Sakakibara, Eisuke 416
Sakamoto, Yoshikazu 296
Sakiya, Tetsuo 652
Samuels, Richard J. 324, 325
Sanderson, Fred H. 936
Sano, Yoshihiro 902
Santora, Joseph C. 749
Sasaki, Naoto 750, 827
Saso, Mary 437
Sato, Hideo 870, 892, 893, 937, 938
Sato, Kazuo 645, 751
Sato, Ryuzo 494
Sato, Sadayuki 598
Sato, Tadao 35
Saxonhouse, Gary R. 937, 938
Schmiegelow, Michele 493
Schonberger, Richard J. 752
Schooler, Carmi 100
Schwendiman, Gary 724, 725
Seidensticker, Edward G. 53
Sekiguchi, Shiro 753
Sengoku, Tamotsu 779
Seo, K.K. 726
Sethi, Narendra K. 754
Sethi, S. Prakash 464, 755, 756
Shapiro, Isaac 871
Sherman, Noah 942
Shibata, Tokue 543
Shiels, Frederick L. 872

Author Index

Shigaki, Irene S. 105
Shilling, David 356
Shimabukuro, Yoshiaki 757
Shimaguchi, Mitsuaki 614, 615
Shimahara, Nobuo K. 83
Shimeall, Warren G. 941
Shimokobe, Atsushi 438
Shimpo, Mitsuru 465
Shinohara, Miyohei 425, 439, 440, 441
Shioda, Nagahide 544
Shirai, Taishiro 843
Shiratori, Rei 289
Shishido, Toshio 494
Siegel, Nancy L. 942
Sigur, Gaston J. 863
Simonis, Heide 442
Simonis, Udo Ernst 442
Sinha, Radha 495
Smith, Charles 443
Smith, Philip R. 446
Smith, Robert J. 166, 167
Snyder, Wayne 496
Sobel, Robert 943
Somkid, Jatusripitak 611
Sorenson, Jay B. 363
Stalk, George, Jr. 679
Steinhoff, Patricia G. 158
Stening, Bruce W. 696
Steslicke, William E. 115, 116
Steven, Rob 168
Stevens, Charles R. 202, 203
Stevenson, Harold 106
Stockwin, J.A.A. 290, 314
Sueno, Akira 574
Sugano, Takuo 927
Sullivan, Jeremiah J. 758
Sumiyoshi, Keyi 815
Suttmeier, Richard P. 291
Suzuki, Norihiko 777
Suzuki, Yoshio 236, 545, 546
Swain, David L. 183
Swanson, Carl L. 756

T

Taira, Koji 444, 445, 520, 844, 944
Takagi, Haruo 759
Takezawa, Shin-ichi 646, 846
Tamura, Kyoko 64
Tan, Hong W. 877
Tanaka, H. William 497
Tanaka, Hideo 204
Tanaka, Hiroshi 780, 781
Tanaka, Kakuei 498
Tanaka, Tsutomu 496
Tang, Roger Y.W. 620
Tanikawa, Hisashi 243
Tasca, Diane 945
Tateishi, Norifumi 499
Tatsuta, Misao 244, 245
Taylor, Allen 946
Taylor, Jared 131
Tazawa, Yutaka 58
Teramoto, Y. 714
Thrush, John C. 446
Thurow, Lester C. 760
Thurston, Donald R. 99
Tiedemann, Arthur E. 31
Tomatsu, Hidenori 196
Tomita, Nobuo 303
Tomoda, Yasumasa 75
Toyama, Kozo 499
Tracy, Phelps 809
Trezise, Philip H. 898
Tsuji, Kiyoaki 292
Tsuji, Yoshihiko 214
Tsurumi, Kazuko 169
Tsurumi, Yoshihiro 447, 562, 584, 599, 761
Tsurutani, Taketsugu 293, 315, 316, 873
Tung, Rosalie L. 600, 762, 947

U

Uchida, Mitsuru 317
Uchino, Tatsuro 448
Ueda, Taizo 435

Ueda, Yoshio   763
Uekusa, Masu   803
Uenohara, Michiyuki   521
Uesugi, Akinori   208
Ui, Jun   193
United States International Trade Commission   656
Upham, Frank K.   238
U.S. Congress. House. Committee on Foreign Affairs. 948
U.S. Congress. House. Committee on Foreign Affairs. Subcommittee on Asian and Pacific Affairs.   874
U.S. Congress. House. Committee on Foreign Affairs. Subcommittee on Foreign Economic Policy.   949
U.S. Congress. House. Committee on Science and Technology. Subcommittee on Science, Research and Technology.   950
U.S. Congress. House. Committee on Ways and Means. Subcommittee on Trade. 951, 952, 953, 954
U.S. Congress. Joint Economic Committee.   522, 551
U.S. Congress. Joint Economic Committee. Subcommittee on Economic Goals and Intergovernmental Policy.   955
U.S. Congress. Joint Economic Committee. Subcommittee on International Trade, Finance, and Security Economics.   820, 956
U.S. Congress. Joint Economic Committee. Subcommittee on Monetary and Fiscal Policy.   500
U.S. Congress. Senate. Committee on Banking, Housing, and Urban Affairs. Subcommittee on International Finance and Monetary Policy.   957
U.S. General Accounting Office.   501, 502, 958
U.S. Industry and Trade Administration.   959

V
Valeo, Francis R.   294
Vandenbrink, John   764
Van Zandt, Howard F.   449, 523, 633
Varley, H. Paul   59
Vaughan, Francis T.   628
Vernon, Raymond   962
Versagi, Frank J.   845
Viksnins, George J.   963
Vogel, Ezra F.   170, 171, 524, 525, 810

W
Wagatsuma, Hiroshi   107, 111
Wakabayashi, Mitsuru   765
Wallace, William McDonald   766
Ward, Robert E.   295, 296
Washington Researchers, Ltd.   647
Watanbe, Masao   60
Watanuki, Joji   297
Weeramantry, C.G.   109
Weil, Frank A.   964
Weinstein, Franklin B.   927
Weinstein, Martin E.   364
Welch, Theodore F.   61
Wetherall, William O.   112
Wheatley, John J.   616
Wheeler, Jimmy W.   430
Wheelwright, Steven C.   767
White, James W.   143, 194, 195, 298
White, Merry I.   84, 85

Author Index

Whitehill, Arthur M. 846
Wilbur F. Monroe Associates, Inc. 965
Williamson, Jeffrey G. 406
Wimberley, Howard 466
Woodall, Brian 506
Worlton, W.J. 184
Woronoff, Jon 450, 451, 625, 626, 768
Wray, Harry 20
Wright, Richard W. 629
Wright-Boulton, J. 452
Wu, Yuan-li 503

Y

Yagi, Eri 183
Yamamoto, George K. 467
Yamamura, Kozo 504, 940
Yang, Charles Y. 769
Yao, Jiro 505
Yasaki, Edward Y. 657
Yashiro, Naohiro 800
Yazawa, Makoto 242
Yoshida, Shigenobu 864, 898
Yoshihara, Kunio 453, 585
Yoshikawa, Akihiro 504
Yoshikawa, Seichi 507
Yoshino, M.Y. 586, 601, 617, 618
Yoshitomi, Masaru 454, 547, 548
Young, Alexander K. 587, 588
Young, Marna Jo 664
Yui, Tsunehiko 554

Z

Zeugner, John F. 95
Zimmerman, Mark 634
Zysman, John 883, 884

TITLE INDEX - BOOKS
The references below are to entry numbers.

A
Adaptation and Education in Japan 83
Amaeru: The Expression of Reciprocal Dependency Needs in Japanese Politics and Law 278
America Versus Japan 519
American Attitudes toward Japan, 1941-1975 857
The American Automobile Industry: Rebirth or Requiem? 649
American Education Through Japanese Eyes 848
American Poetry and Japanese Culture 861
The American Samurai: Blending American and Japanese Managerial Practices 680
The Anatomy of Dependence 122
The Anatomy of Japanese Business 751
The Anatomy of Self: The Individual versus Society 123
Ancestor Worship in Contemporary Japan 166
The Antimonopoly Laws of Japan 208
Antitrust in Japan 205
Appendix to the Report of the Japan-United States Economic Relations Group 913
Arms, Yen & Power: The Japanese Dilemma 344
The Art of Japanese Management: Applications for American Executives 743
As the Japanese See It: Past and Present 36
The Asian Alliance: Japan and United States Policy 863
Asia's New Giant: How the Japanese Economy Works 488
Authority and the Individual in Japan: Citizen Protest in Historical Perspective 156

B
Basic Economic and Social Plan: Toward a Vigorous Welfare Society, 1973-1977 473
Becoming Japanese: The World of the Pre-School Child 103
Beef in Japan: Politics, Production, Marketing & Trade 653
The Behavioral Science of Leadership: An Interdisciplinary Japanese Research Program 733

Beyond National Borders: Reflections on Japan and the World 426
Biographical Dictionary of Japanese History 12
Blind Partners: American and Japanese Responses to an Unknown Future 864
A Book of Five Rings 736
Breaking the Barriers 575
Building a New Japan: A Plan for Remodeling the Japanese Archipelago 498
Business and Society in Japan: Fundamentals for Businessmen 435
Business in Japan: A Guide to Japanese Business Practice and Procedure 559
Business Negotiations with the Japanese 947

C
Case Studies of U.S. Service Trade in Japan 878
The Challenge of Japan's Internationalization: Organization and Culture 127
Changes in the Japanese University: A Comparative Perspective 92
Child Development and Education in Japan 106
Choices for the Japanese Economy 479
Civil Procedure in Japan 216
Classes in Contemporary Japan 168
Comeback: Case by Case: Building the Resurgence of American Business 524
Communism in Japan: A Case of Political Naturalization 339
Comparative Productivity Dynamics: Japan and the United States 816
The Competition: Dealing with Japan 430
Competitive Edge: The Semiconductor Industry in the U.S. and Japan 927
Concise Dictionary of Modern Japanese History 10
Conflict in Japan 158
Consensus Management in Japanese Industry 757
The Constitutional Case Law of Japan: Selected Supreme Court Decisions, 1961-70 229
Contemporary Industrial Relations in Japan 843
Contemporary Japanese Budget Politics 533
The Contemporary Japanese Economy 409
The Control of Imports and Foreign Capital in Japan 627
Coping with U.S.-Japanese Economic Conflicts 893
Corporate Strategy & Structure: Japan and the USA 764
Country to City: The Urbanization of a Japanese Hamlet 462
Credit and Security in Japan: The Legal Problems of Development Finance 243
Crime Control in Japan 70

Title Index - Books

Current Exchange Rate Relationship of the U.S. Dollar and the Japanese Yen: Hearing 951
Current Legal Aspects of Doing Business in Japan and East Asia 221
Currents in Japanese Cinema 35

D

The Death Penalty in Japan: Report 69
Democratizing Japan: The Allied Occupation 296
Development in the Japanese Industrial Structure since Oil Crisis 643
The Development of Industrial Relations Systems: Some Implications of Japanese Experience: Report 836
The Development of Japanese Business, 1600-1980 554
Development Planning: Lessons from Japanese Model 411
Discord in the Pacific: Challenges to the Japanese-American Alliance 869
Doctors in Politics: The Political Life of the Japan Medical Association 115
Doing Business with the Japanese 894
Dojo: Magic and Exorcism in Modern Japan 133

E

The Economic Analysis of the Japanese Firm 801
Economic Development & the Labor Market in Japan 844
The Economic Development of Japan: A Quantitative Study 412
Economic Development of Modern Japan 419
Economic Policy and Development: New Perspectives 494
Economic Statistics Annual 376
Economic Survey of Japan 396
Economic Surveys: Japan 428
Economic Views from Japan: Selections from Economic Eye 471
Education and Equality in Japan 76
Education and Japan's Modernization 73
The Education and Training of Industrial Manpower in Japan 773
Education in Japan: A Century of Modern Development 72
Educational Choice and Labor Markets in Japan 75
Educational Policies in Crisis: Japanese and American Perspectives 77
Educational Policy and Planning: Japan 87
Election Campaigning: Japanese Style 308
The Emerging Japanese Superstate: Challenge and Response 402
Empire of Signs 38
Entrepreneur and Gentleman: A Case History of a Japanese Company 574
Environmental Law in Japan 237
Environmental Policies in Japan 191

The Era of High-Speed Growth: Notes on the Postwar Japanese
   Economy 408

F
Factors Which Hinder or Help Productivity Improvement in the
   Asian Region: National Report--Japan 817
The False Promise of the Japanese Miracle: Illusions and Reali-
   ties of the Japanese Management System 756
Family Planning in Japanese Society: Traditional Birth Control
   in a Modern Urban Culture 101
The Fifth Generation: Artificial Intelligence and Japan's Com-
   puter challenge to the World 654
The Financial Development of Japan, 1868-1977 535
The Flaw in Japanese Management 759
Flexible Automation in Japan 675
For Harmony and Strength: Japanese White-Collar Organization
   in Anthropological Perspective 807
Forecast for Japan: Security in the 1970's 354
Foreign Enterprise in Japan: Laws and Policies 576
Foreign Investment and Japan 621
Form, Style, Tradition: Reflections on Japanese Art and Society
   32
The Fracture of Meaning: Japan's Synthesis of China from the
   Eighth through the Eighteenth Centuries 56
The Fragile Blossom: Crisis and Change in Japan 256
Fragile Interdependence: Economic Issues in U.S.-Japanese Trade
   and Investment 933
Freedom of Expression in Japan: A Study in Comparative Law,
   Politics, and Society 215
From Bonsai to Levi's: When West Meets East: An Insider's Sur-
   prising Account of How the Japanese Live 44
The Future Course of U.S.-Japan Economic Relations 898
The Future of World Economy and Japan 397

G
Getting Your Yen'$ Worth: How to Negotiate with Japan, Inc.
   925
The Growth Potential of the Japanese Economy 410
Guide to Japanese Taxes 247
Guide to Quality Control 828
Guides to Japanese Culture 53

H
The Hidden Sun: Women of Modern Japan 181
High Technology and Japanese Industrial Policy: A Strategy
   for U.S. Policy Makers 903
The Historical Development and Operational Form of Corporate
   Reporting Regulation in Japan 228

Title Index - Books   273

A History of Christianity in Japan   134
A History of Japan   16
A History of Political Institutions in Japan   270
Honda Motor: The Men, the Management, the Machines   652
The Honorable Elders: A Cross-Cultural Analysis of Aging in Japan   163
The Honorable Elders Revisited: A Revised Cross-Cultural Analysis of Aging in Japan   164
The Horizon Concise History of Japan   4
How Japan Innovates: A Comparison with the U.S. in the Case of Oxygen Steelmaking   671
How Japan Works   713
How the United States and Japan See Each Other's Economy: An Exchange of Views between the American and Japanese Committees for Economic Development   382
How to Beat the Japanese at Their Own Game   935
How to Do Business with the Japanese   634
How to Find Information about Japanese Companies and Industries   647
Human Resources in Japanese Industrial Development   775

I
IBM vs. Japan: The Struggle for the Future   943
Improvements in the Quality of Working Life in Three Japanese Industries   646
In Search of a New Industrial Relations Model: Summary of 1984 White Paper on Labor Management Relations   839
An Industrial Geography of Japan   642
Industrial Groupings in Japan   589
Industrial Growth, Trade, and Dynamic Patterns in the Japanese Economy   440
Industrial Organization in Japan   803
Industrial Policy: Case Studies in the Japanese Experience   502
Industrial Policy: Japan's Flexible Approach   501
The Industrial Policy of Japan   487
Industry and Business in Japan   645
Information Societies: Comparing the Japanese and American Experience   145
Innovations in Management: The Japanese Corporation   734
Intangible Factors in Japanese Corporate Strategy   683
The Intellectual Property Law of Japan   239
An Intersection of East and West: Japanese Business Management   682
An Introduction to Japanese Civilization   31
Introduction to Japanese Law   201
The Invisible Link: Japan's Sogo Shosha and the Organization of Trade   586
An Invitation to Japanese Civilization   43

Island of Dreams: Environmental Crisis in Japan   190

J
James D. Hodgson, U.S. Ambassador to Japan, 1974-1977, Speaks on the U.S. Trade Deficit with Japan   907
Japan   377
Japan: A Case of Catching Up   638
Japan: A Comparative View   42
Japan: A Country Study   21
Japan: A Historical Survey   9
Japan: A Postindustrial Power   22
Japan, America, and the Future World Order   859
Japan-America Dialogue: A Survey of Organizational Activities   855
Japan: An Anthropological Introduction   39
Japan: An Economic Survey, 1953-1973   372
Japan and a New World Economic Order   480
Japan and America: A Comparative Study in Language and Culture   64
Japan and Its World: Two Centuries of Change   24
Japan and the United States: Challenges and Opportunities   847
Japan and the United States: Economic and Political Adversaries   909
Japan and Western Civilization: Essays on Comparative Culture   51
Japan as Capital Exporter and the World Economy   548
Japan as Number 1: Lessons for America   170
Japan, Asian Power   11
Japan at the Brink   483
Japan at the Polls: The House of Councillors Election of 1974   304
Japan Business: Obstacles and Opportunities   578
Japan Company Handbook   640
Japan: Divided Politics in a Growth Economy   290
Japan Echo   26
Japan Economic Almanac   395
Japan: Economic and Social Studies in Development   442
Japan: Economic Growth, Resource Scarcity, and Environmental Constraints   427
Japan Electronics Almanac   661
Japan Examined: Perspectives on Modern Japanese History   20
Japan: From Prehistory to Modern Times   8
Japan: Geographical Background to Urban-Industrial Development   407
Japan in the 1980s   289
Japan in the Passing Lane   774
Japan in the Year 2000: Preparing Japan for an Age of Internationalization, the Aging Society, and Maturity   476

Title Index - Books

Japan: Industrial Power of Asia 387
Japan: Its History and Culture 17
Japan: Miracle '70: A Business Guide to the World's Third Economic Power 379
Japan: New Industrial Giant 393
Japan Prepares for Total War: The Search for Economic Security, 1919-1941 369
The Japan Syndrome: Symptoms, Ailments, and Remedies 450
Japan: The Coming Economic Crisis 451
Japan: The Facts of Modern Business and Social Life 432
Japan: The Fragile Superpower 45
Japan, the Government-Business Relationship: A Guide for the American Businessman 516
Japan: The Intellectual Foundations of Modern Japanese Politics 281
Japan: The New Superstate 394
Japan: The Paradox of Progress 144
Japan: The Story of a Nation 18
Japan Today (R. Buckley) 3
Japan Today (K.A. Grossberg) 46
Japan Today: A Westerner's Guide to the People, Language and Culture of Japan 61
Japan: Tradition and Transformation 19
The Japan-U.S. Assembly: Proceedings of a Conference on Japan-U.S. Economic Policy 916
Japan vs. the West: Implications for Management 744
Japan Yesterday and Today 5
The Japanese 57
The Japanese: A Cultural Portrait 130
Japanese-American Relations in the 1970s 849
Japanese and American Economic Policies and U.S. Productivity: Hearings 500
Japanese and Americans: Cultural Parallels and Paradoxes 41
Japanese and U.S. Inflation: A Comparative Analysis 538
Japanese Annual of International Law 240
The Japanese Approach to Product Quality: Its Applicability to the West 827
The Japanese Are Coming: A Multinational Interaction of Firms and Politics 599
The Japanese Auto Industry and the U.S. Market 648
The Japanese Automobile Industry: Technology and Management at Nissan and Toyota 651
The Japanese Automotive Industry: Model and Challenge for the Future? 650
Japanese Blue Collar: The Changing Tradition 834
Japanese Business: A Research Guide with Annotated Bibliography 761

Japanese Business Etiquette: A Practical Guide to Success with
  the Japanese   632
Japanese Business Law and the Legal System   220
The Japanese Business Leaders   571
The Japanese Challenge   639
The Japanese Challenge and the American Response: A Symposium
  917
The Japanese Challenge: The Success and Failure of Economic
  Success   403
The Japanese Challenge to U.S. Industry   635
Japanese Cinema: Film Style and National Character   34
The Japanese Company   686
Japanese Culture   59
Japanese Culture: A Study of Origins and Characteristics   48
Japanese Culture and Behavior: Selected Readings   125
The Japanese Diet and the U.S. Congress   294
Japanese Economic Development: A Short Introduction   453
Japanese Economic Growth: Trend Acceleration in the Twentieth
  Century   424
Japanese Economic Studies   399
The Japanese Economic System: An Institutional Overview   386
The Japanese Economy   366
The Japanese Economy and Business System: Patterns and Influences upon Growth   383
The Japanese Economy in International Perspective   381
The Japanese Edge: The Real Stories behind a Sogo Shosha--One
  of Japan's Unique New Class of Global Corporations   581
The Japanese Educational Challenge: A Commitment to Children
  85
Japanese Electoral Behavior: Social Cleavages, Social Networks
  and Partisanship   310
The Japanese Electronics Industry   659
Japanese Employment and Employee Relations: An Annotated Bibliography   699
The Japanese: Everyday Life in the Empire of the Rising Sun
  120
Japanese Exports to the United States: Analysis of "Import-Pull" and "Export-Push" Factors   965
Japanese Finance: A Guide to Banking in Japan   530
Japanese Finance: Markets and Institutions   532
Japanese Financial Policies and the U.S. Trade Deficit   905
The Japanese Financial System in Comparative Perspective: A
  Study   537
Japanese Folk Literature: A Core Collection and Reference Guide
  62
Japanese Industrial and Labor Policy: Hearing   522
Japanese Industrial Competition to 1990   437
Japanese Industrial Policy   482

Title Index - Books

The Japanese Industrial Society: Its Organizational, Cultural, and Economic Underpinnings 416
The Japanese Industrial System 732
Japanese Industrialization and Its Social Consequences 644
The Japanese Islands: A Physical and Social Geography 431
The Japanese Language in Contemporary Japan: Some Sociolinguistic Observations 65
The Japanese Legal Advisor: Crimes and Punishments 235
The Japanese Legal System: Introductory Cases and Materials 204
Japanese Management: Cultural and Environmental Considerations 724
Japanese Management, 1970-1981: A Selected Guide to Periodical Literature 749
Japanese Manufacturing Techniques: Nine Hidden Lessons in Simplicity 752
The Japanese Marketing System: Adaptations and Innovations 617
The Japanese Mind: The Goliath Explained 118
The Japanese Money Market 534
Japanese Mythology 63
Japanese National Government Publications in the Library of Congress: A Bibliography 29
Japanese Organization Behaviour and Management: An Annotated Bibliography 696
The Japanese Party System: From One-Party Rule to Coalition Government 337
Japanese Patterns of Behavior 124
Japanese Policy and East Asian Security 873
Japanese Policy and Nuclear Arms 363
Japanese Political Culture: Change and Continuity 152
Japanese Politics--An Inside View: Readings from Japan 271
Japanese Politics: Patron-Client Democracy 268
Japanese Private Economic Diplomacy: An Analysis of Business-Government Linkages 622
Japanese Productivity: A Study Mission Report 811
Japanese Productivity: Lessons for America: Hearing 820
Japanese Quality Circles and Productivity 826
Japanese Radicals Revisited: Student Protest in Postwar Japan 326
Japanese Religion: A Survey 138
Japanese Religion in the Modern Century 140
Japanese Religion: Unity and Diversity 135
The Japanese School: Lessons for Industrial America 79
Japanese Securities Regulation 242
The Japanese Social Structure: Its Evolution in the Modern Century 147
Japanese Society (T. Ishida) 153
Japanese Society (C. Nakane) 161

Japanese Society Today 148
Japanese Society: Tradition, Self, and the Social Order 167
The Japanese Steel Industry: With an Analysis of the U.S. Steel
  Import Problem 668
Japanese-Style Management: Its Foundations and Prospects 715
Japanese Tax Policy: Hearing 551
Japanese Technology: Getting the Best for the Least 188
Japanese Trade Policy Formulation 563
The Japanese Trade Surplus and Capital Outflow 557
Japanese-U.S. Business Negotiations: A Cross-Cultural Study
  924
Japanese Voluntary Restraints on Auto Exports to the United
  States: Hearings 52
The Japanese Way: Contemporary Industrial Relations 834
The Japanese Way of Doing Business 689
Japanese Women: Constraint and Fulfillment 178
The Japanese Working Man: What Choice? What Reward? 772
Japan's Commercial Empire 625
Japan's Commission on the Constitution: The Final Report 231
Japan's Cultural History: A Perspective 58
Japan's Decisive Decade: How a Determined Minority Changed
  the Nation's Course in the 1950s 7
Japan's Economic Growth and Educational Change, 1950-1970 446
Japan's Economic Policy 468
Japan's Economic Security 552
Japan's Economy and Japan-U.S. Trade 1982: 100 Questions and
  Answers 477
Japan's Economy and Trade with the United States: Selected
  Papers 955
Japan's Economy at the Crossroads: 30 Years of Transition 398
Japan's Economy: Coping with Change in the International En-
  vironment 486
Japan's Financial Markets: Conflict and Consensus in Policy-
  making 536
Japan's Food Prospects and Policies 936
Japan's Foreign Policy 345
Japan's General Trading Companies: Merchants of Economic Devel-
  opment 582
Japan's High Schools 97
Japan's Invisible Race: Caste in Culture and Personality 111
Japan's Market: The Distribution System 605
Japan's Militant Teachers: A History of the Left-Wing Teachers'
  Movement 98
Japan's Minorities: Burakumin, Koreans, Ainu, and Okinawans
  112
Japan's Modern Myth: The Language and Beyond 66
Japan's Multinational Enterprises 601

Title Index - Books

Japan's New Middle Class: The Salary Man and His Family in a Tokyo Suburb 171
Japan's Nuclear Option: Political, Technical, and Strategic Factors 358
Japan's Options for the 1980s 495
Japan's Outcastes: The Problem of the Burakumin 110
Japan's Parliament: An Introduction 250
Japan's Political System 295
Japan's Postwar Defense Policy, 1947-1968 364
Japan's Postwar Economy: An Insider's View of Its History and Its Future 448
Japan's Public Policy Companies 513
Japan's Response to Crisis and Change in the World Economy 493
Japan's Search for Oil: A Case Study on Economic Nationalism and International Security 503
Japan's Technological Challenge to the West, 1950-1974: Motivation and Accomplishment 672
Japan's Trade Liberalization in the 1960s 564
Japan's Wasted Workers 768
Journal of Japanese Studies 27

K
Kaisha, the Japanese Corporation 679
Key to Japan's Economic Strength: Human Power 600
Keys to Success in Japan's Industrial Goods Market 609
Kikkoman: Company, Clan and Community 569
Kodansha Encyclopedia of Japan 28
Koreans in Japan: Ethnic Conflict and Accommodation 114

L
The Labor Economies of Japan and the United States 378
Labour Law and Industrial Relations in Japan 241
The Labor Market in Japan: Selected Readings 422
Labor Relations in Japan Today 837
Law and Trade Issues of the Japanese Economy: American and Japanese Perspectives 940
Law in Japan: An Annual 200
Lay Buddhism in Contemporary Japan: Reiyukai Kyodan 137
Learning to Be Japanese: Selected Readings on Japanese Society and Education 74
Legal Aspects of Doing Business with Japan, 1985 226
Lessons from Japanese Development: An Analytical Economic History 406
Listening to Japan: A Japanese Anthology 37
The Local Politics of Kyoto 320
A Long-Term Outlook of Japanese and U.S. Economies, 1980 912

M

Made in Japan: Akio Morita and SONY 663
Making It in Management--The Japanese Way 694
Management and Industrial Structure in Japan 750
Management and Worker: The Japanese Solution 782
Management by Japanese Systems 725
Management Career Progress in a Japanese Organization 765
The Management Challenge: Japanese Views 760
Management in Japan and India, with Reference to the United States 726
Manager Revolution! A Guide to Survival in Today's Changing Workplace 707
Manpower Policy in Japan 797
Market Share in Japan 641
Marketing Channels in Japan 614
Marketing in Japan: A Management Guide 618
Marketing Opportunities in Japan 606
The Matsushita Phenomenon 658
Miracle by Design: The Real Reasons behind Japan's Economic Success 704
MITI and the Japanese Miracle: The Growth of Industrial Policy, 1925-1975 514
The Mitsui Bank: A History of the First 100 Years 527
Mitsui: Three Centuries of Japanese Business 593
Modeling Japanese-American Trade: A Study of Asymmetric Interdependence 932
The Modern History of Japan 1
Modern Japan: Aspects of History, Literature and Society 2
Modern Japanese Organization and Decision-Making 810
The Modern Samurai Society: Duty and Dependence in Contemporary Japan 159
Modernization and Stress in Japan 149
Modernization and the Japanese Factory 728
Monetary Factors in Japanese Economic Growth 505
Monetary Policy in Japan 540
Money and Banking in Contemporary Japan: Its Theoretical Setting and Its Application 545
Money, Finance, and Macroeconomic Performance in Japan 546
Monthly Finance Review 539
Multinationalism, Japanese Style: The Political Economy of Outward Dependency 597
Mutual Images: Essays in American-Japanese Relations 854

N

Never Take Yes for an Answer: An Inside Look at Japanese Business for Foreign Businessmen 556
The New Competition 611
New Economic and Social Development Plan 1970-1975 474

Title Index - Books

New Economic and Social Seven-Year Plan 475
Nihongo: In Defence of Japanese 67

O

100 Million Japanese: The Postwar Experience 274
Outline of Japanese Judicial System 233
Outline of Social Insurance in Japan 794

P

The Pacific Alliance: United States Foreign Economic Policy and Japanese Trade Recovery, 1947-1955 882
Pacific Partnership: United States-Japan Trade: Prospects and Recommendations for the Seventies 888
Parliamentary Democracy in Japan 254
Partners in Prosperity: Strategic Industries for the United States and Japan 904
Party in Power: The Japanese Liberal-Democrats and Policy-Making 336
Party Politics in Japan 329
Patterns of Japanese Economic Development: A Quantitative Appraisal 425
Patterns of Japanese Policymaking: Experiences from Higher Education 89
Peasants, Rebels and Outcastes: The Underside of Modern Japan 150
People and Productivity in Japan 819
Perspectives on U.S.-Japan Economic Relations 946
Police and Community in Japan 68
Policy and Politics in Japan: Creative Conservatism 490
Policy and Trade Issues of the Japanese Economy: American and Japanese Perspectives 504
Political Change in Japan: Response to Postindustrial Challenge 293
The Political Culture of Japan 286
A Political History of Japanese Capitalism 388
Political Implications of Cityward Migration: Japan as an Exploratory Test Case 194
Political Leadership in Contemporary Japan 341
Politics and Economics in Contemporary Japan 279
Politics and Government in Japan 277
Politics in Japan 287
Politics in Postwar Japanese Society 297
The Politics of Japan's Energy Strategy: Resources, Diplomacy, Security 485
The Politics of Labor Legislation in Japan: National-International Interaction 838
The Politics of Regional Policy in Japan: Localities Incorporated? 325

The Politics of Trade: U.S. and Japanese Policymaking for the GATT Negotiations 881
Postwar Japan: 1945 to the Present 14
The Postwar Japanese Economy: Its Development and Structure 420
The Price of Affluence: Dilemmas of Contemporary Japan 458
Productivity and Quality Control: The Japanese Experience 830
Prologue to the Future: The United States and Japan in the Postindustrial Age 160
Psychological Dimensions of U.S.-Japanese Relations 860
Psychology of the Japanese People 128
Public Administration in Japan 292
Public and Private Self in Japan and the United States: Communicative Styles of Two Cultures 117
Public Finance in Japan 543

Q
Quality Control Circles of Work: Cases from Japan's Manufacturing and Service Sectors 825

R
R&D Management Systems in Japanese Industry 670
Recent Economic Trends in Japan in 1977 433
The Relation between Final Demand and Income Distribution, with Application to Japan 385
Religion in Changing Japanese Society 139
Religions of Japan: Many Traditions within One Sacred Way 136
Report of the Japan-United States Economic Relations Group 914
Responses to the Japanese Challenge in High Technology: Innovation, Maturity, and U.S.-Japanese Competition in Microelectronics 883
Reviews of National Policies for Education: Japan 86
The Rise of Modern Japan 6
Robotics/Artificial Intelligence/Productivity: U.S.-Japan Concomitant Coalitions 674
Robotization: Its Implications for Management 676
Robots in Manufacturing: Key to International Competitiveness 673
Robots in the Japanese Economy: Facts about Robots and Their Significance 677
The Role of Technical Information in U.S. Competitiveness with Japan: Hearings 950
The Roots of Modern Japan 13

S
Saints and Samurai: The Political Culture of the American and Japanese Elites 249
Saving in Postwar Japan 526

Title Index - Books

Science and Society in Modern Japan: Selected Historical Sources 183
Science and Technology in Japan 182
A Season of Voting: The Japanese Elections of 1976 and 1977 313
Securities Regulation in Japan 245
Selected Readings on Modern Japanese Society 467
The Self-Made Man in Meiji Japanese Thought: From Samurai to Salary Man 154
Semiconductor Trade and Japanese Targeting: Hearing 957
Shadows of the Rising Sun: A Critical View of the "Japanese Miracle" 131
Shinohata: A Portrait of a Japanese Village 455
Shinto: Japan's Spiritual Roots 141
A Short Economic History of Modern Japan 367
The Silent Power: Japan's Identity and World Role 25
64K Dynamic Random Access Memory Components from Japan: Determination of the Commission 656
Smaller Is Better: Japan's Mastery of the Miniature 126
Smart Bargaining: Doing Business with the Japanese 902
Social Change and Community Politics in Urban Japan 195
Social Change and the Individual: Japan before and after Defeat in World War II 169
Social Structures and Economic Dynamics in Japan up to 1980 146
Socialization for Achievement: Essays on the Cultural Psychology of the Japanese 121
Sogoshosha: Engines of Export-Based Growth 584
The Sogo Shosha: Japan's Multinational Trading Companies 588
Sogo Shosha: The Vanguard of the Japanese Economy 585
The Sokagakkai and Mass Society 143
The SONY Vision 662
Sources of Japanese History 15
Standard Trade Index of Japan 561
Strategic Management in the United States and Japan: A Comparative Analysis 762
Strategy and Structure of Japanese Enterprises 722
The Strategy of Japanese Business 876
Structural Adjustment in Japan, 1970-82 637
Structural Changes in Japan's Economic Development 441
The Structure and Operation of the Japanese Economy 370
Suburban Tokyo: A Comparative Study in Politics and Social Change 248
Supplemental Report of the Japan-United States Economic Relations Group 915

T

Tax and Trade Guide: Japan   246
Teachers and Politics in Japan   99
Technology Transfer and Foreign Trade: The Case of Japan, 1950-1966   562
The Textile Wrangle: Conflict in Japanese-American Relations, 1969-1971   892
Theory, Law and Policy of Contemporary Japanese Treaties   350
A Theory of Japanese Democracy   269
Theory Z: How American Business Can Meet the Japanese Challenge   739
The Thorn in the Chrysanthemum: Suicide and Economic Success in Modern Japan   151
The Threat of Japanese Multinationals: How the West Can Respond   595
Three Decades in Shiwa: Economic Development and Social Change in a Japanese Farming Community   465
Tokugawa Religion: The Cultural Roots of Modern Japan   132
Tokyo and Washington: Dilemmas of a Mature Alliance   872
Total Quality Control for Management: Strategies and Techniques from Toyota and Toyota Gosei   824
Toward a New International Economic System: A Joint Japanese-American View   890
Toward Industrial Democracy: Management and Workers in Modern Japan   840
Towards an Integrated Social Policy in Japan   162
Trade with Japan: Hearings   953
Tradition and Change in Postindustrial Japan: The Role of the Political Parties   330
Tradition and Modern Japan   30
Training Japanese Managers   690
Transfer Pricing Practices in the United States and Japan   620
The Turning Point in Economic Development: Japan's Experience   413
Two Hungry Giants: The United States and Japan in the Quest for Oil and Ores   962

U

Uneasy Partnership: Competition and Conflict in U.S.-Japanese Trade Relations   889
The United States and Japan: An Economic, Cultural and Political Thicket   908
United States Foreign Economic Policy toward Japan: Hearings   949
The United States-Japan Economic Problem   880
United States-Japan Economic Relations: Hearings and Markup   948
United States-Japan Relations: Hearings   874

Title Index - Books

United States-Japan Trade: Issues and Problems 958
United States-Japan Trade Relations: Hearings 954
United States-Japanese Relations: The 1970's 849
Urban Policies in Japan: A Review 192
U.S. Export Opportunities to Japan 959
U.S.-Japan Automobile Diplomacy: A Study in Economic Confrontation 896
U.S.-Japan Economic Relations: A Symposium on Critical Issues 960
U.S.-Japan Economic Relations Yearbook 961
U.S.-Japan Strategic Reciprocity: A Neo-Internationalist View 867
U.S.-Japanese Agricultural Trade Relations 887
U.S.-Japanese Competition in the Semiconductor Industry: A Study in International Trade and Technological Development 884
U.S.-Japanese Economic Relations: Cooperation, Competition, and Confrontation 945
U.S.-Japanese Economic Relations: Hearings 956
U.S.-Japanese Energy Relations: Cooperation and Competition 853
U.S.-Japanese Relations: What Should the Future Hold? 875

V
Venture Businesses in Japan and VB Promotion Policies 603
Venture Capital in Britain, America and Japan 619

W
The Waves at Genji's Door: Japan through Its Cinema 33
What Is Total Quality Control? The Japanese Way 829
White Paper on Japanese Economy 374
The Whole Japan Book 23
Why Has Japan "Succeeded"? Western Technology and the Japanese Ethos 417
Why the Japanese Have Been So Successful in Business 702
Willing Workers: The Work Ethics in Japan, England, and the United States 779
With Respect to the Japanese, a Guide for Americans 119
Women in Changing Japan 177
Work and Lifecourse in Japan 776
Work, Mobility, and Participation: A Comparative Study of American and Japanese Industry 771
Workers and Employers in Japan: The Japanese Employment Relations System 841
Working Women in Japan: Discrimination, Resistance, and Reform 172
World Trade War 626

Y
Yakuza: The Explosive Account of Japan's Criminal Underworld 71
The Yen/Dollar Agreement: Liberalizing Japanese Capital Markets 897

Z
Zen 47

TITLE INDEX - ARTICLES
The references below are to entry numbers.

A
"Adopting Japanese Management: Some Cultural Stumbling Blocks" 692
"The Age of New Middle Mass Politics: The Case of Japan" 280
"Aggregate Images of American and Japanese Products: Implications on International Marketing" 612
"Analysis of the Newly Amended Commercial Code of Japan" 217
"Anatomy of Japan: The Bureaucrats" 260
"Anticompetitive Practices in the Distribution of Goods and Services in Japan: The Problem of Distribution 'Keiretsu'" 608
"Antimonopoly Law of Japan--Potential Consequences of International Contract Violations under Article 6" 207
"Antimonopoly Law of Japan Relating to International Business Transactions" 210
"Antitrust Aspects of U.S.-Japanese Trade" 899
"An Appraisal of Japanese Financial Policies" 547
"Aspects of Nonverbal Communication in Japan" 52
"Aspects of the Legal, Political and Policy Issues That Will Confront the U.S.-Japan Trading Community during the Remainder of the 1980's" 895
"Awarding Bonuses the Japanese Way" 783

B
"Behind Japan's Success" 508
"Beliefs and Attitudes of the Japanese Left during the Early 1970s" 333
"'Big Business' and Education Policy in Japan" 88
"Bonus Payments, On-the-Job Training, and Lifetime Employment in Japan" 793
"Budget Policy and Economic Stability in Postwar Japan" 496
"The Bureaucratization of Policymaking in Postwar Japan" 283
"Business Groups in a Market Economy" 590

C
"Can U.S. Business Survive Our Japanese Trade Policy?" 926
"Causes and Patterns in the Postwar Growth" 439
"Changes in Japanese Small Business" 602
"Changes in the Yen Valuation and Japan's Distributive Mechanism" 544
"Changing Characteristics of the Japanese Employment System" 790
"The Changing Fortunes of Japan's Progressive Governors" 284
"Changing Roles of the Sogo Shoshas, the Manufacturing Firms, and the MITI in the Context of the Japanese 'Trade or Die' Mentality" 517
"Child Behavior and Child Rearing in Japan and the United States: An Interim Report" 100
"Child Care Practices in Japan and the United States: How Do They Reflect Cultural Values in Young Children?" 105
"The Chips Are Down: Legal Implications of Alleged Japanese Unfair Practices in the United States Semiconductor Industry" 942
"Come Along, It's Time to Join the Human Race" 623
"Communication and Decision Making across Cultures: Japanese and American Comparisons" 741
"Comparing R&D Strategies of Japanese and U.S. Firms" 832
"Comparison of Selected Work Factors in Japan and the United States" 842
"The Conception of Nature in Japanese Culture" 60
"Concepts and Methodology of Regional Development" 438
"Conservative Dominance in Japanese Politics" 259
"Constitution and Obscenity: Japan and the U.S.A." 230
"Consumerism and Japan's New Citizen Politics" 155
"Cooperation and Control in Japanese Nursery Schools" 96
"Corporate Divorce--Japanese Style" 225
"Corporate Taxation in Japan" 550
"Corporation, Culture and Environment: The Japanese Model" 389
"The Costs of the Consensual Myth: Antitrust Enforcement and Institutional Barriers to Litigation in Japan" 211
"The Crisis of Japan's Liberal Democratic Party" 338
"Critical Choice for Japan: Cooperation or Conflict with the United States" 447
"A Critique of Theory Z" 758
"Culture and Communication in the Modern Japanese Corporate Organization" 685
"Culture and the Management of Time: A Comparison of Japanese and American Top Management Practice" 693

Title Index - Articles

D

"A Decade of Japanese Diet Elections, 1967-1976: Conservatism and Radicalism Reevaluated" 305
"Decision Making--Eastern and Western Style" 718
"Decision Models and Japanese Foreign Policy Decision Making" 346
"Demystifying Japanese Distribution" 615
"Determinants of Administrative Control: A Test of a Theory with Japanese Factories" 809
"Determinants of Female Labor-Force Participation" 179
"Disintegrative versus Integrative Aspects of Interdependence: The Japanese Case" 624
"Distribution in Japan: Problems and Changes" 604
"Doctors, Patients, and Government in Modern Japan" 116
"Dollar Crisis" 414

E

"Economic Concentration and Monopoly in Japan--A Second View" 808
"Economic Growth and Intergenerational Change in Japan" 459
"The Economic Growth of Japan" 365
"Economic Planning in Postwar Japan" 484
"Economic Planning in Postwar Japan: A Case Study in Policy Making" 509
"'Ecstasy Years'--Old Age in Japan" 165
"Education in Japan" 78
"Educational and Cultural Trends in Japan Today" 82
"The Emergence of Japan's Multinationalism: Patterns and Competitiveness" 596
"An Empirical Study on Ideal Personal Characteristics of Japanese OR/MS Leaders" 719
"Employment and Wages" 405
"Enforcement of Japanese Securities Legislation" 244
"Establishing a Joint Venture Company in Japan: Legal Considerations" 223
"Exchange Rate Policy in Japan: Leaning against the Wind" 542
"Export Control and Export Cartels in Japan" 209
"Exports and Economic Growth: The Case of Postwar Japan" 371

F

"Facing Up to the Trade Gap with Japan" 877
"Factors Stimulating Technical Progress in Japanese Industries: The Case of Computerization in Steel" 667
"Fair Trade Commission vs. MITI: History of the Conflicts between the Antimonopoly Policy and the Industrial Policy in the Post War Period of Japan" 507
"The Family as a Firm and the Firm as a Family in Japan: The Case of Kikkoman Shoyu Company Limited" 568

"The Fifth Liberalization of Capital Movements into Japan" 470
"A Financial Comparison of Japanese and U.S. Manufacturers" 664
"Focus: Industrial Japan '84" 443
"Focus on Japan: Nakasone's Post-Industrial Society" 380
"Foreign Capital in Japan" 472
"Formal Management Relations Practices in Japanese Business and Industrial Organizations" 697
"Formation of the Management System in Meiji Japan: Personnel Management in Large Corporations" 712
"Fragile Blossom, Fragile Superpower: A New Interpretation?"" 55
"Functional Alternatives and Economic Development: An Empirical Example of Permanent Employment in Japan" 784
"The Future of Japanese Nationality: An Essay in Contemporary History" 348

G
"Ghost-Hunting: Local Party Organization in Japan" 332
"The 'Gikan' Question in Japanese Government: Bureaucratic Curiosity or Institutional Failure?" 291
"The Governmental Advisory Commission System in Japan" 282
"The Grand Strategy of Japanese Business" 738
"Group Rights and Individual Rights in Japan" 108
"Growth of Japanese Exports" 558
"A Guide to the Study of Japanese Law" 196
"Guided Free Enterprise in Japan" 525

H
"A Hidden Cause of America's Trade Deficit with Japan" 901
"High Personal Saving Rate and Changes in the Consumption in Postwar Japan" 529
"The House of Councillors Election in Japan: The LDP Hangs in There" 317
"How Japan Competes" 392
"How Japan Manages Declining Industries" 636
"How Japanese Business Treats Its Older Workers" 753
"How Japanese Executives Manage the New Zaibatsu" 706
"How to Negotiate in Japan" 633
"Human Rights in Japan: Some Protections and Problems" 109

I
"Ie Society as a Pattern of Civilization" 129
"Images of Conflict Resolution and Social Control: American and Japanese Attitudes Toward the Adversary System" 197
"The Impact of Economic Growth Policies on Local Politics in Japan" 321

"Index of Selected Bilateral Treaties: United States and Japan" 856
"Industrial Planning in Japan" 511
"Industrial Policy and Employment in Japan" 520
"The Industrial Targeting Practices of Japan and the Domestic Machine Tool Industry" 900
"The Influence of Social Structure and Culture on Human Behavior in Modern Japan" 40
"Injured Industries, Imports and Industrial Policy: A Comparison of United States and Japanese Practices" 497
"Innovation: Japan Races Ahead as U.S. Falters" 185
"Inside the Tokyo Ministry of Finance: The Most Powerful Men in Japan" 531
"An Integrated Management System: Lessons from the Japanese Experience" 709
"Interfirm Relations in an Enterprise Group: The Case of Mitsubishi" 591
"An International 'Wall Street' Sprouts in Tokyo" 541
"The 'Internationalization' of the Japanese Economy" 478
"Internationalization of the Japanese General Trading Companies" 587
"Introduction to Joint Venturing in Japan" 628
"Is Japanese Government Really Centralized?" 285
"Is Japanese Management Really So Different?" 731

J
"Japan after the 'Oil Shock': An International Resource Pauper" 444
"Japan and the Nuclear Non-Proliferation Treaty" 362
"Japan and the U.S.--The Security Agenda" 852
"Japan as a Highly Developed Mass Society: An Appraisal" 54
"Japan, China and the United States: Economic Relations and Prospects" 928
"Japan Faces Its Future: The Political Economics of Administrative Reform" 275
"Japan in 1982: Doing Nothing Is Best?" 252
"Japan in the Computer Age" 655
"'Japan Inc.'--The Total Conglomerate" 518
"Japan Is Opening Up for 'Gaijin' Who Know How" 577
"Japan--Is the Market Open? A View of the Japanese Market Drawn from U.S. Corporate Experience" 964
"Japan: Its Industrial Policies and Corporate Behavior" 492
"Japan '78: Time for Reflection, Kabuki-Style" 261
"Japan: The Problem of Success" 456
"Japan-United States Trade Friction: The Reciprocity Issue" 921
"Japan-U.S. Economic Relations" 918
"Japan--Where Operations Really Are Strategic" 767

"Japanese-American Economic Relations in Crisis" 937
"A Japanese-American Economic War?" 885
"Japanese-American Relations" 938
"Japanese and Western Quality: A Contrast in Methods and Results" 716
"Japanese Antitrust Enforcement after the Oil Embargo" 212
"Japanese Business Entities" 219
"Japanese Business Ideology and Labor Policy" 729
"The Japanese Cabinets, 1885-1973; an Elite Analysis" 257
"A Japanese Card?" 868
"The Japanese Communist Party after Fifty Years" 331
"The Japanese Communist Party's Recent Election Defeats: A Signal of Decline?" 307
"The Japanese Company Controversy" 701
"Japanese Culture and the Business Boom" 449
"Japanese Defense in the 1970s: The Public View" 353
"Japanese Economic Growth: The Human Equation" 384
"Japanese Economy in the Seventies" 418
"Japanese Education: How Do They Do It?" 84
"The Japanese Employment System" 788
"A Japanese Explains Japan's Business Style" 681
"Japanese Fair Trade Commission Review of International Agreements" 206
"Japanese Foreign Economic Policy: The Domestic Bases for International Behavior" 489
"Japanese Foreign Investment Regulation: Semantics and Reality" 222
"The Japanese General Trading Company: Model for the United States" 579
"Japanese Law and the Japanese Legal System: Perspectives for the American Business Lawyer" 202
"The Japanese Legal Milieu and Its Relationship to Business" 224
"Japanese Management--A Critical Review" 737
"Japanese Management: An American Challenge" 747
"Japanese Management Philosophy: Can It Be Exported?" 721
"Japanese Management Practices. Part 1." 755
"Japanese Management Practices and Productivity" 710
"Japanese Management: Tradition under Strain" 700
"Japanese Managerial Behavior and 'Excessive Competition'" 678
"The Japanese Managerial Scene: An Introductory View" 754
"The Japanese Method of Preparing Today's Graduate to Become Tomorrow's Manager" 780
"Japanese Multinational Enterprises: Potential and Limits" 598
"Japanese Participative Management--Or How 'Ringi Seido' Can Work for You" 735
"A Japanese Pilgrimage" 373
"Japanese Politics in Transition?" 334

"Japanese Politics of Advice in Comparative Perspective: A Framework for Analysis and a Case Study" 266
"Japanese Politics of Equality in Transition: The Case of the Burakumin" 113
"Japanese Postwar Attitudes towards International Trade and Investment" 469
"The Japanese Private University" 90
"Japanese Productivity: Adapting to Changing Comparative Advantage in the Face of Lifetime Employment Commitments" 812
"Japanese Quality Circles: A Managerial Response to the Productivity Problem" 822
"Japanese Quality Management" 703
"Japanese Regulation of Foreign Transactions and Private-Law Consequences" 218
"Japanese Security Policies and the United States" 357
"The Japanese Spirit of Enterprise, 1867-1970" 390
"Japanese Supercomputer Technology" 184
"Japanese Taxation of the Foreign Income of Japanese Corporations" 548
"Japanese Technology at a Turning Point" 185
"Japanese Technology: Successes and Strategies" 186
"The Japanese Textile Industry: Structural Adjustment and Government Policy" 512
"Japanese Treaty Patterns" 349
"Japanese Universities and Students Today" 94
"Japanese-U.S. Relations and the Security Treaty: A Japanese Perspective" 857
"Japanese Views on Industrial Organization" 806
"The Japanese Way" 799
"Japanese Women and Party Politics" 173
"Japanese Women and the Dual-Track Employment System" 174
"Japanese Women in the Politics of the Seventies" 175
"Japanese World of Work: An Interpretive Survey" 798
"Japan's Beleaguered Ruling Party" 342
"Japan's Bureaucratic Edge" 865
"Japan's Computer Industry" 657
"Japan's December 1983 House of Representatives Election: The Return of Coalition Politics" 299
"Japan's 'Double' Elections" 300
"Japan's Economic Future" 436
"Japan's Economy" 421
"Japan's Economy: End of the Miracle?" 460
"Japan's Foreign Policy" 347
"Japan's Global Engagement" 886
"Japan's Growth Economy: Joy and Anguish" 461
"Japan's Images and Options: Not a Challenger, but a Supporter" 360
"Japan's Industrial Groups" 592

"Japan's Industrial Policy: Instruments, Trends, and Effects" 491
"Japan's Nakasone Government" 265
"Japan's Non-Nuclear Policy: The Problem of the NPT" 361
"Japan's Nuclear Allergy" 355
"Japan's 'PXL' Decision: The Politics of Weapons Procurement" 359
"Japan's Quantitative Restrictions on the Importation of Agricultural Products" 922
"Japan's Search for Food Security" 375
"Japan's Strategy for the '80s" 400
"Japan's Synergistic Society: How It Works and Its Implications for the U.S." 434
"Japan's Technological Challenge to the West: At a New Crossroads" 429
"Japan's 35th House of Representatives Election: The LDP Toys with a Return to 1954" 301
"Japan's 34th General Election: Cautious Change Amidst Incremental Instability" 303
"Japan's Trade Problem and the Yen" 553
"Joint Venture Problems in Japan" 629
"Judicial Review in Japan: The Strategy of Restraint" 232
"The Judicial System of Japan" 234

K
"The Komeito and Local Japanese Politics" 318
"Komeito: Sokagakkai-ism in Japanese Politics" 340

L
"The Late-Developer Hypothesis: An Evaluation of Its Relevance for Japanese Employment Practices" 785
"The LDP in Transition? Mass Membership Participation in Party Leadership Selection" 315
"Learning from the Japanese" 821
"Learning from the Japanese: Prospects and Pitfalls" 687
"Learning from the Japanese: What or How?" 727
"Learning to Do Business with 'Japan, Inc.'" 523
"The Liberal Democratic Party Revisited: Continuity and Change in the Party's Structure and Performance" 335
"Liberalization and Japanese Trade in the 1970s" 555
"Lifetime Commitment in Japan: Roles, Norms, and Values" 795
"The Lifetime Employment System in Japan: Its Reality and Future" 791
"Litigation and Moral Consciousness in Japan: An Interpretive Analysis of Four Japanese Pollution Suits" 238
"Local Politics in Japan: The Changing of the Guard" 324
"The Local Public Personnel System in Japan" 322
"Lockheed and Japanese Politics" 251

Title Index - Articles

M
"Male Female Wage Differentials in Japan: A Rational Explanation" 800
"Management Can Learn from Japan" 691
"The Management of Innovation in Japan: Seven Forces That Make the Difference" 815
"The Management of Innovation in Japan: The Tetsuri Way" 730
"The Management of Innovation in Japan: Why It Is So Successful" 745
"Management Responsibility to Minority Shareholders in Japan: Derivative Suit in West-East Melting Pot" 227
"Management Styles: American Vis-a-Vis Japanese" 769
"Marketing and Antitrust in Japan" 607
"Marketing in Japan: Problems and Possibilities for American Business" 616
"Maternal Strategies for Regulating Children's Behavior" 102
"The Mazda Turnaround" 573
"The Meaning of Work: American and Japanese Paradigms" 684
"Meeting the Japanese Economic Challenge" 368
"Mega-Research Investment for Japanese Microelectronics" 660
"Mergers and Economic Concentration in Japanese Manufacturing Industry" 665
"Minerva and the Crane ('Tsuru'): Birds of a Feather? Comparative Research and Japanese Political Change--A Review Article" 253
"The Missing Leader: Japanese Youths' View of Political Authority" 276
"Modern Japanese Law as an Instrument of Comparison" 203
"More about Late Development" 789

N
"The Narita Conflict" 255
"National Culture-Business Relations: United States and Japan Contrasted" 565
"National Policy and Company R&D in Japan" 521
"Negotiating and Administering an International Sales Contract with the Japanese" 630
"Negotiating Contracts with the Japanese" 631
"New Employee Education in Japan" 781
"A New Era of Japanese Politics: Tokyo's Gubernatorial Election" 316
"A New Look at 'Lifetime Commitment' in Japanese Industry" 796
"New Thinking in Japanese-American Trade" 879
"The 1981 Administrative Reform in Japan" 262
"The 1975-76 Debate over Ratification of the NPT in Japan" 263
"The 1973-1978 Stagflation in Japan: A Watershed?" 445
"The 1969 General Election in Japan" 309
"Non-Western Work Organizations" 802

"Nuclear Power and Japan's Proliferation Option" 352

O
"On Living with Your Past: Style and Structure among Contemporary Japanese Merchant Families" 466
"Organization Development in Japan" 720
"Organizational Paradigms: A Commentary on Japanese Management and Theory Z Organizations" 740
"'Over-Loan' and the Investment Behavior of Firms" 528

P
"Participative Management Practice and Work Humanisation in Japan" 688
"Patience in Human Relations: Key to Doing Business in Japan" 763
"The Performances of Merging Firms in Japanese Manufacturing Industry: 1964-75" 666
"Permanent Employment in Japan: Facts and Fantasies" 786
"Personal Value Systems of Japanese Managers" 698
"Political Corruption and Social Structure in Japan" 267
"Politics-Economics-Public Policy Linkages in Japan, 1965-1969" 258
"The Politics of Criminal Law Reform: Japan" 236
"The Politics of Economic Relations between the United States and Japan" 910
"The Politics of Electoral Reform in Japan" 311
"Postwar Japanese Political Leadership: A Study of Prime Ministers" 288
"Power and Trade in U.S.-Japanese Relations" 944
"The Price of Success: Japan Revisited" 457
"Procedural Fairness to Foreign Litigants as Stressed by Japanese Courts" 198
"Productivity Lessons from Japan" 818
"Promotion Patterns in a Japanese Trading Company" 583
"A Proposition on Efficient Decision-Making in the Japanese Corporation" 708
"Prospects for United States-Japan Trade Relations" 920
"Protest Movements in Japan: A New Politics" 327
"The Psychological Interdependence of Family, School, and Bureaucracy in Japan" 80
"Public Opinion Trends in Japan" 49
"Public Policy in the Japanese Prefectures: The Impact of Environment, Politics, and Resources upon Policy Formation" 319
"Public Servants and Public Interests in Contemporary Japan" 832

Q
"Quality Circles: Japanese Success Story" 823

R

"R&D in Japan: A Future That Will Challenge the U.S." 831
"The Race of American and Japanese Personal Computer Manufacturers for Dominance of the US Market" 613
"The Really Important Difference between Japanese and Western Management" 714
"A Reassessment of Japan's Naval Defense Needs" 356
"Recent Changes in Long Range Corporate Planning in Japan" 572
"The Reemployment of Retired Government Bureaucrats in Japanese Big Business" 515
"The Reform of Japanese Higher Education" 93
"Regulation of Resale Price Maintenance in Japan" 214
"Relative Profitability of the US and Japanese Steel Industries" 669
"Restricting the Supply of Japanese Automobiles: Sovereign Compulsion or Sovereign Collusion?" 923
"A Review of Recent U.S.-Japan Economic Relations" 939
"The Rise of Tokyo as an International Financial Center" 415
"The Risen Sun: Japanese Gaullism?" 871
"The Roles of Japanese Industrial Policy for Export Success: A Theoretical Perspective" 481

S

"SALT, the NPT, and U.S.-Japanese Security Relations" 850
"A Sampling of Japanese Economic Issues--A Review Article" 391
"The Secret of Japan's Export Prowess" 560
"The Secret of Japan's Success" 510
"The Secret Weapon of Japanese Business" 766
"Secrets of Japanese Success" 452
"Sex Discrimination in Employment: The Legal Status of the Working Woman in Japan" 176
"Sheathing the Sword of Justice in Japan: An Essay on Law without Sanctions" 199
"Shifting Alignments in Japanese Party Politics: The April 1974 Election for Governor of Kyoto Prefecture" 314
"Should the United States Restrict Technology Trade with Japan?" 931
"Significant Differences between Japanese and American Businesses" 567
"The Singularities of Japanese Pollution" 193
"Small Group Activity at Musahi Semi-Conductor Works" 814
"Socio-Economic Development and Political Democracy in Japanese Prefectures" 273
"Sociological Studies in Japan: Prewar, Postwar, and Contemporary Stages" 157
"Sogo Shoshas and Japan's Foreign Economic Relations" 580
"Some Aspects of the Contemporary Japanese Family: Once Confucian, Now Fatherless?" 107

"Some Japanese Views on United States-Japan Relations in the 1980s" 866
"Some Principles Governing the Thought and Behavior of Japanists (Contextualists)" 50
"The Sources of Japanese Economic Growth: 1955-71" 423
"Spin-Out Employees in Japanese Business Society: Their Problems and Prospects" 777
"'Spiritual Education' in a Japanese Bank" 778
"Statistical Evidence on the Diversification of Japanese Large Firms" 570
"The Steel Dumping Issue in Recent U.S.-Japanese Relations" 919
"Strategic Planning for the Protection of U.S. Technology and Intellectual Property in the Trade Relationship between the United States and Japan" 941
"The Structure of the Japanese Family" 104
"Sumitomo: How the 'Keiretsu' Pulls Together to Keep Japan Strong" 594
"Supply Management: The Economic Key to Survival in the 1980s" 454
"Systems Outputs, Social Environment, and Political Cleavages in Japan: The Case of the 1969 General Election" 306

T
"The Tanabata House of Councillors Election in Japan" 302
"Tanaka Kakuei, Structural Corruption, and the Advent of Machine Politics in Japan" 272
"Technology and Size as Determinants of the Organizational Structure of Japanese Factories" 804
"The Textile Negotiations: A Failure to Communicate" 891
"The Textile Negotiations: Japan's Point of View" 929
"The Theory of Institutionalization: Permanent Employment and Tradition in Japan" 787
"There *Is* Such a Thing as a Free Ride" 351
"Tokyo Metropolitan Assembly Election--1973" 312
"Tokyo: The Overpopulated Megalopolis" 189
"Tokyo's Governor Minobe and Progressive Local Politics in Japan" 323
"Trade Friction, Administration Guidance and Antimonopoly Law in Japan" 499
"Tradition and Politics in Studies of Contemporary Japan" 298
"Tradition, Modernization, Education: The Case of Japan" 81
"Trustbusting in Japan: Cartels and Government-Business Cooperation" 213
"'Tsukiai'--Obligatory Personal Relationships of Japanese White-Collar Company Employees" 770
"Type Z Organization: Stability in the Midst of Mobility" 805

U

"Understanding Behavior in Japan's Academic Marketplace" 91
"Unemployment in Japan: Policy and Politics" 792
"United States-Japanese Economic Relations" 930
"United States-Japanese Relations: A Japanese View" 870
"United States Protectionism in Economic Relations with Japan" 911
"Urbanization and Political Participation: The Case of Japan" 328
"U.S. and Japanese Economic Growth, 1952-1974: An International Comparison" 401
"U.S.-Japanese Bilateral Trade and the Yen-Dollar Exchange Rate: An Empirical Analysis" 906
"U.S.-Japanese Nuclear Relations: Structural Change and Political Strain" 862
"U.S.-Japanese Trade: Perceptions and Reality" 963

V

"Value Change and Partisan Change in Japan: The Silent Revolution Revisited" 264
"The 'Venture Boom' and Japanese Industrial Policy" 506
"Violence at Yoka High School: The Implications for Japanese Coalition Politics of the Confrontation between the Communist Party and the Buraku Liberation League" 343

W

"What Accounts for Japan's High Rate of Growth?" 404
"What American and Japanese Mangers Are Learning from Each Other" 748
"What American Labor/Management Can Learn from Japanese Unions" 845
"What Can We Learn from the Japanese? The Puzzle of Higher Education in Japan" 95
"What Is Japan, and What Is Not Japan?" 566
"What Makes Japanese Car Manufacturers So Productive?" 813
"What Makes Japanese Products Better?" 717
"What the United States Has to Do to Compete with Japan" 934
"What We Can Learn from Japanese Management" 695
"White Collar Human Resource Management: A Comparison of the US and Japanese Automobile Industries" 746
"Why Japanese Business Is Losing Its Halo" 464
"Why Japanese Factories Work" 711
"Will Success Spoil Japanese Management?" 723
"Winds of Change: Economic Realism and Japanese Labor Management" 705
"Women in Japan Today" 180
"Workplace Harmony: Another Japanese 'Miracle'" 846
"The World's Champion Marketers: The Japanese" 610

Y
"'Yasukuni Jinja Hoan': Religion and Politics in Contemporary Japan" 142

Z
"Zen and the Art of Management" 742

SUBJECT INDEX
The references below are to entry numbers.

A
Administrative reform 262, 275, 490
Advisory commission system 282
Aged 163, 164, 165, 794
Aging workers 456, 476, 686, 753, 790, 839
Agricultural trade 887, 922, 936
Ainu (see Minorities)
All-Japan Prefectural and Municipal Workers' Union (see Jichiro)
Allied Occupation 8, 18, 228, 274, 296
Amae 122, 278, 416, 689
Amaeru 278
Amai 278
AMES 673
Ampo Crisis 326
Ancestor worship 166
Arab Oil Embargo 444, 445, 503, 538
Art 32, 379
Asukata, Ichio 341
Automated Manufacturing Equipment and Systems (See AMES)
Automobile exports 923, 952
Automobile negotiations 896

B
Blue collar employees 834
Bonuses 783, 793
Buddhism 135, 139, 417

Buraku Liberation League 113, 343
Burakumin (see Minorities)

C
Cabinet 257, 288, 525
Canon Company 600
Child behavior and rearing 100, 102, 103, 105, 106
China, Cultural influence of 19, 56
Christianity in Japan 134, 139
Cinema 33, 34, 35
Citizen protest 155, 156, 327
Clean Government Party (see Komeito)
Commission on the Constitution 231
Communication 117, 145, 741, 742
Communication, Nonverbal 38, 52, 117
Confucianism 135, 417, 452, 736, 778
Crime control 70

D
Death penalty 69
Decision-making 383, 685, 695, 696, 702, 714, 727, 741, 742, 750, 755, 772, 802, 810, 818, 836
Declining industries 497, 501, 502, 512, 636, 812

Defense Agency 359
Derivative suit 227
Diet 250, 267, 294, 305, 308, 309, 329, 509, 525
Doctors 115, 116

E
Economic liberalization 222, 469, 470, 472, 555, 564, 897
Education
  and career options 75
  and modernization 73, 79, 446
  and social equality 76
  and tradition 81, 92
  psychological effects of 80, 85
Educational reform 78, 93
Electoral reform 311
Employees, Training of 690, 772, 773, 775, 778, 781, 793, 798, 819
Environmental pollution 189, 190, 191, 193, 221, 237, 238, 394, 429, 460, 461, 464, 473

F
Fair Trade Commission 206, 207, 214, 507, 607
Family planning 101
Federation of Economic Organizations (see Keidanren)
Fifth Generation Computer Systems 654, 670
Film (see Cinema)
Final demand 385
Folk religion 133, 135, 139
Food supply 375
Ford Motor Company 649
FTC (see Fair Trade Commission)
Fuchu 248
Fukuda, Takeo 261, 341

G
General trading companies (see Sogoshosha)
Gikan 291
Group oriented social organization (see Ie society)

H
High technology industries 491, 903, 950
Hitachi Company 572
Honda Company 652
House of Councillors 300, 302, 304, 313, 317
House of Representatives (Japan) 299, 300, 301, 303, 313
Hyogo prefecture 332

I
IBM 743, 942
Ie society 129, 411
Income distribution 372, 385
Industrial groups (see Keiretsu, Zaibatsu)
C. Itoh Company 586
ITT 743

J
Japan/United States compared
  Aged 164
  Automated manufacturing 673
  Automobile industry 771
  Bonuses 565, 567
  Business-government relations 519
  Child rearing and behavior 100, 102, 105
  Communication 117, 145, 741
  Conflict resolution 197
  Corporate organization 805
  Corporate strategy 764
  Culture 41, 45, 64, 123, 864

Decision-making 741
Declining industries 497
Diet and Congress 294
Economic growth 368, 401, 404
Economic performance 373
Economies 430
Education 77, 79
Employment characteristics 784
  Industrial relations 841, 842, 845, 846
  Industrial systems 803
  Industrial robots 673, 674
  Inflation 538
  Labor economies 378
  Management 693, 700, 726, 746, 748, 762, 769
  Manufacturers 664
  Marketing 612, 613
  Mutual perceptions 382, 854, 867, 914, 924
  Obscenity cases 230
  Organization development 720
  Permanent employment 786
  Political culture 249
  Postindustrial age 160
  Price stabilization 538
  Productivity 816, 818
  Public advisory bodies 266
  Public policy 319
  Research and development 832
  Steel industry 669, 671
  Transfer pricing 620
  White collar employees 746
  Work ethic 684, 771, 779
Japan Teachers Union (see Nikkyoso)
Japanese Communist Party 307, 331, 339, 343
JCP (see Japanese Communist Party)
Jichiro 833

K
Kanazawa 466

Kanebo Company 712
Kanegafuchi Spinning Company (see Kanebo Company)
Kao Soap Company 730
Kayaba Industry Company 830
Keidanren 525
Keiretsu 370, 591, 592, 594, 608, 808
Kigyoshudan 591
Kikkoman Corporation 568, 569
Komeito 318, 340
Kono, Yohei 341
Koreans (see Minorities)
Kyoto 314, 320

L
Labor market 75, 422, 637, 686, 791, 800, 841, 844
Lay Buddhism (see Reiyukai Kyodan)
LDP (see Liberal Democratic Party)
Liberal Democratic Party 259, 263, 299, 300, 301, 306, 315, 317, 334, 335, 338, 342, 509, 536, 922, 935
Lifetime employment (see Permanent employment)
Lockheed Scandal 251, 272, 313, 342

M
Managers 583, 698, 707, 765, 777, 780
Marubeni Corporation 581, 586
Marxist parties 333
Matsushita Electric Company 658, 743, 823
Matsushita, Konosuke 658, 694
Mazda (see Toyo Kogyo)
Merchant families 466
Middle class 171
Miki, Takeo 338

Ministry of Finance 525, 531, 536
Ministry of International Trade and Industry 212, 213, 499, 507, 514, 517, 525
Minobe, Ryokichi 323, 343
Minolta Camera Company 830
Minorities 108, 110, 111, 112, 113, 114
MITI (see Ministry of International Trade and Industry)
Mitsubishi Corporation 586, 591, 813
Mitsui & Company 586, 593
Mitsui Bank 527
Modernization 2, 3, 6, 13, 19, 22, 39, 153
  and education 73, 79, 81
  and stress 149
  and suicide 151
  and tradition 30, 32, 81, 144
  and values 169
  psychological effects of 40
Monetary policy 540, 545
Money market 534
Moral Re-Armament 7
Morita, Akio 663
Musahi Semiconductor Works 814
Musahino 248

N
Nakasone, Yasuhiro 78, 265, 347, 380
Narita Conflict 255
Natural resources 427, 552
Nature, Concept of 60, 455
Nemawashi 810
Nikkyoso 98, 99
Ninagawa, Torazo 314, 320
Nippon Electric Company 521
Nippon Steel Corporation 830
Nissan Motor Company 600, 651

Nissan Steel Corporation 600
Nisshin Steel Company 830
Nissho-Iwai 586
NPT (see Nuclear Non-Proliferation Treaty)
Nuclear Non-Proliferation Treaty 263, 361, 362, 850
Nuclear weapons 352, 353, 355, 358, 363

O
Oil Cartel Criminal Case 212, 213, 499
Okayama prefecture 318, 462
Okinawans (see Minorities)
Organized crime (see Yakuza)

P
Parliament (see Diet)
Participative management 688, 735, 757, 798, 819
Patron-client democracy 268
Permanent employment 416, 456, 682, 686, 691, 695, 697, 700, 705, 737, 755, 759, 777, 784, 786, 787, 788, 791, 793, 795, 796, 799, 807, 810, 812, 834, 836
Police 68
Public administration 292
Public finance 543
Public policy companies 513
PXL Decision 359

R
R&D (see Research and development)
Reductionism, Cultural 126
Reiyukai Kyodan 137
Research and development 521, 660, 670, 730, 831, 832, 876
Rincho 275
Ringi seido (see Participative management)

S

Salaryman (see White collar employees)
Samurai tradition 159, 680, 736, 778
San Francisco Peace Treaty 858
Saving 365, 384, 410, 411, 526, 529, 537, 551, 818
Science, History of 183
Scientific research programs 182
Semiconductor industry 400, 883, 884, 927, 942, 957
Seniority wage system 701, 755, 791, 799, 836
Shinohata 455
Shinto 135, 139, 141, 417, 736
Shiwa 465
Showa Boeki 574
Social classes 168, 388, 467
Social conflict 158, 197, 388
Social insurance 473, 475, 479, 794
Social policy 162
Social structure 40, 147, 148, 161, 456, 457, 462, 465, 467
Society of the Friends of the Spirits (see Reiyukai Kyodan)
Sogoshosha 380, 517, 567, 579–589, 597, 600, 601, 762
Soka Gakkai 135, 143, 340
SONY Corporation 600, 662, 663
Student protest 255, 326
Sueno, Akira 574
Sukyo Mahikari 133
Sumitomo Corporation 586, 594, 823
Supercomputer technology 184
Supply management 454, 492

T

Takashima 462
Tanaka, Kakuei 251, 272, 313, 341
Taoism 135
Tax policy 551
Taxation, Corporate 549, 550
TDK Electronics Company 830
Tenrikyo 135
Tetsuri 730
Textile Dispute 891, 892, 929
Textile industry 501, 502, 512, 637, 817
Theory Z 739, 740, 758, 759
Tokyo 189, 248, 312, 316, 323, 326, 415
Tokyo Stock Exchange 392, 541
Toyo Kogyo 573
Toyota Auto Body Factory 771
Toyota Gosei 824
Toyota Motor Company 651, 774, 813, 824
Trade 387, 469, 481, 499, 553, 555, 557, 558, 560, 561, 562, 564
Trade policy 563
Trade surplus 523, 547, 553, 557, 930
True-Light Supra-Religious Organization (see Sukyo Mahikari)
Tsukiai 770
Turning point theory 413

U

Uji 194
Unemployment 451, 792
Unions 685, 704, 772, 807, 815, 833, 834, 836, 840, 845
United Airlines 743
United States Congress 294
Urbanization 189, 192, 194, 195, 304, 328, 407, 429, 460, 462, 488

U.S.-Japan Mutual Security
    Treaty 868

V
Venture business 443, 506,
    603
Venture capital 443, 619
Vertical principle theory
    161

W
Wacoal Corporation 830
White collar employees 154,
    171, 746, 768, 770, 807
Women 178, 180, 181
    and employment 172, 174,
        176, 179, 380, 800
    and politics 173, 175
    and sex discrimination
        172, 174, 176
    and tradition 177

Y
Yakuza 71
Yasukuni Shrine 142
Yawata-Fuji steel merger 806
Yen 403, 534, 542, 544, 553,
    905
Yen-dollar exchange rate
    879, 897, 905, 906, 951,
    954
Yoka High School 343

Z
Zaibatsu 518, 590, 592, 706
Zen 47, 736, 742, 743, 778